SOS:

The Story Behind the Army Expedition to Borneo's 'Death Valley'

To our rescuers

SOS

The Story Behind the Army Expedition to Borneo's 'Death Valley'

Lieutenant Colonel Robert Neill
and Major Ron Foster

C

Century · London

First published by Century 1995

1 3 5 7 9 10 8 6 4 2

First published in the United Kingdom in 1995 by
Century Limited
Random House, 20 Vauxhall Bridge Road,
London SW1V 2SA

Random House Australia (Pty) Limited
20 Alfred Street, Milsons Point, Sydney,
New South Wales 2061, Australia

Random House New Zealand Limited
18 Poland Road, Glenfield
Auckland 10, New Zealand

Random House South Africa (Pty) Limited
PO Box 337, Bergvlei, South Africa

Random House UK Limited Reg. No. 954009

A CIP catalogue record for this book is
available from the British Library

ISBN 0 7126 7528 0

Typeset in Times by
SX Composing Ltd, Rayleigh, Essex
Printed in Great Britain by
Mackays of Chatham PLC, Chatham, Kent

Acknowledgements and Credits

We are indebted to the following people and organisations whose efforts led to our successful extrication from Low's Gully and our subsequent safe return to the UK:

The Royal Malaysian Armed Forces – in particular Brigadier General Hussin bin Yussof, Lt Col Yahya bin Hains and members of 16 Battalion Royal Malay Regiment, Captain Izhar bin Hassan, Lieutenant Gabriel Joel and the rescue helicopter crews. The Sabahan Police Force and Frontier Scouts. Director, Park Rangers and Guides – Kinabalu National Park. Major Nick Cooke and staff – Outward Bound School, Kota Kinabalu. The villagers of Kampongs Melangkap Kappa and Tamis. Doctor Heng Aik Cheng and his staff – Sabah Medical Centre. The Ministry of Defence – various departments contributing to the rescue effort. Colonel Julian Lacey and staff, Headquarters Eastern District, York. Defence Attaché and staff, British High Commission, Kuala Lumpur. Major General John Foley and staff, Headquarters British Forces Hong Kong. Lieutenant Colonel Tony Schumacher. RAF Mountain Rescue Service. Second British Rescue Team. Colonel David Henderson and staff, British Military Hospital, Hong Kong.

In writing this book, we are grateful to all those who gave us a better understanding of the massive efforts made to find us. In particular Lieutenant Commander Mike Elesmore and Flight Lieutenant Richard Mowbray.

We would like to thank Beth Humphries for copy-editing so efficiently and Louise Hartley-Davies and the team at Century for their encouragement, consideration and tolerance in helping to bring this book to fruition. Last, but not least, we thank Duff Hart-Davis wholeheartedly for his help and advice, and whose professional writing skills turned all the various stories into one cohesive account.

Lieutenant Colonel Neill: My personal thanks to Sylvia Dicks for her untiring help in dealing with the multitude of correspondence before, during and after the exercise. I will be eternally grateful to the friends, relations and colleagues who supported Fiona and my family, at home and in Canada, during the dark days when we were missing. In particular, I would like to thank Major David Bentley, whose unenviable task it might have been to tell Fiona that the search teams had failed to find us, and were being called off.

Major Foster: My deepest gratitude for the prayers and thoughts of countless people throughout the world during our period of isolation; to my friends, neighbours and colleagues who gave active encouragement and support to Jeanette and my family during their time of crisis; and that same support to me on my return home.

Map of Malaysia reproduced from *Indonesia, Malaysia & Singapore Handbook 1995* with the permission of Trade & Travel, Bath, England. Map of Sabah reproduced from *Indonesia, Malaysia & Singapore Handbook 1995* with the permission of Trade & Travel, Bath, England. Overview of Low's Gully area reprinted by kind permission of Joe Couchman. Kinabalu annotated aerial photograph (Crown copyright). Abseils into Low's Gully by kind permission of Joe Couchman. Sketch of Low's Gully (Ron Foster). Diagram of Kevin's Cave (Ron Foster).

With the exception of the following all photographs in the two plate sections are Exercise Gully Heights Expedition photographs:

Map of Kinabalu area (Crown Copyright/MOD). Exercise Jungle Heights 3 (Ron Foster). Composite aerial photograph of northern end of Gully (Richard Mowbray). Helicopter shot of top end of the Gully (Richard Mowbray). Aerial view of the southern side of Kinabalu (Richard Mowbray). Foul weather on the northern flank (Richard Mowbray). Somewhere down there were the trapped group (Richard Mowbray). GOT EM! (Richard Mowbray). Crewmen in the bed of the Gully (Ron Foster). Welcoming smiles inside the Sikorsky (Ron Foster). Foster in Kampong (unknown). Neill in Kampong (unknown). The last ones out of the Gully (unknown). Recce group recovering at base of severe waterfall (Robert Mann). All's well that end's well (Roger Scruton).

Contents

Authors' Foreword

In leading an army expedition to Borneo in February and March 1994, our objective was to make the first ever descent of Low's Gully, the precipitous ravine which plunges down the north flank of Mount Kinabalu. If Exercise Gully Heights had gone as planned, one member of the expedition could have composed a first-person account of its progress. But because the party split into two, and a major international rescue operation had to be launched, action became so fragmented that no single viewpoint could cover all the events that took place.

Trapped in the Gully, we were cut off from the rest of the world for more than three weeks, and had no means of knowing what had happened to our reconnaissance group. Nor did we know what enormous efforts were being made to find us, both by the Malaysian authorities and by specialist teams from the United Kingdom.

In describing what happened, we therefore decided to draw from different sources and recount events from the viewpoint of one narrator with an overall command of the scene. This has enabled us to preserve chronological order, and to present our story as a comprehensive day-to-day record of an experience which we were lucky to survive.

This is our account of how the expedition was conceived and planned, of why it split, with such disastrous consequences, and of how British and Malaysian armed forces combined in a large-scale operation to rescue us.

Robert Neill
Ron Foster

York, December 1994

Climbing Glossary

Abseil — *Verb*: to make a controlled descent on a rope over vertical or very steep drops.
Noun: any such descent.

Ascender — See Jumar.

Belay — *Noun*: the means by which a climber attaches himself to the rock with ropes, slings and crabs (see below) to prevent being pulled off by a falling climber.
Verb: to use a belay.

Belay point — Tree, rock or other secure anchor to which a belay can be attached.

Bivvy Bag — Waterproof outer casing for sleeping bag.

Black Marlow — Pre-stretched make of climbing rope.

Crab — Short for Karabiner (see below).

Descender — Alloy figure-of-eight friction device used to control rate of descent on a rope.

Dive Sack — Thick, waterproof sack for keeping kit dry in water.

Figure-of-eight — See Descender.

Jumar — *Noun*: mechanical jamming device with teeth which locks on to a rope, enabling a climber to pull himself upwards.
Verb: to climb a rope using such a device.

JSRCI — Joint Services Rock Climbing Instructor.

Karabiner — Oval-shaped alloy snap/screw link with gate, used, among other things, by climbers and abseilers to clip their harnesses on to a rope, or to attach ropes to belay points. Generally known as a crab.

Kernmantel — Type of climbing-rope.

Prussik Loop — *Noun*: thin kernmantel loop (4mm), tied in a knot, used as a friction device on a rope either to climb up it or stop a climber sliding down it. *Verb*: to climb a rope, using a Prussik loop.

Shunt — Trade name for another jamming device, but without teeth, which can prevent an abseiler sliding down the rope. Also can be used as an ascender.

Sling — A closed loop of climbing tape, often used in belaying.

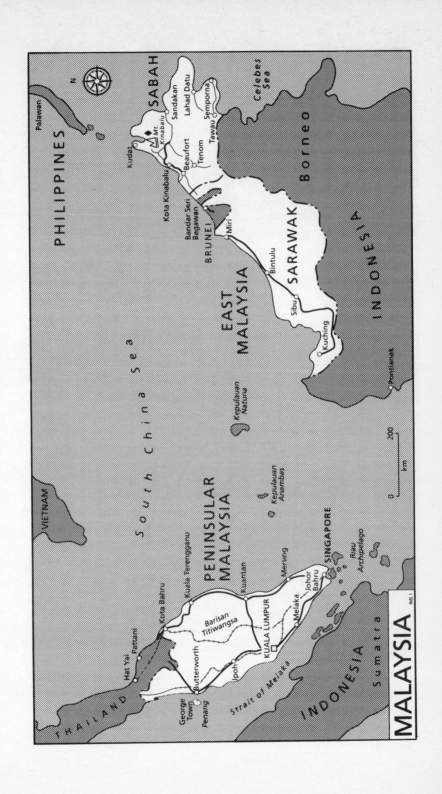

MALAYSIA

IMS 1

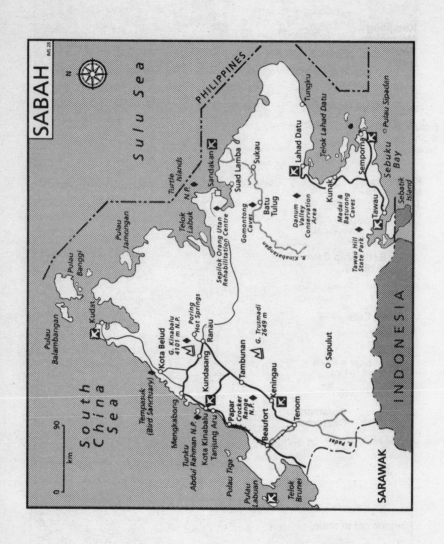

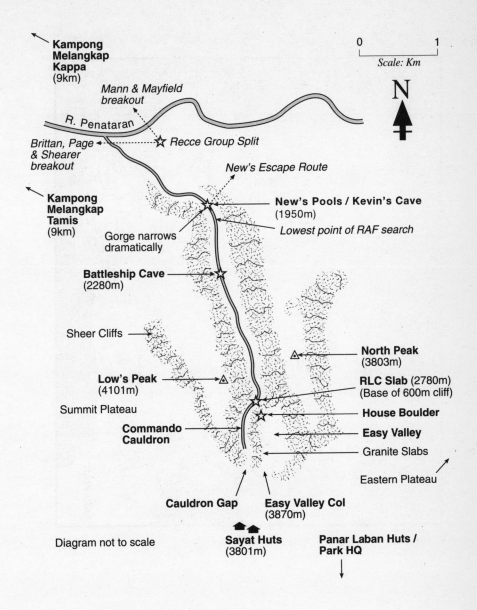

Overview – Low's Gully area

Chapter 1

At Death's Door

As dawn broke on Sunday, 20 March 1994, five men lay in their sleeping bags beneath a dripping granite overhang, 2,000 metres above sea level on Mount Kinabalu, in northern Borneo. Trapped in that dank cave for the past two weeks, they had run out of food and were slowly starving. Their bodies were wasting; their clothes, rotting on them in the damp air, gave off a fetid stink of decay. Their attempts to climb out of the ravine had failed, and their ambition had shrunk to that of conserving energy by keeping warm, and awaiting rescue, or death.

Survivors of a ten-man British Army expedition which had set out to conquer Low's Gully – the immensely steep ravine which plunges down the north side of the mountain – they had lost touch with their own reconnaissance group on 27 February, and did not know what had happened to the five British NCOs who had gone on ahead. Their own descent of the Gully had come to an abrupt halt when deluges of rain had filled the ravine with a thundering torrent and rendered further progress impossible.

Now the leader of the party, Lieutenant Colonel Robert Neill, had grown too weak to launch any more escape bids. His latest attempt to lead a breakout had drained him, and lack of food had prevented him making any substantial recovery. The three Hong Kong soldiers in his charge were equally debilitated. The one man with any strength left was the second-in-command, Major Ron Foster, a burly outdoor enthusiast who had survived best simply because he had started off with most meat on him. Now he became determined to make one last supreme effort: to break out of the Gully and fight his way through the surrounding jungle to summon help. But the officers had eaten the last of their food – a teaspoonful each of meat paste, half a biscuit apiece, and a small amount of coffee.

1

After days of continuous rain, the weather on 20 March was providentially dry. Foster prepared to set off at 0930, having borrowed Neill's lightweight trousers: his own had been washed away by a flood, and Neill had lost so much weight that his would no longer stay up. Foster also took Neill's sleeping bag, which was less bulky than his own, and left much of his heavier equipment behind. Against all good sense, he insisted on taking his video camera. Neill told him he was crazy and tried to make him leave the extra weight behind. 'The bloody thing might throw you off-balance,' he said.

When Foster was ready, he shook hands with each of his fellow-survivors.

'Don't do an Oates on me, Ron,' said Neill.

'Don't worry,' Foster answered. 'I'll be back.'

So he bade his companions farewell, and scrambled out of the cave. 'It was a desolate moment,' Neill recorded in his diary, 'as I doubted whether I would see him alive again.' Ever a realist, for the time being, he gratefully moved into Foster's bed-space and borrowed his sleeping mat, which took some of the sting out of the bare rock floor.

Together with the Hong Kong soldiers, he then made a big effort to collect potentially combustible sticks and leaves, with the aim of lighting a fire if a helicopter should come into view. Everything was sodden, but they brought the best material they could find into the cave, hoping that it would gradually dry out. Neill even thought of putting some inside his sleeping bag, but rejected the idea, since that would have made him wet, and lowered his body temperature.

He was surprised but pleased to notice that the injuries suffered by the party seemed to have cleared up. His own hands, which had threatened to go septic from thorn punctures and other lacerations, had healed; Foster had earlier cracked a rib and gashed a leg, but neither wound was troubling him any longer; Chow had stopped complaining about his back, which had been hit by falling rocks; Kevin Cheung's twisted ankle had also recovered.

The all-round improvement brought home the length of time

the party had been trapped – as did the fact that shrubbery which they had trampled during one of their escape bids was already putting up long new shoots. This made Neill reflect on the speed with which the entire overhang might be grown over, so that if they died in the cave, their bodies would be buried under a green bower, and would probably never be found. An even less welcome development was that flies appeared for the first time, probably attracted by the detritus which had built up in crevices, in spite of the soldiers' efforts to keep the place clean.

With Foster gone, Neill had more time to chat to the Chinese, and to think about things that he had failed to do. He was uncomfortably aware that in England he had left a number of personal and family matters uncompleted. In particular, he had not made an up-to-date will, and now decided that the time had come for him to write some form of last testament in his little notebook, which he had come to value almost more than life itself, and kept in multiple layers of waterproof covering. This was his last link with home, and a record of the expedition, when or if their bodies were found. The wrappings were plastered with stickers bearing the name and address of his wife Fiona, so that in the event of his death the booklet would find its way to her at their home in Yorkshire.

From far back in his days at university, the legal requirements and even the phrases returned to him. 'This is the last will and testament of me, John Robert Neill. . . I hereby revoke all earlier wills and instructions.' Appointing an executor was easy. Fiona would deal with everything. 'I leave everything to my wife, Fiona. This will is written in dire circumstances in a Gully on the north face of Mount Kinabalu. I am of sound mind and body, and this document represents my absolute wishes. Signed: J.R. Neill. Dated: 20 March 1994.'

Then he thought, 'Bloody hell! This isn't active service. I need two people to witness my signature.'

How was he to explain to the Chinese, without alarming them still more, that he needed their signatures? Could he admit that he was preparing for the worst? He need not have worried.

'What are you writing, Robert?' asked Victor Lam, stumbling back into the cave.

3

'It's a letter to my wife – in case we have another accident.'

'Oh – you mean your will! I did mine a few days ago.'

'Cheers, Sport!' said Neill to himself. Nothing like having confidence in your officers!

Victor signed as a witness, then Kevin did the same, and in due course each of them asked Neill to witness wills of their own – pages of (to him) indecipherable Chinese characters. The process did not seem to depress them, and they disclosed that they had already made their peace with their gods some days earlier. Victor, a Christian, showed Neill some prayers written on little cards which his girlfriend Pansie had given him. All the colonel could do in return was to assure them that even if nobody in the Far East had sparked at the fact that they were so long overdue, people in England would be growing more anxious with every day that passed, and an irresistible head of steam would build up behind any rescue attempt, once it got going. He did not mention his deepest inner dread: that a rescue operation had already been mounted and abandoned, because of the extreme difficulty of the terrain.

With his last testament made out and witnessed, he felt more positive, and better able to concentrate on the business of keeping his party going. He also had plenty of time to write. Ever since the group had come to rest in the cave, he had been making long entries in his journal, spurred by the realisation that if nobody survived to tell the tale, his notes might have to recount their slow decline. He had also spent much time talking to Fiona on paper: he spoke to her endlessly in his mind, but in writing he felt that he was actually establishing contact with his wife. The very act of communicating was therapeutic, and helped him retain his mental stability.

'Thank God it's a dry day for Ron's final attempt to escape from this wretched place,' he now wrote:

Well done Ron for having the strength to go for it. Good luck, Old Chap. At least I've given him my altimeter. Privately, I do not think he will make it – and that will be one more death that I will have to come to terms with. He has the

4

will – so do I – but although he is stronger than me, he, too, has had virtually nothing to eat for the past two weeks, and is getting weaker.

We failed to find a way out of the Gully when we were far stronger, defeated by the steepness and the slime on the rock faces, and the vegetation. No matter what we tried to hold on to, it peeled away in our hands and from under our feet, leaving us staring at greasy, black, evil, vertical slab-granite.

And now he has announced that he can no longer lie here, gradually rotting away and waiting for death. He says he has enough strength to go for it, and would prefer to die in the jungle than rot here. I have tried to dissuade him, saying that someone in authority must have registered that the expedition was due to report to Park HQ sixteen days ago. Also that our families had been expecting phone calls soon after that, and it was beyond belief that an official ten-man army expedition could just go missing without anyone pulling their finger out.

We made the decision to remain here, in the defined watercourse of the Gully, where we can be seen from the air, rather than risk certain death further down, because we were well overdue and knew we would not be seen in the jungle. Fat lot of good it has done us. We both wish we had said, 'To hell with it. Let's go for it, and take the consequences' – which is presumably what the recce group said. And they obviously haven't made it out. But to have tried would have been criminal, given the weather and the torrent the Gully developed into. Damn the rain. Damn everything.

I would dearly love to go with Ron, but I'm too weak, and so are the lads. We would only hold him up. Kevin's relatively strong still, but I'm not losing him and the other two after all the near squeaks we have had. Like it or not, I will be held responsible for whatever has happened to the first group, and I have no intention of adding further to the casualty lists. Ron is big enough, old enough and smelly enough to make his own decisions – and he wouldn't listen to me even if I were to order him to stay. Good for you, Ron. You're a bloody good man. I'll miss not having you around.

5

As soon as Neill stopped writing, his gloomy surroundings seemed to close in on him. Everything in the overhang was slimy and wet to the touch, and the constant, rumbling drone of waterfalls sounded cruelly like helicopter rotors. But that sound had been in his ears for so long now that he had learned to discount it, and, in spite of his natural confidence, he had begun to doubt whether rescue would ever come.

Chapter 2

The Mountain

Everyone who has seen Kinabalu agrees that it is an awe-inspiring mountain. At 4,101 metres or 13,455 feet, it rises in solitary splendour to tower above the steaming jungles of Sabah, the most northerly state of the vast island of Borneo, in East Malaysia. Its lower slopes are clad in tropical forest, but its upper ridges and peaks are naked granite, and include many faces of breathtaking steepness. Although the summit of the mountain is 50 kilometres inland, in clear weather it can be seen not only from the coast, but from great distances out to sea; yet it is from close at hand that its jagged battlements, its vast sheets of rock and its precipices make the strongest impression. Anyone who climbs to the top can immediately understand why in ancient time the local Dusun tribes named it 'Aki Nabalu', or 'Home of the Spirits of the Departed'.

In 1769 a British naval officer, Captain Alexander Dalrymple, gave a hint of the impact it makes when he wrote: 'Though perhaps not the highest mountain in the world, it is of IMMENSE height.' In 1844 Admiral Sir Edward Belcher fixed its altitude with fair accuracy at 13,698 feet, from bearings taken at sea. In 1851 it attracted the attention of Sir Hugh Low, British Colonial Secretary on the island of Labuan, south-west of what is now known as Sabah. In February that year he was on his way to 'deal with some Bolanini pirates who had recently ravaged the coast' when he became fascinated by the appearance of Kinabalu, and decided that he could afford two weeks to investigate the mountain. For his march inland he hired forty Dusun porters, who warned him about the lurking spirits; and to protect his party from supernatural beings who might be lurking up there, he took a guide armed with a basket of quartz crystals and human teeth.

7

He later described his journey as 'the most toilsome walk I have ever experienced'. When he reached Paka Cave – a large, overhanging rock about 3,000 metres above sea level – he concluded that 'all beyond was perfectly unknown', since his guides had never climbed so high. Presumably believing that he was close to the summit, he pushed on towards the pair of vertical rock spires now known as the Donkey's Ears. Heading for a gap in the skyline to the right of them, he came up on to a knife-edged ridge, and when he looked over into what is now known as Easy Valley, he could see straight down for 2,000 feet. He found himself gazing into 'a circular amphitheatre . . . the bottom of which, from its great depth and my position overhanging it, was indiscernible'.

On reaching the plateau near the summit, he learned from the Dusuns that the peak was inhabited by a dragon which lived in a cave guarding an immense jewel, and that the top of the mountain was strewn with enormous precious stones which none might touch (perhaps a reference to hailstones). Further, the Dusuns told him that when Chinese first visited the place, they annoyed the dragon by stealing its fire – with the result that the dragon put a curse on all Chinese, and, if any tried to set foot on the mountain, lured them to their deaths.

Having decided that 'the highest point is inaccessible to any but winged animals', Low took out a bottle of Madeira and drank Queen Victoria's health – after which he wrote his name on a piece of paper, put it in the empty bottle and left it there, upturned. His porters thought this was some form of religious ritual, and for years afterwards they insisted that all Europeans climbing to the peak should leave similar messages, to protect the party from evil or disaster.

The second recorded ascent of the mountain was made by Spenser St John, British Consul in Sarawak, in April 1858. Low accompanied him, and because a ship which they hoped would bring them shoes never arrived in the port of Labuan, they began their journey wearing boots. These caused such blisters that both men decided to walk barefoot. Soon Low's feet were in a poor state, so St John went on alone and climbed the South Peak, only to find that the main peak was higher. Three months later he and Low again set off together and reached the summit plateau, whereupon St John climbed the peak which now bears his name. This proved only 12 metres lower than the summit itself; but the highest peak was not named for another thirty years, when John Whitehead, an ornithologist, climbed it and called it after Low.

Legends about Kinabalu continued to thrive. Near the summit there was said to be a lake on which sailed many boats, each with a lamp. The spirits inhabiting the mountain lived on mushrooms, and tended ghostly herds of buffalo. Until recently members of expeditions climbing the mountain had to agree in advance with their porters precisely what sacrifices they would make. The standard requirement was seven fowls and seven eggs, given as offerings at the outset, two gunshots to warn the spirits of the impending invasion, and two further shots discharged in a northerly direction when the summit was reached.

Today Kinabalu is often wrongly described as the highest mountain in South-East Asia; in fact it is the highest between Mount Hkakabo in Northern Burma and the snow-capped peaks of the Pegunungan Maoke range in New Guinea. Yet its bulk and presence make it seem far higher. During the Second World War United States Air force pilots had their maps overprinted with '19,000 feet' in heavy black ink, to keep them well clear of the peak, which is frequently surrounded by clouds.

Such is the mountain which fascinated, and almost killed, the two British Army officers, Lieutenant Colonel Robert Neill and Major Ron Foster, who led the ill-fated Gully Heights expedition of February and March 1994. Both had climbed Kinabalu several times on earlier occasions and knew the summit area well. Yet, thrilled as they were by what one author described as its 'series of peaks shooting upwards like petrified flames', there was one feature which beyond all others gripped their imagination and challenged their audacity: Low's Gully, also named after Sir Hugh – the colossal chasm which falls away from the amphitheatre known as Easy Valley and dives down the northern face of the mountain, falling more than 2,000 metres in a horizontal run of only four kilometres before it evens out into the River Penataran.

9

A vivid description of Easy Valley and the top of the Gully was left by C.M. Enriquez, whose book *Kinabalu: the Haunted Mountain of Borneo* appeared in 1927:

> *The summit of Kinabalu is by no means as flat as one might suppose from certain distant aspects of it, and this is soon evident, for on crossing the plateau, it is found to end abruptly in a horrid abyss – a sort of 'crater'; a veritable 'Devil's Cauldron' of incredible depth, whose walls rise in sheer precipices for thousands of feet. As the outer aspect of Kinabalu is of perpendicular lines, so also is its interior. This gulf in the centre of the mountain is certainly a grand and terrifying sight ... Low's Rift, Low's Chasm, or Low's Abyss would be more appropriate.*

On previous expeditions Neill and Foster had looked down from Easy Valley at the upper end of the Gully, and they had gazed at the terrific walls of rock which soared up on either side of it; but because the ravine is so deep and narrow, and there is no commanding vantage-point above, they had never been able to see down into it. Elementary mathematics showed that its *average* drop was more than one in two; common sense dictated that its bed must consist of waterfalls, pools and fallen rocks, and that in wet weather the stream flowing down it would turn into a ferocious torrent, since it acted as a drain for the enormous catchment area above. In other words, to descend the Gully would require not only a high degree of organisation and physical stamina, but also expertise in abseiling – the technique of going down vertical or nearly vertical drops on ropes. Further, dry weather would be critically important.

Small wonder that in the nineteenth century Spenser St John had dismissed any idea of venturing into the Gully with the ringing observation: 'There was no descending here.' Now, to these two determined officers, it appeared one of the few remaining uncharted wonders of the world – and it demanded their attention.

The reasons why no one had ever gone down the Gully were

not hard to find. Apart from Kinabalu, Borneo has no high mountains, and attracts few climbers: if European or American mountaineers want foreign challenges in the Far East, they tend to head for the Himalayas. Few Malays go climbing as a rule. The Gully had been left alone not because it was too difficult, but simply because no one had got round to tackling it.

Chapter 3

The Leaders

Although alike in the fact that they had both made their careers in the Army, and were members of The Royal Logistic Corps, the leaders of the Gully Heights expedition came from very different backgrounds.* In 1994 Robert Neill was forty-six – a tall man, slim and wiry, with dark hair and an angular face with deep-set eyes, which reflected a strong, focused nature, softened by a wide smile and easy laugh. The son of a doctor in Gloucester, he went to Kelly College, the public school at Tavistock, on the edge of Dartmoor, where he discovered his love of the outdoors. He joined the Army straight from school, and after Sandhurst was commissioned into the Gloucestershire Regiment. He transferred to the Royal Army Ordnance Corps when he was medically downgraded after his hearing had been damaged by the close passage of a Carl Gustav 84mm anti-tank missile; but then he decided to further his education, passed two more A levels through a correspondence course (on top of the four which he already had), and at the age of twenty-five won a place at Exeter University, where he read law. By this time he had earned various mountain leadership qualifications, which he put to good use when posted as a training officer to Germany.

Part of his arrangement with the Army was that he would spend a month in uniform during each long vacation, and in two successive summers he took parties of soldiers mountain-hutting in the Allgäu Alps of Bavaria. Then, on getting his degree, he was posted to the Royal Marines, and had a rude reintroduction to soldiering in the form of the Commando or Green Beret

* The Royal Logistic Corps was formed on 5 April 1993 from the former Royal Corps of Transport, the Royal Army Ordnance Corps, the Royal Pioneer Corps, the Army Catering Corps and the Postal and Courier Service of the Royal Engineers. Neill and Foster had both been in the RAOC.

course. Anyone who wanted to serve in the Commando Logistic Regiment had to pass this, and it included much abseiling and rope-work on the cliffs of south Devon, as well as in various Dartmoor quarries excavated by prisoners during the Napoleonic wars. Neill spent several winters in Arctic Norway, where he was able to pursue his interest in skiing, and over the years maintained his fitness with a wide range of energetic pursuits.

In 1972 he married Fiona Wallace, who had been working in the computer unit at the university, and in due course they had two sons, Alexander, born in 1975, and James, born in 1977. In his private life Neill was always equable, and had a ready sense of humour. Army colleagues found him relaxed, mild-mannered and slow to anger: certainly he was no military maniac. But when in command (according to his second-in-command, Ron Foster) he tended to appear rather reserved and formal. Once on an earlier expedition, also to Kinabalu, he had disconcerted Foster by taking an unsympathetic attitude when the latter had been smitten by altitude sickness. Nevertheless the two were old colleagues and friends, who understood each other well, and were united by their preference for individual sports.

Ron Foster was fifty-four: a powerfully built, burly man, with a warmer, more accommodating personality than Neill's, and a career of formidable physical activity behind him. Born in Scunthorpe, the grandson of a coal merchant, he had grown up in Lincolnshire during the Second World War, and had learned the value of thrift from an early age. At the age of ten he began delivering newspapers, and quickly realised that if he got up early enough, and moved fast enough, he could cram two rounds into the same morning.

At Barton Grammar School he gained six O levels – enough to have made it worth his staying on. But he chose to leave when he was just sixteen, and after a seven-month stint delivering coal, which did much to build up his physique, he joined the Ordnance Survey as a cartographical draughtsman and surveyor. With National Service still in existence, he expected to be called up any time after his eighteenth birthday, but because the system was running down and disorganised, it was not until he was almost twenty-one that the summons came. He then enlisted in the RAOC, expecting to serve for two years, but after only three months he signed on as a regular soldier, and made his career in the Army. In August 1960 he married Jeanette Windle: for two bitterly cold winters they lived in a caravan at Andover, but survived this ordeal happily, and later they had two children, a boy and a girl, Vaughan and Kerry.

From childhood Foster had been keenly interested in outdoor pursuits: camping with the Scouts, a walking tour in Luxembourg, and above all cycling, for which he developed a passion. At the age of sixteen he once rode 180 miles in a day, and by the time he joined the Army he was covering 300 miles a week in training. Over the next twenty-five years he won fifteen individual army championships at a variety of events, from 1,000-metre sprints to 100-mile time trials on the road, and although he gave up competitive cycling at the age of forty-five, he continued to 'amble through the lanes for fun'.

His career took him to Aden, Sharjah in the Trucial States, and Germany, where he discovered the joys of orienteering; but it was a summer camp at Penhayle Camp, in Cornwall, which introduced him to what the Army calls 'adventurous training'. There he abseiled for the first time, and was elated by the 'sheer exhilaration of going off a cliff and landing on the rocky shore below'. Mountain walking led to Alpine skiing, and a course with German Alpine troops at Mittenwald in Bavaria taught him the art of movement and survival at high altitude. Soon he himself became a Joint Services ski instructor: racing for the first time at the age of forty, he won the RAOC individual title in 1981, and Alpine instruction grew to be his first love.

* * *

It was service in Hong Kong that put Neill and Foster in direct contact with Kinabalu. Neill went out to the Far East in October 1980 as a newly promoted major, posted as second-in-command of the Composite Ordnance Depot in Kowloon, and in December that year he took his family to spend Christmas with

14

friends in Brunei. As they sailed out to a beach party in a launch, he suddenly became aware of a huge mountain brooding over the sea on the northern horizon. Even at a range of 150 kilometres, it made an impressive sight, with the only clouds in the whole of the wide blue sky gathered round its summit. His hosts told him that it was called Kinabalu, that it was over 4,000 metres high, and that it was in Sabah, at the northern tip of Borneo. It formed the centrepiece of the Kinabalu National Park, and was a recognized tourist destination, since, in spite of its great height, ordinary hikers could walk up it.

Back in Hong Kong, Neill found his memory dwelling on the sight. Kinabalu had reawakened his hunger for mountains, unassuaged since his last visit to the Austrian Alps four years earlier. The fact that it was relatively close to Hong Kong made him all the keener. It also stirred his latent interest in Borneo, which had gripped his imagination in childhood and always made him think of headhunters, with their rows of human skulls along the rafters of their longhouses.

As a boy, if asked to point out Borneo on a map, he might not have been able to put a finger straight on it; but he knew that it was the third biggest island in the world, that much of it was covered by jungle, and that orang-utans were only one of the many species which inhabited its steaming, tropical forests. He also associated Borneo with Conan Doyle's novel *The Lost World*, in which the redoubtable Professor Challenger leads an expedition to a plateau cut off from human life by its encircling cliffs, and there discovers dinosaurs still living. Neill knew perfectly well that the story was set in South America, but even so he thought of Borneo as a lost world in its own right, so far away did it seem.

As an officer cadet at Sandhurst, studying recent conflicts in which the British Army had been involved, he took a close interest in the campaign known as Confrontation, in which some 17,000 British, Australian and New Zealand servicemen had helped fight off the attempt at a Communist takeover launched by President Soekarno of Indonesia during the 1960s. Much of the campaign took place in dense jungle, through which guerrillas were infiltrating into Sabah – then known as British North Borneo – and Sarawak, after they had crossed the border from Kalimantan, the Indonesian province which forms a large part of Borneo.

Interest in Kinabalu brought Borneo into sharper focus, and Neill began looking for an opportunity to get to know the mountain at first hand. Research told him that the Kinabalu National Park had been created in 1964, and that over the next fifteen years good tourist facilities had been opened up. By 1980 a serpentine trail led all the way to the summit, with seven shelters and drinking-water points along it; a Park Headquarters had been built 1,560 metres above sea level, and closer to the top were several huts in which hikers or climbers could take refuge: Panar Laban (Place of Sacrifice) at 3,360 metres, and Sayat Sayat (a species of shrub found near the mountaintop) at nearly 4,000. Lower down were miles of graded trails along which the walking was easier. The fauna and flora, he learned, were incredibly rich, many of them unique to that environment: over 300 species of birds, 28 of squirrels, 1,000 of orchids, 450 of ferns, 27 of rhododendrons, and nine of that extraordinary order *Nepenthes*, the pitcher plant, which had fascinated Low – a botanical killer which traps, drowns and digests insects or larger creatures in leaves specially developed for the purpose. Not to be missed was the parasitic *Rafflesia pricei*, the largest flower in the world, with fleshy red blooms nearly half a metre across.

The more Neill read about Kinabalu, the more he became fascinated – and the result was the expedition called Jungle Heights 1, which he launched from The Composite Ordnance Depot in March 1981.

The first proposal for a foray to Malaysia came from a warrant officer called Paul Hughes, an old friend from Commando days, who suggested that they should take a party to Gunung Tahan, another mountain standing in its own national park, in West Malaysia. Neill liked the idea; but he deferred the trip because it proved too difficult to organise in the time available, and he switched his immediate aim to Kinabalu.

So it was that he organised and led a party of ten – seven

16

British, including Hughes, and three Hong Kong soldiers – who ascended the mountain and spent several days exploring the summit area, where they discovered a wonderful adventure playground, spectacularly beautiful and blessedly cool after the moist tropical heat at sea level. The expedition succeeded in all its aims, and revealed to its members that the top of the mountain offered extensive possibilities for rock-climbing and exploration; but the main effect of the trip was to whet Neill's appetite for an attack on the most striking of Kinabalu's unique features: Low's Gully.

Gazing from the Col into Easy Valley, he had seen the top end of the mighty ravine, and – so far as he could discover – nobody had ever succeeded in going up or down it. A discussion with the park authorities suggested that no one had even tried. People either just went to the peak, or did some rock-climbing in the summit area. Here was a terrific challenge – a genuine first to be attempted. Even as he looked at the swooping faces of smooth, bare granite, and the chasm vanishing out of sight, the hair on his neck was prickling, and he knew he would return.

The next expedition he led – Jungle Heights 2 – went to Gunung Tahan, his original target. Again, it was successful, and it formed a useful part of his own long-term training cycle. Then Jungle Heights 3, in November 1982, took him back to Kinabalu.

His aim, this time, was nothing less than to climb the mountain from the north by going up Low's Gully – an undertaking which (he later agreed) he considerably underestimated. He took as his second-in-command Ron Foster, who was then a Warrant Officer Class One, with the appointment of Conductor RAOC. Paul Hughes had been posted back to the United Kingdom, and Foster, a like-minded enthusiast, was glad to help organise the expedition. The party consisted of ten men, three of them Hong Kong soldiers, all from the Composite Ordnance Depot, and during the three months before setting out they put in regular days of special fitness training, designed to ensure that all ranks were capable of carrying a 22-kilo pack for at least eight hours and 20 kilometres a day, with a rise and fall of up to a thousand metres, over difficult terrain.

Their aim was to ascend the River Penataran – the main watercourse fed by Low's Gully, and in effect its continuation through the lower reaches of the mountain – and to carry on up the Gully as far as possible – a passage which they hoped would be made easier by some aerial photographs they had acquired. Foster never forgot his first sight of the mountain. The party was driving from Kota Belud, a small market town, towards the start of their trek, when someone called out and the driver pulled off the road. There, 25 kilometres away but dominating the southern horizon, stood the gigantic bulk of Kinabalu, with a few fleecy clouds round its summit. To Foster it looked like 'an impregnable fortress, majestic, magnificent and magnetic', which filled him with awe, and also with trepidation at the scale of the task they were about to attempt.

His apprehension was well founded. After violent struggles with the torrent in the River Penataran and with the jungle on either bank, he and his colleagues had to turn back on only their third day. Not only did the river prove to be in spate; the nature of the watercourse itself, with its huge, rounded boulders, made further upstream progress impossible. The sides of the gorge through which the river hurtled were too precipitous for the explorers to climb out and work round impassable stretches – and all too soon it became apparent that lack of time would undermine their efforts. Because of the limitations imposed by flights, they had only fourteen days away from Hong Kong, and the fixed time-frame imposed a very tight programme. They had taken only seven days' rations with them, and clearly were not going to reach their goal within that period. It was Foster – arguably the more cautious of the two – who suggested that they should turn back, and Neill agreed, though not without misgivings, as he would have liked to keep trying for a bit longer.

Apart from Neill, none of the party had been up the mountain before, so at least they had a secondary objective on which to fall back. Forced to retreat, they returned to their start-point in record time by the end of Day Five, swept downstream by the power of the current; on their way they saw a small poisonous coral snake, which they were glad to avoid. Their swift recovery

18

gave them time to go round by road and climb Kinabalu by the conventional route. Once on the Col, they went down into Easy Valley and reconnoitred the top end of Low's Gully from there. Looking up at the cliffs to the east, they saw some ropes nearly 300 metres up, dangling 30 or 40 metres over the edge, and wondered what story they could tell. Were they connected with the rumours that a Japanese expedition had abseiled part of the way down? Park Headquarters were not explicit on the subject.

In an article which he wrote for his Corps gazette, Foster decided that 'although the main aim of the expedition had not been acheived, it had been a rewarding and exciting experience'. Neill, at the end of his official report, put up a 'suggested plan for a future expedition to Low's Gully', pointing out that seven days were not long enough to tackle such a challenge, that no man could comfortably carry more than seven days' food, and that it might be a good idea for volunteer porters to accompany the main team for a certain distance upriver, carrying extra food before falling back.

After the exercise Neill was swimming in the sea of Brunei when he trod on a stringray – the most excruciatingly painful experience he had ever had: it felt as if a six-inch nail had been driven into his foot, and the pain slowly seared up his leg until it reached his upper thigh. Injections in the foot brought the poisoning under control, but six months later the wound was still open, because the sting has a triangular barb, and its venom makes flesh fester.

To his disappointment, Neill was posted to Germany before he could have another crack at his favourite target. But by then others had caught the bug, and Exercise Jungle Heights 4 took place less than a year later, in August 1983. The basic aim was similar – to ascend the Penataran – but this time the team split into two, and one half went down Easy Valley to meet those coming up. Foster was again a member; but once more the expedition was foiled by lack of time, and degenerated into a two-day trek up the tourist trail. Since no official report was published, and contemporary notes were lost, few details survive; but an important point was that the radios which the

19

party took proved a dismal failure, as did the flares, which did not go high enough to be seen from any distance. All attempts to establish radio or visual communication between the two halves of the expedition proved futile.

Thereafter, with both Neill and Foster posted away from the Far East, army interest in Low's Gully dwindled, and although the depot in Hong Kong encouraged people to go to Kinabalu, they concentrated on climbing the tourist route to the summit. Foster remained, if not exactly haunted or obsessed by the mountain, at least with a feeling of personal challenge; and five years on, in May and June 1988, he joined six men and one officer of the 17/21 Lancers (motto: 'Death or Glory') in Exercise Kinabalu Triangle. Once again, the aim was to force a passage up the Penataran river, but the group's luck was out: although they thought they had chosen the dry season, they found the river in spate, and on the first day Foster cut his hand badly on a submerged rock. Next morning the party agreed to split in two: one group of four men went on, while the other turned back to seek treatment for the injury, before climbing Kinabalu by the usual trail.

The river party continued to battle upstream for four more days, but were forced to abandon their attempt due to the same difficulties as before, principally the weight of water in the torrent, and the unscalable cliffs on either bank, but also leeches and fire ants. Not being equipped for climbing, they penetrated a couple of kilometres beyond the farthest point reached on Jungle Heights 4, but turned back when they met a gigantic boulder more than 20 metres high, and returned to Kota Kinabalu, in the words of their own report, 'suffering from rashes, cramps, bites and badly bruised feet'. The first group, meanwhile, had reached the summit via the tourist trail and again explored Easy Valley.

In spite of all these setbacks, Foster retained his determination to conquer Low's Gully. He was tantalised by a claim made by the leader of the 1988 expedition that his team had 'reached Low's Gully', and fascinated by a photograph of the colossal boulder which had blocked their path. Gradually he had come to realise that long stretches of the river and a large section of the

Gully had yet to be tackled. Early in 1992 he proposed to Neill that they should mount yet another expedition. By then he was out of the Regular Army and running his own financial services business, but he had been commissioned as a captain in the Territorial Army, with a commitment to put in a fortnight's camp every year, as well as various training weekends; and this gave him the chance to continue outdoor pursuits, and to encourage other TA soldiers in the same line.

Over the past ten years he and Neill had seen little of each other: Foster was second-in-command of South West District Ordnance Company, based at Deepcut, near Camberley, and living in Tewkesbury, while Neill had been posted, on promotion to lieutenant colonel, to Headquarters Eastern District in York, and had moved from Devon to a farmhouse in North Yorkshire. Yet the two had kept in touch, and were both still physically very active: from time to time they had talked about another assault on Low's Gully, and now Foster's proposal rapidly brought them back into harness. Their first idea was to make yet another attempt at climbing the Gully, and they were convinced they could manage it provided the weather remained dry. After further reflection, however, they decided that an ascent was beyond the capabilities of a small-scale, unit expedition such as they were planning, and they settled instead for a shot at going down. As Neill remarked, it was a novel scheme for a mountaineering expedition: go up the easy way and come down the hard.

In proposing their plan to the appropriate authorities, they were encouraged by the knowledge that the Army actively promotes adventurous training, and welcomes initiatives of the kind they were launching. The official Ministry of Defence document on the subject declares that adventurous training 'develops those qualities of loyalty, team spirit, discipline, self respect, courage, fitness, resourcefulness, adaptability and good humour which are defined as the qualities of the soldier'. Participation in adventurous training is reckoned to add 'an extra dimension to a soldier's life . . . by placing him in an environment where he has to become accustomed to danger, hardship and

challenge within the increasing restraints of peacetime service.
. . . It is invaluable in developing character and training potential
leaders.' The regulations governing expeditions run to more than
twenty printed pages, but two of the most important rules (from
the organisers' point of view) are, first, that personnel taking part
are considered to be on duty, and second, that as many soldiers
as possible should be given the chance to participate, novices
being considered 'as important as experts'.

Unlike large-scale Joint Services expeditions, their project
would not rank very highly, and would not attract major support.
Nevertheless, there was little doubt that their initiative would
receive official blessing, especially as their own knowledge of
Mount Kinabalu was so extensive.

Chapter 4

Building the Team

Serious planning began in the autumn of 1993; but before that Foster carried out an important reconnaissance mission in the Far East. In May and June, together with Jeanette, he visited Hong Kong and Sabah, principally for a holiday, but also to collect information. Since finance was certain to be one of the expedition's major problems, it was an enormous help to Neill that Foster – now a civilian who put on uniform only for his TA activities – made this long trip at his own expense.

At the headquarters of the Kinabalu National Park he met the chief warden, Eric Wong Hon Fui, and obtained verbal assurance that there would be no problem about getting permission to descend Low's Gully. Another useful contact was Francis Liew Shin Pin, Assistant Director of the Sabah Parks, who told him, among other things, that if he liked he could hire a helicopter to go and reconnoitre the Gully – at about £2,000 an hour.

His most valuable discovery – made through Wong – was that Robert New, an English property consultant living in Sabah, had already traversed the Gully at least part of the way down. In fact he had made three attempts to descend it, the last a major effort in May 1991 – but had been defeated every time. Foster had met New briefly before the start of Exercise Jungle Heights 4 in 1983, and then again in 1988, on Exercise Kinabalu Triangle. New's exploits, and in particular his trip of May 1991, became a key factor in Foster's and Neill's planning.

New himself was in his forties, very tall – the best part of two metres (about six foot four) – married to a Sabahan, and as friendly as he was elongated. What Foster could not appreciate, when he talked to him, was the extent to which he unconsciously played down his own capabilities, and made little of the ordeals he had been through during his last attempt on the Gully.

New purported to be no more than averagely fit, claimed that he did not even jog regularly, and ascribed such success as he had had in the Gully to his climbing companion, Steve Pinfield, who (he said) was much more of a professional. But New's record spoke for itself: he had climbed difficult routes in the Alps, in Norway and Uganda, and had ascended Kinabalu by the tourist trail more than fifty times, once carrying his thirteen-month-old son to the summit on his shoulders.

Neill and Foster later heard that New became involved with Low's Gully only when Pinfield began looking for someone to replace his original partner, Mike Elesmore, who returned to Wales in 1986. He made his first attempt on the Gully in 1988, but abandoned it when rain set in and the level of the water began to rise. His second expedition, in 1990, had to be aborted when Pinfield fell and dislocated a shoulder: he slid out of control down a tremendously steep incline, and had he not managed to deflect himself to one side and grab some vegetation, he would have hurtled on over a cliff, almost certainly to his death.

Their third attempt, in May 1991, lasted six days and ended in limited victory. Again Pinfield was the leader: after descending the ravine for three days, he and New came to twin pools lying in a narrow V of rock, and decided that to proceed further would be impossibly dangerous. Rather than risk going on down the watercourse, they climbed the right-hand face of the Gully, with considerable difficulty, and after three more days fighting their way through the jungle, emerged at a village called Melangkap Kappa, about ten kilometres north of the mountain.

Talking to James Sarda, a journalist on the Sabah *Daily Express*, New had emphasised the risks of the undertaking. He made it clear that although the Gully was negotiable in dry weather, it became lethal in the wet, since it acted as a drain for the huge catchment area of Easy Valley, and the trickle of water flowing down it rapidly became a torrent, in which men would have no chance. He described his 'great sense of isolation and helplessness in the face of such a dramatic landscape', and remarked that if there had been an accident, 'nobody was going to know or rescue you'. He had told the Park authorities what he was doing, and had given them a date on which he hoped to reappear. 'But frankly, what could they do even if we didn't show up by then? They wouldn't know exactly where we were. Even if they could locate us, they would not be able to get at us, because you can't get a helicopter in there.' But even allowing for all these difficulties, New said that he would certainly consider making another attempt, but that he would need to be better equipped.

In spite of his cautionary remarks, Foster came home much encouraged; not until later did he realise that he himself had perhaps been rather naive, and that New's self-effacing nature had led him to play down his experience, which in fact had been fairly traumatic.

Back in England, Foster showed Neill copies of two articles from the Sabah newspaper which described New's exploits. Neill found these reassuring: he was delighted to learn that someone had pioneered part of the route, and that New was by no means an Olympic athlete. It seemed that a complete descent of the Gully should be within the capabilities of a well-equipped team. The reports also confirmed what Neill had already tentatively decided: that he would be wise to take along a good army rock-climber, with proper qualifications, probably an instructor, who would be able to lead on difficult sections of the route. Common sense apart, army regulations would demand the inclusion of such a specialist.

What remained unclear was the distance which New had managed to penetrate down the Gully before being forced out. He had said that the twin pools (which Neill and Foster from now on called New's Pools) were 'one day's walk in dry weather' from the bottom of Easy Valley. What lay between them and the Penataran river? This was the key question which Neill hoped to resolve. It struck him that New had been most unwise to attempt the Gully with an Alpine-style party only two strong. Standard mountain drill lays down that in case of accident one member of the party stays with the injured person, while a third goes for help, preferably accompanied by others. Clearly the Army would never approve a two-man expedition (Neill plus Foster –

combined age 100 exactly!). He was already thinking in terms of ten people, if only for reasons of safety, since he knew from his own experience that even four strong, fit soldiers cannot carry a casualty on a stretcher very far over difficult country.

He was also reassured, rather perversely, by the fact that New and Pinfield had got themselves into serious trouble by failing to take water containers. They had assumed that water would always be abundant – as indeed it was for as long as they remained in the bed of the ravine. But when they tried to break out through the jungle, they found none, and became dangerously dehydrated. A mistake as basic as that, Neill reckoned, gave further evidence that they were by no means infallible. On Exercise Jungle Heights 3 he had found that two water bottles per man were the absolute minimum; and whenever the team was within easy reach of water, they could of course empty the bottles, saving themselves a significant amount of weight.

Neill also noted the need for strong, flexible waterproof containers, in which kit could be wrapped and sealed if it became necessary to swim through rock pools. Earlier expeditions had taught him the paramount importance of being able to keep clothes and equipment dry. Sealable bags would also act as useful buoyancy aids when swimming.

Reading and rereading New's account, Neill found only two references to abseils during the descent of the upper part of the Gully; and since the two men had had only two ropes, none of the drops could have been greater than the length of a single rope – 50 metres.* It seemed clear that the upper end of the Gully was less steep than Neill had supposed; down to the point at which New and Pinfield climbed out, abseiling did not appear to have been a significant factor. They certainly had not had to do any free abseils – drops in which one swings out clear of the rock,

* In abseiling, the usual technique is to run a rope round a belay point such as a tree or rock, or thread it through a karabiner, so that it will run freely when one end is pulled. If climbers are to recover their ropes for further use, they must double them every time they do an abseil, so that they can pull them down afterwards. Thus one 50-metre rope will suffice for a 25-metre drop, and two 50-metre lengths for a 50-metre abseil.

or inwards beneath overhangs. Both of these are tricky for men wearing heavy packs, as the weight tends to turn a climber upside-down, unless he is wearing a chest harness. A more serious threat appeared to be that of being washed down the Gully by floods – and against this the team would have to take all possible precautions.

They would need to practise techniques for ascending the sides of the ravine in a hurry: one of the tasks of the reconnaissance party would be to fix ropes whenever the ground demanded it, so that if a sudden flood came down, the others would be able to clip on and climb to safety.

New's journey had taken six days; and since part of it had been by an emergency route, which was presumably longer than the direct route, Neill reckoned that, with a good team and the right equipment, the same six days would suffice. Adding four days 'for the fudge factor', he arrived at a maximum probable duration for the descent of ten days. He knew from previous experience that this was the longest period for which the party would be able to carry its own food, for much climbing equipment would be needed, and packs were going to be an enormous weight anyway.

The newspaper reported New as saying that success depended more on 'knowing what you are doing and making the right decisions as you go along than on actually being supremely fit, because you're not going fast or racing against time'. What you needed, he said, was 'basic physical strength and lots of stamina'. The apparent simplicity of New's descent – certainly as reported in the Sabah newspaper – also increased Neill's determination to include some relative novices in his team. Abseiling with beginners is a time-consuming process, which frays nerves all round, at least initially, but his aim was to take a team of mixed ability, as he had on earlier expeditions, and this now definitely seemed feasible. As he remarked, there was no point in taking 'only the gladiators': better that less experienced, younger men should develop their skills. Apart from anything else, recruiting would be easier if he did not have to look exclusively for men with a fistful of qualifications.

In August 1993 Neill travelled to Foster's home in Tewkesbury to discuss plans in greater detail. Together the two men went through other relevant articles, including one about the climbers from Sarawak who had gone missing on the mountain in 1988, and whose bodies had never been discovered. They found the story easy enough to believe, since they had seen for themselves that vegetation on the upper slopes consisted of incredibly dense bushes such as rhododendrons, whose matted trunks and branches would have defied a battalion of chain-saws, and in the river itself the power of the water was such that bodies would soon have been pounded to pieces and washed away.

Foster had recently acquired a new 8 mm video camera, and this possessed amazing powers of magnification when held a few inches away from a document, map or photograph. Trying it on one postcard-sized shot of Easy Valley, taken from a vantage-point near Low's Peak on an earlier trip, they felt their insides churn as they examined the vast granite slabs that plunged vertically downwards before vanishing out of sight. But even with this new magic eye they could not see into the waterfalls, which to anyone on or near the peak are in dead ground, hidden beneath their flanking cliffs; yet they found the view distinctly awesome, and hoped that New's route did not go anywhere near one particular cliff face, which as Neill put it, looked 'bloody steep and slippery, with an ominous, slate-grey sheen which indicated wet and slime, and threatened bum-rash or worse to an unsuspecting climber'.

Anxious to glean every possible scrap of information, they searched for the 'boulder as big as a house' from which New had started his descent. They knew that when their own team abseiled, they would not be able to afford to leave ropes in place, but would have to arrange things so that they could pull most or all of them down. For one thing, ropes were very expensive – about £100 apiece – and for another, they would probably be needed again and again. Besides, if the team returned to base without them, the quartermaster would have a sense-of-humour failure; if you lose kit and die, you are forgiven, but woe betide you if you leave kit behind and survive. They also pored over their aerial photograph, which had been damaged by water on an earlier expedition, but had survived sufficiently intact to be usable.

In Kota Kinabalu New had told Foster that he thought it might be possible to find a scrambling route out of the Gully, back up into Easy Valley, and now the two officers searched their photographs minutely with the video camera to see if they could identify any fault-lines in the rock which could be useful to them. They found there was something eerie about peering at that immense cliff face, thousands of miles away, from the comfort of an English living-room, reckoning that probably no one had observed it in such detail before, and thinking that, with luck, they themselves might be on it in a few months' time.

Close scrutiny of maps and photographs helped them define the aim of the expedition precisely:

To complete the first descent of the north face of Mount Kinabalu, Sabah, by means of Low's gully. Thereafter, to follow the River Penataran to Kampong *(the village of) Melangkap Kappa, the nearest roadhead.*

They did not stake everything on being first down the Gully. If they managed that, they would regard it as the icing on the cake. Nevertheless Neill hoped that by advertising his expedition as the first descent he would be more likely to attract sponsorship, as well as more than usually generous funding from the Army. As for choosing a name, he and Foster considered 'Gully Depths', which in many ways would have been appropriate, but somehow lacked the right ring. In the end they decided on 'Gully Heights', which carried an echo of Jungle Heights, the mother of all Neill's Kinabalu expeditions.

How long should they allow for the trip? Above all, they were determined that the expedition should not be curtailed by lack of time, as all previous ones had been. New's trip had taken six days. They were unlikely to cover the ground in less, especially as they had no intention of being forced out of the Gully, like New. The addition of four days for unexpected hold-ups brought the total to ten. Allow a week for travel, a week for shaking out before and after the expedition, and four days for climbing the mountain in the first place . . . and it became clear that the party would be away for a month. There would be a chance to see a bit of Sabah and renew acquaintance with Hong Kong: the prospect, especially in the middle of an English winter, looked rosier by the minute.

The date of the expedition to some extent chose itself. Planning would take six months; and this, together with the fact that the wettest months in East Malaysia are November to January, ruled out the rest of 1993. On Jungle Heights 1, which had taken place in March, the weather had been perfect, with no rain at all. For various reasons both officers wanted to be back in England by April. So the preferred start-date came down to late February or early March 1994.

As to the size of the party – both men favoured a maximum of ten, including themselves. On earlier expeditions they had found that ten was an ideal number – manageable, small enough to engender good team spirit, yet large enough to deal with an emergency. An even number made it simple for members to pair off and share essential equipment like tents and cooking stoves.

The aim was that all the British soldiers taking part should be from The Royal Logistic Corps, that being the organisers' parent corps, and preferably from Eastern District, where Neill himself was stationed. Soon, however, it became clear that there were not enough RLC soldiers in his immediate area to make this hope realistic, and he decided to open the expedition to RLC personnel serving elsewhere in the UK. Then, since Foster was a member of the Territorial Army, Neill threw it open to members of the TA as well.

From the start, one of his prime concerns was to keep costs down, as he did not want to land members, particularly the more junior ones, with huge bills. Since the main expense was going to be air fares, a great deal depended on whether or not he would be able to secure CNFP (Concessionary Non-Fare Paying) flights from London to Hong Kong and on to Brunei, where the British Army maintains a training base at Seria.

CNFP flights are the Royal Air Force equivalent of civilian standby tickets, with the added advantage that, for personnel on authorised adventurous training exercises, they are free. The theory is that if there are spare seats on an aircraft which is going to fly anyway, they might as well be usefully filled by servicemen who are considered to be on duty. The big drawback is that a team leader never knows until the last moment whether or not he is going to get the seats he wants, or a proportion of them, on the dates he wants. In the final minutes before take-off – even if a plane has begun taxiing – men may still be taken off a flight to make room for late arrivals with higher priority. The result is that the organisers of Service expeditions cannot rely on securing CNFP seats, and have to make alternative air bookings at normal market rates, usually requiring substantial deposits – for, according to the rules, nobody is allowed to cancel an expedition, once it has been authorised, simply because free flights are not available.

The full return fare to Hong Kong would be over £400 per head, and that from Hong Kong to Brunei the same again. (Brunei is 170 kilometres south-west of Kota Kinabalu, the capital of Sabah.) It was not reasonable to ask private soldiers or corporals to find such large amounts, especially if they were married, with houses and families of their own. The hope was always that these fares could be avoided, but there remained a chance that at least some members of the expedition would have to pay. The organisers did everything they could to raise funds from two main sources – the Army itself, and private sponsors.

In the event, by persuasive advocacy, Neill managed to wring a generous contribution of £2,300 from central funds. He also received £700 from the Regimental Headquarters of The Royal Logistic Corps, and £300 from the Ulysses Trust, which encourages the Territorial Army in worthwhile endeavours. This amounted to over £300 per head, enough to cover all expenses except air fares. At the same time, Foster set about trying to attract sponsorship from commercial firms, but with the economic recession at its nadir this proved impossible.

The largest number of men that Neill could hope to fly free

from the United Kingdom was ten, for a rule limited the number of CNFP seats to ten for any one party; but in any case, at an early stage he had decided to offer up to three places to soldiers based in Hong Kong. (Apart from other considerations, they would not need passages from London.) Since all members of the expedition were to be from The RLC, any Chinese who joined would automatically come from the former ordnance depot in Hong Kong, which by then was known as Supply Services. Having himself served in Hong Kong and taken Chinese soldiers on his earlier expeditions, Neill felt sure that Lieutenant-Colonel David Kerr, the Supply Services' Commanding Officer, would appreciate an offer of adventurous training for his soldiers.

Neill also saw that it would be natural and convenient for his new team, as it passed through Hong Kong, to base itself on his old unit, and sort itself out in the barracks there. Civilian flights from Hong Kong to Brunei and Sabah were frequent, and he hoped that even if the party could not obtain CNFP passages, they might be able to take advantage of some group fare scheme for the second leg of their journey.

Fortunately he was stationed in a headquarters which had all the usual office facilities – word-processors, fax machines, photocopiers – needed for wrestling with the red tape which inevitably obstructs such projects. He typed most letters himself, using a word-processor, but was lucky to have the help of a wonderfully efficient and experienced clerical officer, Sylvia Dicks.

His first task was to clear the trip with his own Commanding Officer, Colonel Ossie Hall, who thought it a splendid idea. A firm believer in letting people exercise their initiative, Hall had flown over Kinabalu in a helicopter years ago and had organised several expeditions of his own. As word leaked out that an exotic trip was in prospect, hopeful officers began to lurk in the corridor outside Neill's door – only to be told, in the friendliest terms, to think about planning some jaunt of their own, rather than trying to climb aboard a bandwagon that was already rolling.

On 6 September 1993 Neill wrote to Kerr, in Hong Kong, to say that he was assembling a team 'to attempt a descent of Low's

Gully on the northern flanks of Kinabalu': he asked if the expedition might stage at the depot on its way through to Brunei, and offered three places to Hong Kong soldiers. On 15 September Kerr replied, saying that 'accommodation should be no problem', and asking for more details, so that he could canvass volunteers.

Neill's next task was to put in the Adventurous Training Form A (ATFA), so that the process of obtaining political clearance could begin. When parties of servicemen travel abroad, the Ministry of Defence seeks clearance, via the Foreign and Commonwealth Office, from the countries they propose to visit, even if they are going entirely as civilians, without uniforms, weapons, radios or any other form of military equipment. Hence the mass of detail demanded in the ATFA. Having filled in such forms before, Neill knew that it was essential to give dates of travel, border-crossing points and other specific information; but he also remembered the value of including a more comprehensive description of the activity proposed, and an assessment of why it seemed worth while. Evidently his formula hit the right note, for the form whizzed its way up the system without blowbacks.

On the personal front, he took steps to update his own proficiency in abseiling and climbing techniques so that he would be confident, and also competent to instruct others, should the need arise. He realised that the boulders and rock walls of Low's Gully could well be slimy with water, algae and moss, and that flash floods might suddenly make it necessary for the party to use ropes in the wet. In other words, caving techniques might also come in useful. He therefore made contact with Major Tom Parker, Commandant of the School of Adventurous Training at Ripon, and in two visits to the school was brought up to date with the latest developments in the field. Parker agreed that although Neill himself held a mountain leadership certificate, he would do well to include a qualified rock-climbing instructor in his party.

The two men discussed at length the equipment that the party would need, the first essential being rope. Ordinary climbing rope, known as Kernmantel, is what its manufacturers call 'dynamic': it is designed to stretch by up to 10 per cent of its length in the case of a fall. By doing this, it absorbs some of the kinetic energy of a plummeting body and is less likely to break when it goes taut; also, the person falling is not nearly cut in two, since the strain on his body is taken up more gradually, as on that of a bungee-jumper. But since the expedition was interested principally in abseiling rather than in climbing, Parker suggested that non-dynamic ropes might be better. An abseiler does not want to bounce around as he goes down a cliff: his aim is to make his way down steadily and deliberately, putting as little strain on the rope as possible. Non-dynamic rope (usually Black Marlow in the Services) is generally used when abseiling from helicopters, and Neill put in for a supply of it, only to find that none was available at that moment, so he had to settle for Kernmantel instead.

Under Parker's direction, he then turned his attention to devices for descending, and first to the alloy figure-of-eight familiar to most soldiers – a piece of kit which works well as long as an abseiler keeps hold of his rope. Because there was a chance that members of the expedition could be hit by falling rocks, or, as Parker put it, of 'being attacked by venomous snakes and other creepy-crawlies as they abseiled past their lairs', he recommended taking some device which would lock if anyone let go of a rope, and in particular an item known as a Stop, made by the French firm Petzl. As for ascenders – devices which only slide up a rope, and dig in if pressure is applied in the opposite direction – here there was little choice. Conscious of the need to keep packs as light as possible, Neill opted for a version which dispensed with the luxury of a handle.

After much discussion of climbing harnesses, it was decided that besides a standard waist harness, everyone should also have a chest harness: an unconscious abseiler unbalanced by a heavy pack might turn upside-down on his rope and slide out of a normal waist harness. After a good look round the army depot at Thatcham, near Newbury, which held the loan-pool of adventurous training equipment, Neill did not find the sort of lightweight harnesses he was after, so he was thrown back on the

Petzl catalogue, which illustrated some excellent lightweight chest harnesses – and down they went on the list. Modern, lightweight climbing helmets were another essential, as were slings and karabiners, the latter generally known as 'crabs', very light, and made of modern alloys, yet able to withstand enormous breaking strains. Specialist climbing kit, such as chocks and bolts, would be chosen by the party's rock-climbing expert, once Neill had briefed him about likely hazards.

* * *

In November Neill signed on for a five-day refresher TR & A (top-rope and abseil) course on climbing techniques, based at the Adventurous Training School at Ripon, within easy reach of gritstone cliff faces in North Yorkshire. Then, thinking that it would be useful if his second-in-command did the course as well, he suggested to Foster that he too should apply for a place. Since most of the twenty-odd soldiers on the course were junior NCOs or young officers at the start of their climbing careers, they tended to look on the two older officers as some sort of novelty. Nikki Charlton, their competent sergeant-instructor, made it clear that she would love to join the Kinabalu party, but thought it unlikely that she would be able to get time off – and in any case, she was a member not of The Royal Logistic Corps, but of the Army Physical Training Corps. Besides, Neill was aiming for an all-male expedition, if only to make practical details like tent-sharing easier.

The trainees were soon swinging on the ends of ropes over spectacular drops, fast remembering what they thought they had forgotten. All week the temperature hovered near zero, the wind howled over the Brimham Rocks and the Cow and Calf rocks on Ilkley Moor, and rain constantly found its way inside waterproofs. In the evening Neill and Foster practised knots and discussed the expedition. One afternoon, as they were preparing to abseil from a high point overlooking Ilkley, gravity suddenly compelled Foster to take a line different from the one he had been fancying: the rope appeared to be dragging him to his right.

He lost his footing and swung sideways a few feet below the top of the crag, before coming to a stop by a large protruding rock. Neill, who had been supervising the safety rope, was also jerked off his feet, right to the edge of the cliff, before he too was halted by his own belay. Nicki was filming with Foster's video camera and recorded the whole incident on tape, including her own shriek of alarm as she saw her students – and her career as a rock-climbing instructor – fast disappearing over the edge.

One 25-year-old lance corporal on the course showed particular interest in the proposed expedition. A good-humoured redhead from the north-east, Steve Page was a member of The RLC Mobile Display Team, part of the recruiting organisation. He was short, stocky and strong, if slightly overweight, and he had joined the course so that he could become qualified to throw would-be recruits off the tops of abseil scaffolding towers at recruiting stands around the country. Neill did not immediately promise him a place, because Page was not certain whether or not he would be available; but Neill asked him to stand by, and Page said that he would see if he could take time off in February.

On 15 November Neill wrote to the Director of National Parks in Sabah, saying that he was hoping to bring out a party of ten people in the last week of February 1994, 'not only to climb Mt. Kinabalu but also to explore the summit area and Low's Gully'. He enquired about the procedure for obtaining permits to climb the mountain, and asked whether it was possible to hire guides or porters. This letter – he discovered later – reached its destination, but was never answered.

Meanwhile, he had made contact with his former colleague from Hong Kong days, Paul Hughes, who had been his second-in-command on Jungle Heights 1, the original expedition to Kinabalu. By then Hughes had left the Regular Army and was administering a Territorial Army unit on the outskirts of his native Plymouth, and so in effect was a serving member of the TA in the south-west. When Neill telephoned and offered him a place, he declined, jokingly recalling that he had no head for heights, but promised to look around not only his own unit, 383 Command Petroleum Troop, but also 'the Squadron' for suitable recruits. By 'the Squadron' he meant the Ordnance Squadron of the Commando Logistic Regiment, a regular unit which provided 3 Commando Brigade with all its logistic requirements, and in which he and Neill had served together during the 1970s. There he soon identified a man who he thought would be suitable.

This soldier was Lance Corporal Richard Mayfield, aged 25 and married, with two young children, a military storeman by trade, but also a qualified Joint Services Rock-Climbing Instructor, described by Hughes as 'mustard keen' on all forms of rock work. A second candidate produced by Hughes, from his own unit, was Sergeant Bob Mann, who worked as a sprayer in the dockyard, and put in a lot of time with the Territorial Army: in his thirties, he was also married with a young son, and keen on outdoor pursuits. Neill, delighted to have found two volunteers so quickly, especially men so reliably recommended, agreed to take them on, provided that they proved suitable during a training weekend he was planning to hold on Dartmoor.

Up in the north-east he telephoned a dozen small RLC units with whom he had direct connections, offering to send details of the expedition if any soldiers were interested. These overtures produced only one more recruit: 26-six-year-old Lance Corporal Peter Shearer, from a Royal Engineers regiment stationed in Cambridgeshire. When the offer arrived, he was away on a long weekend in the Scottish hills – in itself a good sign – but as soon as he returned he volunteered enthusiastically and sent Neill a mass of photocopied pages from his mountain log-book.

This meant that Neill had four possible starters. Foster had identified another – Martin Meighan, a senior warrant officer based in Oxfordshire who was just coming to the end of his 22-year army career. So they had five, plus the two officers. If three Hong Kong soldiers were forthcoming, as he hoped, the party was already up to strength.

On 19 November Neill sent out his first sitrep (situation report) to potential starters. This confirmed that he had received military clearance from the Ministry of Defence ('a big hurdle, in view of relations with Malaysia'), and that details of the exercise had been sent to Brunei and Kuala Lumpur for political clearance.

Under the heading 'Finance' he reminded everyone that individuals were required to contribute a minimum of one-third of the expedition's costs. After setting out various theoretical sums, he continued:

You do not need the brains of an economist to realise that we will need to put in more than the minimum of £250 that I have used for planning purposes. Personally, I am planning on putting £400 into expedition funds, and will rely on credit cards for horrors. I recommend you do the same. Every individual MUST have his own credit card, just in case, for flights: we must have the capability of moving as individuals. Thirty paid days in Hong Kong and Sabah for about £400 has to be a bargain – let alone the challenge of the Gully!

Under 'Medical' he wrote:

Take your own first aid seriously, as the Gully has plenty of potential for injuries, and Sabah doesn't have a mountain rescue service. We will have to rely on self-help. We are covered by the Army for hospitals etc . . . Dentist: get sorted out now, as Sabah dentists only use pliers!

Under 'Briefing' he wrote that he wished to meet all members, 'for obvious reasons', and to have a training day on the ropes. He asked everyone to stand by for a weekend at Plymouth, with a training session 'probably on the Dewerstone on Dartmoor'. In a paragraph on equipment he reminded members that the temperature in Sabah would probably range from zero Celsius on the summit of the mountain to over 30 degrees (with very high humidity) at sea level. He urged everyone to go on the TR & A course which he and Foster had just attended.

* * *

The dates for the training weekend were set as 17 and 18 December. Beforehand, Neill telephoned Mayfield, introduced himself, and explained that he wanted to use the occasion to make sure that all the volunteers were as proficient at climbing and abseiling as they had claimed. The corporal was full of enthusiasm, and offered to organise all the equipment required. A day or two later he rang back and confirmed that he thought the Dewerstone, a granite crag overlooking the River Plym, would be as good a spot as any, especially as it was close to Bickleigh Viaduct, a remnant of the old Great Western Railway line, which offered the chance of an impressive 140-foot free abseil.

The UK members of the expedition met on Friday evening, except for Shearer, who was on unavoidable duty, and Meighan, who had suddenly been offered a job interview. Their rendezvous was the TA Centre in Plymouth, where Paul Hughes had put two classrooms at their disposal and produced camp-beds. Mayfield had laid out the climbing kit for the next day: Neill was pleased and impressed to see that nothing had been forgotten. He was becoming overburdened by administrative details, and found it a relief to have something done for him with complete efficiency. Soon the men were exclaiming over the slides of Kinabalu which Neill had brought with him, and as they got their first glimpses of the mountain, enthusiasm for the venture mounted rapidly. A TA cook prepared a meal for the group, and later in the evening, after a long briefing, they piled into a minibus and drove into Plymouth, where they had a second supper.

The Dartmoor weekend was the first occasion on which Neill and Foster had seen most of their recruits, and it gave them a chance to assess abilities at first hand. They also wanted to judge levels of commitment: the chances were that every member might have to contribute a good deal of money.

Richard Mayfield was dark-haired, tall, slim and well proportioned, with broad shoulders – the classic rock-climbing build. At the age of twenty-five, he was proud of his Commando background, and openly confident in his own rock-climbing ability. He was obviously very fit. Neill was slightly surprised that he was still a lance-corporal, but thought he looked very promising.

Also from Plymouth came Sergeant Bob Mann, who knew Mayfield from living in the same area. Aged thirty-seven, he was half-way between the younger lads and the two leaders; mentally he was more in tune with the older men. A humorous character, with a broad Devon accent, he was thin, dark, wiry and not very tall – probably the lightest member of the group. He had never done any adventurous training on the scale proposed, but because he had passed the Commando course and had seen service in Norway, Neill knew that he would be familiar with rope-work. Mann was full of enthusiasm, and always ready with a joke; he looked like a good man to have along.

The third man new to Neill was Corporal Hugh Brittan, aged twenty-four, who came from the same unit as Page, and had been brought along by him. As the eleventh recruit, he was only a potential member of the team, being first reserve. Physically, he was the most impressive member of the party: good-looking, tall, broad in the shoulders, he had an air of considerable self-assurance. He was also quick-witted, with a dry sense of humour. Neill saw that he was a well-organised man: he had a mobile telephone with which to keep in touch with his girlfriend(s) and maintain the momentum of his social life.

Within the military environment of the United Kingdom, relationships between the leader of the expedition and his men were still formal. The soldiers showed a certain deference in the presence of a colonel whom they had only just met, and addressed Neill as 'Sir' or 'Boss'. Foster, however, decided to break the ice, and invited them to call him by his first name – a common practice in adventurous training circles.

In the morning they drove out to Bickleigh Viaduct, which seemed to be in excellent shape, considering that it was nearly a hundred years old, and soon they were swinging beneath its tall brick arches. Mann confessed that he was no lover of heights, but that did not stop him committing himself to the abseil and putting his faith in a 10mm-thick nylon rope and an alloy descender. Rain began to fall, but no one was deterred. Mayfield revised everyone in the technique of ascending the ropes using prussik loops and mechanical jamming devices known as Shunts, which he had decided would be more suitable than jumars: less could go wrong with these, and they would be easier for the Hong Kong soldiers to master.*

Soon the team was practising on the nearby 180-foot face of the Dewerstone – and because the mist was down, they could hear, but not see, the River Plym roaring in spate below them. The rock was granite – the same as on Kinabalu – and glistened with water, so conditions were admirably realistic.

Because one rope became wedged in a crack near the top of the crag, and took some time to free, they returned to their minibus later than planned, as the winter dusk was falling. The purpose of the day had been achieved: Mayfield and the two officers were satisfied that everyone was competent on the ropes. Having found a pub, they settled into the bar, and Neill described his plans for the expedition.

He had already realised that he, Foster, Meighan and probably the Hong Kong soldiers would not be able to keep up with young men as fit as Mayfield and Brittan, who were twenty or thirty years younger than the officers. He also saw that to make the fittest travel at the pace of the slowest would be a sure remedy for frustration, and that the ebullient energy of the young men – already evident from their training session – would have to be harnessed for the good of the expedition as a whole.

Neill outlined his idea of how the expedition would operate. Because the group was going to be one of mixed abilities, and the young British NCOs were likely to be fitter and more experienced than the Hong Kong soldiers, the team would work in two halves on the harder phases of the descent. The British, taking advantage of Mayfield's expertise, would set up ropes on difficult sections, while he and Foster would concentrate on bringing the Hong Kong soldiers down. Every now and then the recce party would report back, and the expedition would go on down in one unit until another reconnaissance became necessary.

* One advantage of shunts is that they are more versatile than jumars, in that they can be used to ascend double as well as single ropes. Also, there is no risk of them damaging the rope, whereas jumars have teeth which can fray the rope's mantle, or outer covering. If anyone were to be hit by a falling rock in the middle of an abseil, the shunt would lock his chest harness and prevent him turning turtle.

Neill called this his 'elastic band' principle: the younger members of the expedition would have plenty of chance to use their initiative, but he would remain in control and dictate the overall pace of progress. He told the NCOs that he had no intention of going down the Gully first: that was likely to be their job. He and Foster would concentrate on the Chinese soldiers; whenever necessary, he would lead the second, slower group, and Foster, as second-in-command, would probably bring up the rear. In summary, he said that it would be a single expedition, but everyone would have plenty of flexibility.

This plan – which was only tentative at that stage – went down extremely well with the NCOs. They saw that they would have a chance to get on with the job in hand, and be able to make decisions of their own – something increasingly rare, for soldiers of their rank, in the modern Army. In their eyes, this was an exceptional opportunity.

Discussion moved on to details of equipment. Head-torches were added to the list, and Mayfield undertook to identify the most suitable make of rucksack. They then talked about what would happen if anyone got hurt. Neill confirmed that there was no rescue service in the Kinabalu National Park, so that the party would have to be self-sufficient, and, as on previous expeditions to Sabah, rely on safety in numbers. If it proved impossible to carry an injured man out, two or three would stay with him while others went for help. They did not consider the possibility of the entire party becoming stuck in the Gully: from New's experience, they knew that there was at least one way out of the ravine.

Later, Neill could not remember whether or not they discussed the possibility of taking flares. Foster believes they did, but the idea was quickly dropped. For one thing, the sides of the Gully were so high that no ordinary flare would clear them; and since there was no human habitation in sight of the ravine, there would be nobody to see distress signals. For another, Neill knew that flares, like gas canisters, would be banned from commercial aircraft. But the group certainly did discuss radios. One strong objection to them was their weight and bulk, and that of extra batteries. For a radio network to be effective, they would have to leave a party on top of the mountain to act as a base station, and also to place manned relays all down the Gully – something that would be feasible for a full-scale Joint Services expedition, but not for a small group. Another problem was that the Malaysian authorities might well object to the importation of military equipment, and ban its entry.

What really finished the idea of radios, however, was the fact that they had signally failed to work on a previous Jungle Heights expedition. Even though the party had managed to import them, and had set up a station in Easy Valley at the head of the Gully, they had not been able to make contact with the rest of the expedition coming towards them up the Penataran river. Had they managed to establish a direct line of sight, the radios might have worked; as it was, they were defeated by the tremendous granite walls of the mountain, and by the fact that the Gully turns a sharp corner just at its steepest point.

Another idea was that members of the expedition should buy small walkie-talkie sets when they passed through Hong Kong. These might have been invaluable for keeping the two groups in contact with each other, but revised travel schedules cut out any time for shopping in the Colony, so no radios were bought there. Nor could Neill and Foster find anything suitable in Kota Kinabalu.

Having read the account of New's descent (which Neill had sent them), and talked about conditions in the Gully, team members were asked for their ideas on what should be taken. Mayfield undertook to specify all the technical climbing equipment. Everyone sat around with notebooks, and Neill asked for volunteers to assume various responsibilities, his aim being partly to integrate the members into the expedition, and partly to remove some of the administrative load from his own shoulders.

All in all, he thought that he had the makings of a first-class team, and he drove back to York feeling pleased. Having completed the initial paperwork, all he needed was some good men, and his team was coming together nicely. The best feature so far was that he had found a highly competent JSRCI: so pleased was he, in fact, that he wrote a note of gratitude to Paul Hughes, who had produced Mayfield for him.

On previous expeditions he had always brought members together over a number of months, so that he could get to know them, and they him, and he could gauge everyone's strengths and weaknesses. This time, however, because the individuals were all mature NCOs with a fair bit of experience, including adventurous training, he was not worried by the fact that they would be unable to train together as a team. With people coming from all over the country, this was a luxury he would have to forego. Yet they all seemed to get on well with each other. He knew that the two men missing – Shearer, whom he had met already, and Martin Meighan, whom Foster had recruited – would slot in easily enough. He was also confident that the Hong Kong lads would fit in, as they had on previous expeditions, even though they would probably prefer to stick together because of language difficulties, their preference for different rations, and their ability to draw strength from each other. Experience had shown him that they performed much better working as a group than as individuals.

Apart from making travel arrangements, his priorities now were to order the equipment and rations. Soon after Christmas he summoned the team for a second training weekend, this time in Yorkshire. By now Meighan had dropped out, for personal reasons, but had agreed to continue acting as the expedition's quartermaster, and to look after the stores at his base in Bicester. This allowed Neill to offer a firm place to Brittan, who accepted, giving him seven starters from the United Kingdom – exactly the number he wanted. (Brittan also took his advice, and enrolled on a TR & A course in Wales.)

On 16 January Foster wrote to Robert New in Sabah, confirming that the expedition hoped to arrive in Kota Kinabalu on about 20 February, and inviting him to join the party. 'We would be very pleased if you were able to come with us,' wrote Foster. 'I know you seemed reluctant about another attempt, but this expedition has sufficient equipment, knowledge and provisions to succeed.' He also asked New to mark an enclosed map with the route by which he escaped from the Gully, and said that he and Neill hoped to call on him as they passed through Kota Kinabalu on their way to the mountain.

On the evening of Friday 28 January the team assembled at the School of Adventurous Training in Ripon, where Tom Parker had offered them accommodation. They were minus Foster, who by then was working as a ski instructor in Germany. Meighan had drawn out the necessary kit; Mann and Mayfield were to bring up rations from Plymouth, where they had had access to high-calorie food designed for the Arctic. They were then to call in at Bicester on their way, to collect the equipment from Meighan, and bring it up to Yorkshire. The plan was that on the Friday evening all the kit would be issued to individuals and the rations sorted; then on Saturday they would drive out into the Yorkshire Dales to Malham Cove, which has the highest limestone cliffs in England. With its 300-foot faces, it would give them some of the feel of the huge drops they were likely to encounter in Low's Gully.

The party from Plymouth arrived late, delayed by rain and heavy traffic. There was no time that evening for the issue of equipment and sorting of rations, which would take two or three hours; that had to be postponed until next morning.

On Saturday the climbing equipment was broken down into individual kits: ten brand-new, turquoise, top-of-the-range rucksacks with 100-litre capacity, ten dive-sacks, bright red with a yellow band round the top, waterproof but quite heavy because of their high rubber content; ten 50-metre ropes, forty karabiners and so on. Everything was laid out on the floor of a draughty Nissen hut, divided up and labelled with names: Foster, Mann, Hong Kong 1, Hong Kong 2, and so on. The aim was to send as much as possible in bulk by air freight, principally the ropes, which weighed about five kilos apiece, and could, if they went astray, be replaced at the last moment. With them went the equipment for the Hong Kong soldiers. The multicoloured nylon chest harnesses – special, lightweight ones for the slimmer members, and ordinary English ones for Neill and Foster, who could not fit into the slim-fitting models made in Italy – went in individuals' packs. Key smaller items such as prussik loops and

45

jumars, which could not be replaced so easily, also remained with individuals. The three rucksacks for the Hong Kong soldiers, together with all the ropes, went back into boxes with the rations, for direct shipment to Hong Kong. Neill, sorting Foster's kit, found that it took a surprisingly long time to select rations and pack for someone who was not there – as did the corporals who were acting for the Chinese.

With the rations, much personal selection was involved. They could choose from Arctic packs, lightweight, dehydrated packs, and normal packs – in many respects the most appetising – which are heated by boiling in a bag. The standard army ration, designed and packaged to be adequate for one man for one day, came in a box about nine inches square; but most people reckoned that this contained more than they needed. In any case, each man preferred to make up his own selection, stripping the packs down, leaving out what he did not care for, and adding other items from here and there to make up individual sets of food for ten days. Lightness was a prime consideration. The Arctic packs contained the highest food value – nearly 4,500 calories a day – but to save weight some people preferred to substitute lighter freeze-dried rations which they had bought from outdoor shops.

At this stage Neill paired off the members of the expedition so that they could cook in twos, saving gas, and share some essential items of kit such as tents and cookers. Mann and Mayfield, who were both from Plymouth, were one obvious pair. Page and Brittan, from the same unit, were another, as were Neill and Foster. That left Shearer, whom Neill assigned to accompany one of the Hong Kong lads. (The other two would also form a pair.) Neill assumed that the party would not sleep in tents on the mountain or in the Gully, because the terrain was so rough that pitching them would be impossible; but it seemed likely that they would need to camp out at some point, certainly after the expedition proper, so they took very lightweight tents along.

When all the rations were sorted and repacked, they weighed about a kilogram a day for each pair, or just over one pound a head. They were packed into green bags, labelled with the names

46

of the owners, and then re-stowed in boxes for air dispatch. (These bags – supplied to the Navy for use in the dockyard at Plymouth, and brought along by Mann – were of various sizes, but extremely strong and completely waterproof.)

By the time everything had been sorted it was almost midday, and barely four hours of winter daylight were left. The weather was bitterly cold, and a ferocious wind was blowing: Neill decided that in such unpleasant conditions, and with the limited time available, it would be pointless to drive two hours to Malham Cove, and then perhaps not even be able to go out on to the cliffs. Better, he reckoned, to practise on the climbing wall in the school – and this is what they did.

Shearer, who had missed the weekend in Devon, was put through his paces by Mayfield and found proficient. Slim, younger-looking than the rest, not as strong as Mayfield or Page, he spoke with a broad Scots accent and bubbled with enthusiasm. Being a bachelor, and serving with a not particularly warlike unit, he chose to spend frequent weekends in the hills, because he loved trekking, and being out in wild country. Now he was thrilled at the prospect of a trip to such a splendid and faraway mountain. Neill saw him as 'a good, confident sort', and asked him to work out what they should take in the way of first-aid supplies. A further advantage was that Shearer held a certificate as JSMEL (Joint Services Mountain Expedition Leader), a qualification similar to Neill's mountain leadership certificate, and this strengthened the team's credentials.

* * *

More delicate than these physical preparations was the business of obtaining political clearance. Relations between Great Britain and Malaysia were difficult anyway, and the Malaysian government was particularly sensitive about allowing official visitors – that is, anyone except ordinary tourists – into Sabah, apparently because of recent scandals over logging operations. Destruction of the rain forest was having a disastrous effect on indigenous tribes, and local politicians had been accused of taking rake-offs from the sale of timber.

47

In September 1993 Neill had discovered that the Foreign and Commonwealth Office was unable to grant clearance for the expedition, and on a copy of the message bearing this bad news, which he forwarded to Foster, he wrote 'Damn!' After all the work he had already put in, this was a heavy blow – and he felt especially aggrieved when some desk-bound officer in London, with no conception of the effort needed to carve out and plan an expedition of this kind, glibly said, 'Oh well – find something else to do.'

Neill persevered in the hope that things would change – and in the end they did. Later in the year the FCO agreed to accept his application, and instructed him to send it to the military attaché at the British High Commission in Kuala Lumpur for processing by the Malaysian authorities. Weeks passed; then a signal came in from Malaysia asking for the nominal roll of expedition members, which he immediately sent; but final clearance did not arrive until the very day that Neill left England, and he went off without actually setting eyes on it.

As part of his research he made contact with an RAF unit which specialised in aerial photography, and obtained shots not only of Kinabalu, but also of the Penataran, and of the Gully, taken from a great height. The resolution was only moderate, and the Gully itself lay deep in shadow, but the photographs showed ridges and the general lie of the land, and looked as if they might be valuable should the expedition have to break out through the jungle. He also visited the British Library in London to collect details of the fauna the expedition might encounter, and of first-aid preparations to deal with snake bite. By then, like all the members of his team, he had been heavily vaccinated – for typhoid, tetanus, polio, tuberculosis, yellow fever, hepatitis A, Japanese encephalitis and cholera. He had also equipped himself with stocks of Paludrine and Nivaquine tablets, the preventatives against malaria.

The quest for free flights proved difficult and time-consuming, but Neill had the advantage of being able to use a computer in his headquarters. Using this he could tap into the Services' Booking Centre data bank, which showed the availability of flights around the world, and in particular those on British Airways, which held the contract to provide the Armed Forces with a certain number of seats every day to Hong Kong. In due course he saw that the most promising date was 15 February, which was showing a lot of spare seats. He therefore decided the the party would fly that evening.

With prospects looking good, his memoranda to the team took on a jaunty note. On 7 February he sent out a message giving details of the flight, and went on:

Of the 127 species of snakes in Malaysia, only 16 of the land species are venomous, of which only five are fatal to man. All 23 of the sea snakes are venomous, so watch it.

Members were instructed to check in at Heathrow Terminal Four by 1925 hours on Tuesday 15 February. Neill wrote that he would meet them at the airport, and cautioned them to remember their malaria tablets. 'Civilised dress,' he added. 'No jeans.'

Chapter 5

Hiccups in Transit

After more than twenty years' marriage Fiona Neill had developed a fairly wry attitude towards her husband's frequent need to find new challenges. As she remarked, 'A challenge is not something which I myself would actively go in search of.' Army life seemed 'to dish out challenges with astonishing generosity'; and now, having endured months of preparation, she felt acutely depressed when she dropped Robert off in a lay-by on the morning of 15 February 1994, to pick up a lift on his way to Colchester and thence, in the evening, to Heathrow.

The weather was icy, and light snow was falling – but it was not the cold that troubled her most. Her sixth sense, which never failed, told her that he would be away for much longer than he planned. For reasons she could not explain, she was full of foreboding: she also resented the fact that, as usual, he had made his arrangements without seeking her approval, and now was leaving her on her own as the worst of the winter set in.

The best-laid plans. . . At the last minute Neill had got wind of the fact that onward CNFP seats from Hong Kong to Brunei might possibly be available on the evening of the 16th, within a couple of hours of their arrival in the colony. Brunei lay 170 kilometres short of their final destination, Kota Kinabalu, but the chance of free flights was too good to miss. He had therefore asked Foster to leave London twenty-four hours early, so that he could meet the three Hong Kong soldiers and have them ready, in case the onward seats became available. If they could all catch the Brunei flight, it would mean scrapping plans for the three-day stop-over in Hong Kong; but it would land them in their target area with three days in hand, and, of equal importance, with £2,000 saved.

So Foster had arrived at Heathrow on the evening of 14

February. By good fortune he had secured the last seat on the aircraft, when another passenger failed to show, with the result that he travelled free. Reaching Hong Kong at 1710 local time on the 15th, he was met at the airport by a sergeant from the Supply Services depot, who drove him to the officers' mess of his old unit in Blackdown Barracks, close to the airport. But there a nasty surprise greeted him. Major Nigel Ramsden, second-in-command of Supply Services, showed him a fax message from Neill saying that because of a muddle over freight, all the expedition's rations and equipment had missed the vital aircraft. Would he, Foster, please do all he could to replace everything that had gone astray?

In England an operation that should have been perfectly straightforward had turned into a drama of its own. Meighan had had to go through all the expedition's kit and repack it, for Neill had forgotten to remind everyone to take the matches out of their rations, as no combustible material was allowed in unaccompanied baggage. With the matches removed, Meighan had arranged for the heavy equipment and rations to be sent out to Hong Kong as air freight, to await the party's arrival at the Supply Services depot. For the members of the party, it was a major boost to be rid of their heavy gear.

At his depot in Oxfordshire Meighan delivered the consignment to the Traffic branch, which arranges the dispatch of all the stores sent out daily to dozens of service addresses. Traffic would arrange for the expedition's kit to be forwarded to the RAF station which was flying freight to Hong Kong. Critical to the whole operation was a panel on the dispatch form which gave the date by which the consignment was needed at the far end. This was 15 February. Another panel gave the call-forward date, to be inserted by Traffic once the RAF knew what flights were available: as soon as the details were known, Traffic would send the boxes wherever the RAF directed. All this was standard operating procedure, and should have caused no problem.

In fact it caused Neill to lose his cool. He had done all the planning for the expedition on top of his normal job, and the pressure had been intense. Some weeks earlier he had been asked to carry out an inspection in Colchester on 15 February, which would not end until about 1600 on the very evening the main party was due to fly. Awkward as this was, he could not avoid it, and he was in the middle of the inspection when he received an urgent message to telephone the RAF. Leaving the rest of his team to carry on, he made the call – only to hear an RAF dispatch clerk asking why the expedition's kit had not been delivered to the airfield. It was already too late to catch that day's flight, and the next was towards the end of the week.

In a flash Neill saw all his plans going, as he put it, 'to a ball of chalk'. The party would fly that night and arrive in Hong Kong with no ropes, no personal kit for the Chinese soldiers, and no rations. They would have to hang around in Hong Kong, unable to train for lack of equipment, and would miss the onward connection to Brunei. Probably they would have to pay their own fares on the second leg of the journey, and a huge amount of excess baggage. Several of their precious days would be lost. . . .

Over the telephone Neill tore strips off anyone and everyone who might have been responsible for the error. The officer in charge at Traffic, with hundreds of other consignments on his hands, had no special knowledge of the expedition's kit. Half an hour later, it transpired that human error was to blame: some unspeakable storeman had read the 'delivery required' date as the 'call-forward' date.

Resisting the urge to leap into his staff car, drive like the wind and throttle the fellow, Neill dispensed some forceful criticism, followed by an appeal to Traffic to sort things out. The only solution he could see – a long shot – was to have the kit accepted as freight on the British Airways flight which they themselves were taking – and this Traffic somehow managed to arrange. Mightily relieved, Neill thanked the officer in charge and dashed off another fax to Foster, saying that everything was in order after all, and standing him down from the instruction to assemble a second batch of kit in Hong Kong. This message he left with the Commanding Officer of the unit he was visiting, who promised to dispatch it.

Unfortunately, the fax never reached its intended recipient. To re-equip the entire expedition in twenty-four hours was a formidable task; but thanks to his own tireless ingenuity, and the outstanding generosity of all concerned, Foster managed it. Everybody with whom he made contact went out of their way to help him, and during the course of 15 February – a frantic day for him – he managed to beg, borrow or otherwise acquire a complete array of duplicate equipment and rations – not all of it ideal, but adequate.

In England, having completed his army business with a couple of job-appraisal interviews, Neill changed out of uniform in the CO's office, casting off the mantle of staff officer and switching to travel mode. Then he set off through the freezing dusk for Heathrow, driven by Bob McCartney, a major who had been serving in his branch and was on the point of retiring. By then everything seemed to point to Borneo: Bob had flown helicopters there during Confrontation, and was familiar with Jesselton, the old colonial name for Kota Kinabalu: he had even flown in the area of Mount Kinabalu, and reminisced happily about his time in the Far East.

By the time they reached the airport, light snow was falling. Neill was the first of his party to arrive, and used the time to check that all was well with their reservations. Finding everything in order, he relaxed, and presently was delighted to see Mann and Mayfield appear, raring to go, Mann with his video equipment packed into a special yellow case – waterproof, impact-proof and lined with foam padding – which Neill had obtained for him. Soon the other three arrived, clutching their passports and easily identified by their turquoise packs. Then a truck drew up outside, delivering the heavy kit from Bicester: Neill's relief at seeing it knew no bounds, and in a few minutes everything had been safely checked in.

When Neill got confirmation from the Movements NCO that Foster had obtained a CNFP flight the night before, and had been given the last seat on the aircraft, he felt that luck was right behind them, and they moved to the bar for a toast to their departure. Since they had time for only one round, Neill said, 'Right, lads: drinks on me, to mark the start of the expedition.'

As they drank to the forthcoming adventures, they noticed an advertisement for low-alcohol beer hanging over their table. 'How low can you go?' it asked. 'To the Gully!' they cried, deciding immediately to make 'How low can you go?' the expedition slogan – and liberated a copy of the advertisement from a slightly bemused barman.

Neill was keen to split up the large amount of cash that he was carrying, so he divided it into ten and handed out shares. In spite of his instructions, some of the corporals had not got round to equipping themselves with credit cards, so he was glad he had plenty of cash. Because the girl in the currency exchange had never heard of Brunei, Neill abandoned plans for buying Brunei dollars, and got some Hong Kong dollars instead. Then came the usual rush to board: the party was last on to the plane, but there followed the inevitable hanging around as the aircraft waited for a place in the take-off queue – and at last they were away, leaving the snow and ice of the English winter far below.

* * *

Emerging tired and creased at Hong Kong airport fourteen hours later, Neill was greeted by two messages. The first gave him excellent news: that, courtesy of the Services Booking Centre in London, and helped by a little pressure from Foster, they had been awarded ten CNFP seats to Brunei. The men were delighted and at once began speculating as to how they might spend the money thus saved: they were each some £200 better off – a gain of £2,000 for the expedition as a whole. The snag was that the flight left in two hours' time. Far from having a couple of days to shake down and do some training in Hong Kong, the party could not even leave the transit area of the airport.

The second message asked Neill to put in an immediate call to Foster. It was then that Neill discovered that Foster had already booked a whole second issue of kit on to the flight for Brunei. The expedition now had twice as much kit as it needed; but nobody was in a mood to complain, and Neill felt confident that they could sort everything out once they reached their destination.

Airport bureaucracy prevented the two halves of the expedition uniting on the ground. The party from London, trapped in the transit area, waited interminably for the agent from Royal Brunei Airlines to produce their tickets. At the last moment they had to run for the coach which took them on to the waiting Boeing, known to soldiers in Hong Kong as 'The Flying Banana', from its violent yellow livery. It was not until everyone was airborne that Neill had a chance to meet his three Chinese recruits.

All came from the Hong Kong Military Service Corps (HKMSC), but wore RLC cap-badges, and had been working as regimental police at the Supply Services depot. Lance Corporal Cheung Yiu Keung, thirty-two, and the only married man of the three, struck him as fit-looking and competent: he was about 5 feet 8 inches tall, well built and compact – stocky, almost – and had clearly been in the Army for some time. Private Lam Wai Ki was twenty-seven, of typical Cantonese appearance, being tall and slim, and wearing glasses. He was quietly mannered, and appeared thoughtful; Neill soon saw he was a sensitive fellow, acutely aware of the people around him, and of what they thought about him. The third soldier was Private Chow Wai Keung, aged twenty-four, and the most Chinese-looking: of medium height, shorter than Lam and rather slight, he too wore glasses, with circular wire rims, and had a distinctive, almost jarring voice. Neill noticed that he was on the thin side.

They all spoke limited English, which, on reflection, Neill decided was no worse than that of the Hong Kong soldiers he had taken on earlier expeditions. He himself still retained a little Cantonese from his posting in the Far East – and as time went on he realised that the three understood far more than they let on: certainly they could understand English much better than they could speak it.

The flight to Brunei was dry, and the food was dreary, but the British NCOs were entranced by the beautiful air hostesses in their long, sari-like dresses. The travellers got their first glimpse of Borneo a few minutes before landing. Flying due south from Hong Kong, they came in with Kinabalu somewhere out to their left; but the mountain held its secrets. When Neill saw moonlight reflected off the surf below, he immediately thought of the time he had stepped on the stingray, on one of those selfsame beaches. Where the surf stopped a scatter of lights twinkled in a belt along the shore, but further inland inky darkness prevailed.

As the aircraft's doors opened, the damp, cloying heat of the tropical night flooded in to swamp the passengers. The British party had hoped to leave their cold-weather clothes in Hong Kong; but their rapid transit had frustrated that plan, and Neill was still carrying his waxed jacket, which was fine for Yorkshire, but not entirely suitable for Brunei. They were soon sweating profusely.

The huge airport building, lined with marble, left no doubt as to the country's wealth. Neill deliberately went through the immigration control last – just as well; for an official was suspicious of the Chinese. He knew all about Gurkhas; but how did a British Army party, travelling in civilian clothes, come to have these men from Hong Kong in its ranks? After a few difficult minutes Neill managed to convince him that they were all genuine tourists on their way to Mount Kinabalu – but the officials, who were about to pack up for the night, would not stamp their passports. Cheung was worried, because he thought they might have trouble leaving Brunei in a couple of days' time – as indeed they did – and the exchanges reinforced Neill's belief that the countries on the edge of the South China Sea regard all Chinese as potential illegal immigrants.

Already it was 2300 local time, and the next problem was to find accommodation for the night. After a few telephone calls Foster established that there was only one real possibility, the Brunei Hotel in Bandar Seri Begawan, the capital, commonly known as BSB. A friendly young British captain, who had come to the airport to meet some Gurkhas, gave the party a lift in his coach: and in response to a request which Foster had made from the UK, he had brought them some extra ropes from Seria. In twenty minutes they were piling into the hotel, where they tried in vain to haggle over rates. Attempts to bargain led to confusion, but they settled for the business rate of £25 per man.

They were sharing, two or three to a room, but the rooms were air-conditioned, cool and clean, with showers that worked. Exhausted by travel and time changes, they collapsed gratefully into bed.

'What a start!' thought Neill before he fell asleep. Only twenty hours after leaving London, his whole party had reached its target area with no expense. Admittedly they had lost their days in Hong Kong; they had had to go without a few last-minute things like mosquito nets and lightweight sleeping bags, which they would have bought in the Colony; and Neill had had no chance to vet the Chinese. Nor had he been able to make detailed arrangements about the party's return to and through Hong Kong. But now he had time in hand, and he could put the new recruits through their paces in the best possible place – on Mount Kinabalu itself.

* * *

Late the next morning they moved out into cheaper accommodation – the youth hostel in Bandar – and because of the stifling heat they hired a taxi to transport their kit. The hostel had been well fitted out, with expensive tiling, and must have been very smart when new; but, as with so many buildings in the Far East, it had never been maintained, and now was falling apart, with none of the plumbing in working order. Geckos sped about the walls, usefully gobbling up mosquitoes.

The team was assigned cabins with double bunks, and spent most of the day sorting their kit, as well as going on forays into town. Now they went into expedition mode, filling their packs with everything they wanted for the mountain, stripping out the personal possessions they would not need, and repacking the duplicate equipment for return to Hong Kong. The most important task was to sort out the rations for the Chinese soldiers: the food brought from England had been supplemented by the stores Foster had rounded up in Hong Kong, and a selection now had to be made. Neill detailed three of the corporals to see that each of the Hong Kong men had ten days'

57

rations in his pack. At the end of the day some young back-packers appeared at the hostel: rather than throw the spare food away, Neill offered it to them, and they accepted it gratefully.

With all the climbing gear and food, the packs were a prodigious weight – at least 35 kilos, or nearly 80 pounds, and some over 40 kilos. Now that they were away from a military environment, Neill announced that they would drop all formality and behave like a civilian group, always bearing in mind the military structure beneath the surface. In the evening the party went off to explore the delights of Bandar and its night market: the British lads were fascinated to see sugar cane being crushed and the liquid mixed with coconut juice to make a sickly drink, but they were dismayed by the dubious hygiene of the traders, and highly suspicious of the food that was handed out in response to their orders – lumps that looked like squashed toads, and even more unpalatable objects.

Next morning, when they set off at 0700, the heat was already overpowering, and their packs seemed a tremendous weight. At the harbour the team embarked on a 60-foot, passenger-carrying speedboat, powered by huge outboard engines, which bore them swiftly across Brunei Bay to the free port of Labuan, an island off the coast of Sabah. Although part of Malaysia, Labuan enjoys special rights, so that at last it was possible to buy a beer. Steamy heat, two-storey concrete shacks housing Chinese traders, pungent smells from the storm drains – everything was new to the young British soldiers. Neill and Foster went off to the post office to buy telephone cards, so that they could ring ahead to Robert New in Kota Kinabalu, and confirm their reservations at the Travellers' Rest hostel, which Foster had identified as a useful base during his summer reconnaissance. Neill also sent postcards to thank people who had helped the expedition take off, and was delighted to find some which depicted Low's Gully. But the main task was money-changing. He had come out with £3,000 in cash, which he had divided up among his team, and everyone now changed some into Malay ringgits (usually referred to as dollars). Neill himself was still carrying the Hong Kong dollars which he had acquired at Heathrow, carefully wrapped in waterproof polythene and stowed with his passport and credit cards in a body-belt.

Another fast ferry sped them on up the coast: the air-conditioning in the cabin was so fierce that the air was almost uncomfortably cold. Yellow beaches, backed by jungle, flowed past on their right, but a greenish haze hanging over the forest denied them sight of their objective. As they disembarked at the port of Kota Kinabalu in mid-afternoon, small, barefoot boys swarmed round clamouring to carry some of their kit, and seducing one or two of the soldiers into letting them take a small grip or suitcase.

Off they tramped with a large escort, heading for the Travellers' Rest, a hostel on the fourth floor of a jerry-built concrete edifice much favoured by young Australian back-packers. They found themselves in a single large room, with double-decker bunks round the walls, one fan on a stand in the middle of the floor, and a powerful infestation of cockroaches. Page, in the Far East for the first time, let out a roar of disgust when he discovered the state of the kitchen, and when the lads returned from an evening foray, they saw rats the size of cats scurrying about the storm drains. At night, whenever someone came in, he turned the fan to face his own bunk area – so that a few minutes later the other men woke up soaked in sweat. The Hong Kong soldiers, in contrast, were too cold when the fan faced in their direction. Everyone had a rotten night, since the temperature was about 30 Celsius.

Among their final requirements, which they set out to buy in the morning, were cylinders of gas for their cookers. Shearer combed every likely shop in town before he found the right ones. The Chinese set off in search of extra noodles to supplement some of the Western food in their rations. To help make them feel members of the team, Neill assigned them the task of hiring a minibus to take the party to the mountain – an undertaking which required a good deal of haggling in Cantonese or Mandarin. Neill and Foster went to the head office of the Sabah Parks to arrange accommodation on the mountain, while Brittan booked flights back to Hong Kong on 9 March. By then Neill had canvassed ideas about how people would like to spend any spare time after they had left the mountain, and the vote was for returning promptly to Hong Kong, rather than staying in Sabah. Several members of the party tried to telephone their families in England, to say where they were, but failed to get through.

In the evening Robert New collected the two officers and drove them to his home in the smart suburbs north of the town for drinks and a showing of his slides, which Foster recorded on videotape. A shot of New's Pools – the spot beyond which he had thought the Gully too dangerous to continue – showed that the ravine was indeed formidable at that point; but further discussion confirmed Neill in his belief that with a balanced team, sensible direction and proper equipment he would be able to go on down, or, if that proved impossible, to break out through the jungle as New and Pinfield had.

On Sunday 20th February, after an uncomfortable, sweaty night, the party dumped their non-expedition clothes in a locked side-room and boarded their minibus for the mountain. Two hours on the grandly named Trans-Sabah Highway – in European terms a normal road – took them up out of the cultivated coastal plain, into the jungle-clad foothills and on to a plateau, where they got their first awe-inspiring view of Kinabalu itself. In several places the road had been swept away by the downpours of the recent rainy season, and they had to make detours. At a stop in the village of Tamparuli they bought two parangs – long-bladed knives with wooden handles for cutting through undergrowth – in case they had to divert from the watercourse and hack their way out through jungle. As they climbed, the temperature fell steadily from about 35 to 25 Celsius.

In the shadow of the mountain they paused at a wayside stall to buy fruit, and were amazed at the luxuriance of the display. Everyone could recognise the small, green bananas, and huge pineapples which cost the equivalent of 25 pence each; but there were several kinds of fruit which none of the British had seen before, and Neill bought what he thought were melons, only to discover later that they were pumpkins. The young men were scared stiff of buying anything that had not been wrapped in layers of supermarket plastic, and he tried to open their minds by emphasising that out east you have to live on whatever is available locally. No NAAFI around every corner!

At Park Headquarters, 1,560 metres above sea level, the cloying heat of the jungle was left behind, and the temperature was that of a summer day in England. Strange birds were singing and calling in the jungle, and the crystal-clear air gave glorious views. At the entrance to the headquarters stood a cut-out wooden representation of the mountain, like a large picture, showing tracks and salient features, so that visitors could look at it and, simultaneously, at the magnificent view of Kinabalu itself rising behind it. Specific points could be identified from the key. The buildings were modern and well maintained, and the whole place had an air of efficiency; but, as this was Sunday afternoon, there were no officials on duty to issue Neill with the permission he needed to set off for the summit.

Having been to the Park several times before, he and Foster knew where the hostel was, some distance off along a side road that followed the contours, and the party drove straight to it. The place was clean and well-found. Neill then looked round for somewhere to check the proficiency of the Chinese in abseiling techniques: rather than wander off into the headquarters' grounds without permission, and set up ropes on some handy tree, he decided to use the big, overhanging balcony outside their rooms, which was deserted at that time of day. Soon people came along to watch, among them David Powell, a Briton based at the nearby Outward Bound school, who was taking a party of tourists to the summit. Neill was delighted to meet another European involved in outdoor pursuits, especially one with local knowledge.

Having climbed the tourist route up the mountain many times himself, Powell was fascinated by the expedition's plans – but immediately sounded a note of caution. He asked if they realised how difficult and dangerous the Gully was, especially for men carrying packs as heavy as theirs. In particular, he wondered if the Hong Kong soldiers would manage. Neill explained that he

61

and Foster had already been on expeditions to the mountain, and had talked things through thoroughly with Robert New. Besides, their rock-climbing instructor, Mayfield, was fully competent and qualified. If he and Mayfield felt satisfied with the Chinese, Neill said, all would be well; they would progress to the mountain itself and do more training on rock faces, where they would be exposed to the actual danger of being on ropes over big drops. But if they showed no aptitude at all, they would have to be left behind.

In the event, the Hong Kong men responded well to Mayfield's instruction. They had all abseiled before, although not in difficult conditions, and soon made themselves familiar with the equipment which the British had brought. Cheung, the lance-corporal, was the most proficient, but his two colleagues also satisfied Mayfield that they were competent. Mann then gave the party practice in constructing makeshift stretchers: by tying a stone into each corner of a bivvy bag, and others half-way down each long side, it is possible to create handles, and by latticing ropes underneath the bag a hammock-like stretcher can be made. Mayfield also showed the rest of the team how to make an assisted hoist – a system of pulleys, using ropes, with which even a fairly weak single man can lift a heavy casualty up a rock face.

As the park was well geared for entertaining tourists, Neill sent men off to find out what the latest attractions were, and the scouts returned with the news that a video film was available in the modern administration building. The whole team went to see it, and most found out, for the first time, what happened when heavy rain fell on Kinabalu: trickling streams turned into torrents, and waterfalls thundered over vertical drops, so that the entire mountainside turned into a hurtling sheet of water. (Foster had experienced this at first hand in 1988.) The explorers told themselves that if Low's Gully proved to be like that, there was no way they would go down it; but their apprehensions were lulled by the fact that no rain had fallen for several weeks, and the wet season appeared to be over. (During Neill's visit at the beginning of March 1981, not a drop of rain had fallen.) A display of photographs, pieces of rock, and stuffed insects of enormous

62

size helped give newcomers an idea of local flora, fauna, geology and so on; but that information naturally concentrated on the area round Park Headquarters and the summit trail: there was almost nothing on the north of the mountain, and nothing whatever on the Gully.

Foster stayed behind in the hope of being able to arrange a showing of his video film made from New's transparencies, but he could not find anyone to put it on. While he was looking for assistance, a young American botanist showed him a satellite photograph which he spread out on the floor. The picture was more than a metre square, and in colour, and showed Mount Kinabalu, with Low's Gully in deep shadow – a striking image, which Foster recorded on his camera.

Dark fell early, soon after 1830. Neill walked down to the administration building in search of the botanist. The American showed him the aerial photograph too, but it told him little more than they knew already. Everyone then had supper in the canteen, where rice and noodles headed the menu. At least the Chinese were happy, even if some of the British were not so chuffed. There was some discussion as to whether or not they should hire porters in the morning. Local men could be paid to carry baggage up the tourist trail to the Panar Laban huts at 3,360 metres, but Neill felt that he could not book any until he had permission for his party to enter the Gully: he could only hope that the Park Warden would reappear at his office first thing next morning.

After many attempts to telephone home, Neill at last got through, and found Fiona sounding very depressed. Pleased as she was to hear his voice, the weather in Yorkshire was bitterly cold: it was 'grey and dark, with snow flurries and icicles', and she was still having premonitions of disaster. Over a dreadful line, with an obtrusive echo, he tried to reassure her by telling her that he had seen Robert New, and that the abseils were well within the expedition's capability: he said that, being granite, they reminded him of the Dewerstone, and they looked about the same height, no worse. She thought he sounded elated: he told her that the Gully down to New's Pools was going to be

63

easier than he had expected. In her forthright way she thought, 'That's a load of nonsense!' and wished she could 'give Robert New a good smack with my handbag'.

In a further discussion with David Powell, Neill learned that state elections were in progress, and that all Malaysians were required to go back to their own villages to vote. In fact, Powell said, the whole country was in a state of tension, because of the possibility that West Malaysia – Peninsular Malaysia – might start trying to take over from local parties in Sabah. People were uneasy that power might shift to the capital, Kuala Lumpur, and that if this happened, revenues from timber and oil would be siphoned off into central funds.

To Neill, this was bad news: the last thing he wanted was that some anxious defence attaché at the British High Commission in Kuala Lumpur should foresee civil strife in Sabah, and recall the expedition from the mountain at the very moment when it was about to set off. He could well imagine a signal arriving, via the Park Administrator, advising Westerners, particularly foreign soldiers, to leave the country – and this made him anxious to start up the mountain as soon as possible.

Early next morning he used one of the new parangs to cut up the pineapples he had bought the day before, and he handed the pieces round at breakfast. The blade of the big knife was extremely sharp, and sliced away the tough skin of the fruit as neatly as if it had been a scalpel. The British NCOs remained suspicious of Sabah fruit. Having opened up one pumpkin and found it inedible, Neill left the other on the table as a gift to future tourists. Then he and Foster returned to the office to see if Eric Wong had reported for duty. The Chief Warden could not be found, but they bought permits and insurance cover to climb the mountain: permission for the expedition to tackle Low's Gully was a separate affair.

They now had to decide whether or not to hire porters for the initial hike up the tourist trail. If they had gone about it early enough, they could have secured men to carry their ropes and food, thus considerably lightening individual loads. The expense would have been modest – about £10 for a porter carrying 20

64

pounds weight – and after their free flights they had plenty of money. For the moment, though, they still did not have permission for Low's Gully, so they were obliged to hang around.

When Foster telephoned Wong, he turned out to be in the administration building, a kilometre away. Foster reminded him that they had met in the summer, and said that he had now returned with his party: could he come and sort out permission? Wong agreed, and Powell, who had offered to smooth the way if necessary, drove the officers down. When they arrived, however, Wong had someone with him, so the papers were dealt with by his deputy, who raised no difficulties, but took photocopies of their passports and a copy of their itinerary. This said that they would be back at Park Headquarters by 4 March; as a contact address, the document gave that of Major Nigel Ramsden, who had helped Foster so much in Hong Kong. Later, Neill bitterly regretted that he had not insisted on meeting Wong: it would have been hard to do so, because he was a guest in the Park Headquarters – but a personal contact at the outset might have made all the difference when the expedition failed to report back on time.

Emphasising that there was no mountain rescue service, the official required Neill to sign accident indemnity forms, but said, half in jest, that if the party was not back by 4 March, he would come looking for them. He stressed that it was important for the group to check back in when they came off the mountain, and Neill promised that they would of course do so; they would also collect the certificates which tourists receive to show that they have climbed Kinabalu. Later, Neill vividly remembered the official putting away the folder of photocopies in a filing cabinet.

With permission granted, David Powell offered the whole party a lift up to the power station, where the road ended. This would save them a two or three-hour walk, in direct sunlight, on tarmac. It was already after 0900: most of the day's walking parties had already gone off two hours earlier, and porters not already hired had filtered away. In any case, they would have been located a kilometre back at the office which issued climbing permits. Considering that a lift was a better option than porters, Neill accepted Powell's offer with gratitude, and promised to repay his generosity with several beers when the expedition returned to tell their tale.

While the formalities were being completed, Powell drove the rest of the team up to the power station, then returned to take the officers up as well, so that all ten were reunited at the end of the road. They were already 1,850 metres above sea level, but now, with their heavy loads, they faced a climb through almost the same height again, to the rest huts at Panar Laban.

Chapter 6

Conflict

In retrospect, it is clear that the gruelling slog up the tourist trail had a fatally damaging effect on the expedition, and contributed materially to its break-up. By revealing how widely standards of fitness varied within the party, it put one element at loggerheads with the other before the men had had a chance to shake down and develop true team spirit.

The two officers, having climbed the trail several times before, knew that a tough hike lay ahead of them. But they also knew that tourists wearing training shoes, and local porters wearing flip-flops, managed the ascent every day – admittedly without carrying loads as heavy as theirs. Neill, who wanted his men to enjoy the ascent, told them to take their own time and make their way individually to the Panar Laban hut. There was no rush: they had the rest of the day for the climb, and it would be impossible to get lost. The last thing he intended to do was to nanny individuals by giving them detailed instructions about how to tackle a simple trek – from his experience on earlier expeditions, he knew how much people disliked being constantly told what to do.

Even so, he assumed that the men would walk in pairs or small groups, so that they would all have companions to talk to, and could help each other if anyone got into trouble. Since water was available in tanks along the trail, there was no need to carry full bottles, but the packs were extremely heavy all the same.

They left the power station at 0930 on Monday the 21st and Mayfield and Brittan soon forged ahead, followed by Page and Cheung. Neill was glad to see how enthusiastic the NCOs were – they went so fast that they reached the Gunting Lagadan hut, 100 metres above Panar Laban, where they were booked in for the night, after about seven hours. At one of the shelters on the way, over 3,000 metres above sea level, Mayfield felt so fit that he began doing one-arm pull-ups for the benefit of Foster's video camera, which he himself had carried up. The Britons were impressed by the way Cheung kept up with them.

Foster's pack felt to him like one of the hundredweight sacks of coal he used to carry. On his first two ascents of Kinabalu he had been hit by altitude sickness, and knew that if he took the climb slowly, the effect would be minimised – so he deliberately set a moderate pace. Mann, who carried his own video equipment in its yellow case, was also heavily laden. Because of his age, he naturally gravitated towards the two officers, and set out with them. Neill and Foster had told the others that they intended to take all day to climb to their night's lodging, and that they would bring up the rear; as they did not start till 0930, they did not expect to arrive until dusk.

The temperature was comfortable – not more than 15 degrees Celsius – but all members of the party found the ascent extremely hard work. The track, though dry, was very steep, much of it rising in natural steps made by tree roots. For a while Shearer stayed at the back with the officers; then he found the pace irritatingly slow, and pressed on. The Chinese were also ahead. For six or seven hours Neill slogged on, content to bring up the rear with Mann and Foster; but then he saw that nightfall was approaching, and knew he still had quite a distance to go. He realised that, at this rate, they were not going to reach the hut before dark; the weight on their backs was slowing them down more than he had anticipated. The obvious remedy was to lighten his pack, so he took out his rope, which weighed 5 kilograms, and cached it beside the track; he would not need it that night, and, because he had already decided to make the next day a rest day, he would be able to come back down for it in the morning.

As he waited for the other two, he put a brew on beside the track, preparing to greet them with a reviving mug of tea. They arrived before this was ready. When he told Foster and Mann to lighten their loads in the same way as he had, they were initially reluctant, not wanting to lose face; but then they obeyed the order, and unloaded some of their gear into dive-sacks, which they covered with branches.

Starting off again, Neill drew ahead once more, but a few hundred metres up the track he got a shock. There in the middle of the track lay Chow, spreadeagled on his back, propped up on his pack, arms flung out sideways and looking deathly pale. It was as if he had squatted down and rolled on to his back to take his pack off, but had been overcome by the effort. Quickly Neill got the pack off, sat him up and gave him some water. Chow said he felt very tired, and apologised for collapsing. He did not seem sure how long he had been there. Neill told him not to worry. 'You've already done better than I have,' he said. 'I've dumped part of my kit' – and he helped Chow do the same. It transpired that the soldier had eaten and drunk almost nothing during the climb.

Nevertheless, Neill was alarmed that Chow had pushed himself to the point of exhaustion. He was also annoyed that the man had been left on his own: although he had said everyone should go at their own pace and meet at the top, he had assumed that all three Hong Kong soldiers would stay together, for until then they had showed no inclination to split up. Besides, since darkness was already drawing in, he was concerned that no one had come back down to see how the rest of the party was faring. This had nothing to do with military discipline: he felt it was a matter of common mountain sense that members of the party should support each other. The Board of Inquiry later accepted that the men had acted in accordance with their orders.

He waited till Foster and Mann came up, and asked Mann to keep an eye on Chow's pack while he sent someone down to help bring it up. He himself then went on up with Chow. At first the Hong Kong soldier walked with his arm round Neill's shoulder for support because he seemed extremely weak; and the colonel wanted to keep a close eye on him, so that he could observe his recovery rate.

When at last Neill reached the hut, and found Mayfield and

Brittan on the track just outside it, he was fairly short with them. 'For God's sake,' he said. 'What the hell have you been doing? Go back down and help the others in. They won't want you to take their packs, but take them anyway.' Then, discovering the other two Chinese inside the hut, he demanded of them, 'Where's Chow?'

'We don't know.'

'Well, you should know. I've just found him lying knackered on the track. Get a brew on for him, with lots of sugar, and then put him straight into his sleeping bag, because he's suffering from exhaustion. Keep an eye on him, and don't leave him.'

A little later, and well after dark, Foster arrived, utterly drained. David Powell, whose group was staying in the Laban Rata resthouse, only 100 metres down the hill, insisted on carrying his gear the last short stage to the upper hut, despite Foster's protestations that he could manage. Once Neill had seen the others into the hut, he came out with a cup of tea and chatted to Powell, who said he was worried about the ability of the Hong Kong men to cope with the loads they were carrying: given Chow's condition after one day on a tourist track, he expressed strong reservations about taking them into Low's gully. (He evidently did not realise that Cheung had kept up with the leaders, and that Lam had been not far behind.)

For the moment Neill reserved judgement, but agreed that it would be better to defer the party's ascent to the summit; they had originally planned to leave for this at 0300 the next morning. Instead, he said, he would make the next day a rest day, which would allow his men to recoup their strength and recover the equipment which they had cached along the trail.

The Gunting Lagadan hut was maybe ten years old, but well built in wood, with electricity and running water. It had a single big room, a smaller room with primitive cooking facilities, and cabins with bunks, mattresses, pillows and sleeping bags. Since few other people were staying there, the British party had plenty of space: the NCOs had bagged all the rooms at one end of the hut, and had allocated one of them to the officers.

Some time after the stragglers had arrived, Neill went into his room and found Mayfield, sitting on his (Neill's) bed, in conversation with Foster, who was resting in his bunk. Page had made him a brew of coffee, and he was recovering fast. As Neill entered, Mayfield said, 'Can you give me five minutes alone?' Mayfield went on, 'I just want five minutes alone with Ron.' Neill saw that the corporal was serious and tense. 'No,' he said, 'whatever you've got to say, you can say it in front of both of us. I don't have any secrets from Ron. We're all part of the same expedition, and we can't have cliques forming.'

Mayfield repeated his request, and when he got the same answer, suddenly left the room, going along the passage and out of the hut, leaving Neill taken aback by his behaviour, which he felt was unacceptable. He shouted after him, 'Richard – come back! What's wrong with you?' Getting no answer, and seeing Brittan, whom Mayfield had brushed past, he said, 'Go after him and find out what's wrong with him, please. And while you're at it, tell him to find out what time supper finishes, and let us know.' But Mayfield did not return, and when Neill sent another man after him to bring him back, he still did not reappear.

'Good job you came in then!' Foster exclaimed, when Neill returned to his room and shut the door. He felt that Mayfield had been about to quiz him on his fitness. Neill thought that Mayfield might have been affronted by the rather curt way in which he had told him to go down and help the stragglers. Foster had no doubt about his own physical abilities, because he had just spent seven weeks working as a ski instructor in Bavaria, and knew that his heart, lungs and legs were in good shape. Further, he had proved his ability to carry heavy weights over long distances many times in the past. He was confident that he would recover quickly from the climb, and that the worst of the uphill load-carrying was already over.

Nevertheless, the incident left Neill unsettled: it was worrying that his rock-climbing instructor – a key member of the expedition – should lose his self-control over an apparently trivial episode. It subsequently transpired that Mayfield had wanted to talk about the fitness of group members and had sought an opportunity to speak with each of them alone and to pass on to Neill a request from Chow to leave the expedition because of his concerns about his fitness. Mayfield told the Board of Inquiry that he would have been more comfortable talking on a one-to-one basis and felt he had not been taken seriously.

The early arrivals had already had supper, but the stragglers in the party were still hungry. By asking Mayfield to find out what time meals ended in the cafeteria in the lower hut, Neill hoped he would oblige the corporal to come back and rebuild broken bridges. But the ruse failed: Mayfield did not reappear, and it turned out that the last orders had already been taken. Foster, who was back on his feet after thirty minutes and refreshed by an ice-cold shower, brewed up some of their precious rations for himself and Neill, and they ate their supper in the upper hut.

Seeing that the group needed to be pulled together, and in view of the day's various mishaps, Neill put out word that at 2100 he would hold a formal O-group,* at which they would talk over the day and discuss plans for the future. He then walked down the hill for a shower in the resthouse. There, at the far corner of the hut, he saw Mayfield sitting with David Powell's group of British tourists, and suspected that he was discussing the expedition; he did not approach him, because he did not wish to create a scene in front of strangers.

At 2100 the whole team sat down at a table in the big room of the upper hut, including Chow, who had more or less recovered. By now the late arrivals had changed into their tracksuits, as the night air was cold. When general chatter broke out, Neill announced, 'Right – I want this to be a formal O-group. Things have gone wrong, and we need to put the record straight. I'll say what I've got to say, and then we'll go round the table, so that everyone can give his opinion in turn.'

He started by apologising for not hiring porters: with

* O-group is short for Order-group, the military term used when a Commander gives formal orders to his assembled men.

72

hindsight, he said, it obviously would have been better to have had some. But he explained that by the time they started, the porters had all drifted away for the day, and he had not wanted to loaf about at Park Headquarters until the following morning, particularly as local electioneering activity might jeopardise the expedition's chances of going up the mountain. When he pointed out that the lift given them by David Powell had been more or less the equivalent of porters, the men agreed that they would probably have made the same decision.

Neill then expressed disappointment that no one had seen fit to check on where Chow or any of the other stragglers were at nightfall, or had considered finding out about meal times, so that latecomers could get something to eat in the canteen. He would not, he said, tolerate an 'I'm all right, Jack' attitude. He also reminded everyone that, although they were on an expedition, this was also a military exercise, and that after it he would be sending reports on their conduct to commanding officers. He softened what he had just said by adding, 'Don't worry, though. You're all looking good at the moment, and I don't see any real problem.'

Next he raised the question of command and control, in case any of the group had got the wrong idea: he reiterated that the expedition was his, and his alone. It was he who had organised it, he who had invited the other members; Foster was his deputy, and although he was the oldest in the party, Neill had no worries about his fitness. He emphasised that Mayfield was his rock-climbing expert, and that whenever the expedition was in a life-threatening situation, on rock faces or on ropes, he would be king. Everyone else had specific roles: Brittan was the still photographer, Mann the video cameraman, Shearer the diarist, and so on. As expedition leader, he, Neill, was ultimately responsible for everyone's safety.

In conclusion, Neill deliberately raised the fact that levels of fitness did vary widely; but he pointed out that they had already discussed this question in the pub at Plymouth, when he had announced that the expedition was going to be one of mixed ability. He said that at the moment he was not worried by

73

anybody's physical condition (apart from that of Chow, who had obviously overdone it) because the climb up the mountain, which they had already accomplished, was the stiffest stint of uphill load-carrying they were likely to face: once they started down the Gully, apart from strenuous rope-work, it would be more a question of taking care. He pointed out that Cheung had kept up with the leaders – no mean feat – and that Lam had done almost as well.

In any case, he concluded, the members of the group were not engaged in a race. The aim of the expedition was to descend Low's Gully, not to reach the top of the mountain first – and he wanted everyone to enjoy themselves.

When he opened the discussion to the meeting, he asked Mann, on his right, to lead off. The sergeant suggested that the party should split into two: a river group of the less fit, and a Gully group of the young bloods. The first would work upwards along the Penataran, the second downwards, the aim being to meet somewhere in the middle. (He himself, being in between the two, in age and fitness, would have opted for the river party.) The idea was chewed around for a bit, but Neill rejected it, largely on the grounds that it had been tried before, on Exercise Jungle Heights 4 and Exercise Kinabalu Triangle, and had failed, because of the river party's difficulty in ascending steep and slippery rock against a fierce current.

Chow apologised for having collapsed and raised the question of whether he should go on with the expedition. Neill told him not to worry: if anybody was to blame, it was he himself, for not having detailed someone else to keep an eye on him. By the end of the discussion there was general agreement that they should stand by the plan formulated in Devon: their performance on the walk up confirmed that it would make sense for the younger, fitter group to recce on ahead, preparing the way while not going too far ahead, and for the rest – Neill, Foster, Mann and the three Hong Kong men – to come down behind them in tandem. Brittan later quipped to Neill: 'I know what you're afraid of – that we'll get down the Gully before you!'

Once things were decided, Neill confirmed that the next day

74

would be a rest day. His original idea had been that the whole party would leave in the early hours of the following morning and walk up the trail to the summit, to be there for sunrise – a memorable experience which all tourist groups enjoyed as a matter of course, and one he was anxious his own team should not miss. By delaying the visit to the summit by twenty-four hours, he would give everyone a chance to recoup their energy and recover their kit where necessary. They were several days ahead of their original schedule, set in England, and there would be no penalty as far as rations were concerned, because for the time being they could eat in the tourist cafeteria. It was decided that Neill, Foster, Mann and Chow would go down to pick up their dive-sacks, bring them back to the hut, and then relax for the rest of the day. Mayfield, Brittan, Page and Shearer, already entranced by the huge mountain, were eager to explore the summit anyway, and have a look down into the top of Low's Gully from above.

After the meeting, Neill, determined to get to the bottom of Mayfield's behaviour, including his failure to find out the meal times, took him aside to avoid possible grudges building up and to clear the air. 'What was all that about?' he asked. The corporal apologised, but said that he had wanted to see Neill alone to discuss the fitness problem. Neill recognised that the corporal was an independent-minded, free-thinking soldier, and it was partly for this reason that he had selected him in the first place. But as Neill said afterwards, 'Either I got a grip of Mayfield and kept him on board, or I sent him off, scuppering the expedition.' He therefore merely said, 'All right. I'll take that as an apology. Don't do it again. When I ask you to do something, do it, because there's a good reason for it. Let's get on with the expedition.' To which Mayfield replied, 'OK, Boss'.

When the Hong Kong soldiers expressed doubts as to whether they would be able to keep up with the others, Neill explained that they were coming along expressly to be given the chance to excel themselves. They had been selected by their commanding officer for this purpose. Other Chinese soldiers of similar ability had had no difficulty on earlier expeditions.

75

SOS

Besides, he, Neill, would look after them to make sure they got down safely, and the expedition would proceed at the pace of the slowest man.

Later, as everyone turned in for the night, and Neill and Foster lay in their sleeping bags, they discussed the episode with Mayfield. The Colonel said he hoped that he had smoothed things over, and that perhaps, once they started to descend the Gully with Mayfield in his element on the rock, things would improve. His other concern was that the Hong Kong soldiers would be fit and keen in the morning. At intervals during the night he and Foster went into their room to make sure that Chow was all right, and to their relief they always found him sleeping peacefully.

Chapter 7

Easy Valley

On Tuesday 22 February everyone awoke to find the weather brilliant, the sky cloudless, the views stunning – and Chow recovered. The ubiquitous David Powell happened to come past, enjoying the early sunshine; he started chatting with Neill, and in his straightforward fashion again counselled caution, pointing out that the mountain offered other possibilities for energetic endeavour, among them the Eastern Plateau; but Neill still did not feel that he was being over-ambitious, and was inclined to proceed. He asked Powell if he had ever been into Low's Gully, and, on getting the answer, 'No', enquired how he knew it was as horrendous as he claimed. Powell said he was going on the evidence of Robert New. Neill said that he had spent the evening before last *with* New. Had Powell ever been on the River Penataran? No. 'Well,' said Neill, 'I have, and so has Ron Foster – three times, in fact. The mountain won't have changed in ten years. Admittedly I'm ten years older, but I'm happy in the lads I've got with me.'

He went on to say that although he had reservations about Chow, he was sure that between them the whole team would manage all right. As for the technical ability of the Hong Kong soldiers – he said he would take them only if Mayfield was satisfied that they were up to it after putting them through more rope-work on the mountain.

There was no doubt that Powell was trying to be helpful; but although Neill and Foster were grateful for his assistance the day before, and appreciated his interest, they felt that he was on shaky ground when he started trying to influence the course of a military expedition. In their view, this was no time for him to give them a lecture on adventurous training. Beyond the fact that he was a tourist guide, they knew nothing of his background.

At 1100 Neill, Foster, Mann and Chow went back down to collect their kit, as planned. Cheung and Lam decided to have a complete day off, resting and pottering around the hut. The British NCOs wanted to explore the peak area, and decided to take some of their equipment and dump it higher up the mountain, so that they would have less to carry on the pre-dawn ascent next morning.

Away they went, bounding with enthusiasm; but although they had been warned about the effects of the sun at high altitude, they returned in the evening with the winter-white skin of faces, arms and legs burnt. They also came back alight with excitement: it was clear that, besides the sun, they had caught Neill's enthusiasm for the mountain, and had seen precisely why the expedition was going for Low's Gully. They had looked down from the summit into Easy Valley and seen what lay ahead of – or, rather, beneath – them. What Neill did not realise until later was that Mayfield, instead of merely going as far as the Col, had made an initial recce down into Easy Valley on his own.

Mayfield returned well before nightfall, with Neill none the wiser, and the whole team had supper together at the resthouse, where they pushed two tables together to make one big surface. Most of the group were content with local food, but a couple of the Britons insisted on ordering the Malaysian version of sausage, egg and beans, which was far more expensive. Then, just as Page was contemplating his precious plateful, the two tables came apart right beneath it, and the whole lot fell through the gap on to the floor – a mishap which provoked a stream of abuse from him, and mirth in everyone else. Page was far from amused – but the atmosphere was high-spirited; everyone was talking about the challenges which the mountain would have in store for them, and the expedition seemed to have come together.

With military titles and courtesies fast becoming inappropriate, and with the expedition proper about to start, first names became the order of the day. Neill had said, 'Right; lads: we're now in expedition mode. I don't like formality anyway, and to all intents and purposes we're civilians. Therefore my name's

Robert, and Ron Foster is Ron.' Going round the table, he asked everyone to say how he preferred to be addressed. Richard Mayfield was known as 'Rich', Mann as 'Bob', Shearer as 'Pete' and Page as 'Steve'. Brittan, who did not like his Christian name Hugh, preferred to be 'Britt'. Lam's first name was Victor, and Cheung's Kevin. Chow alone appeared to have no European name, and was content to be merely Chow.

As to the next day's programme: Neill asked Mayfield to find a spot where, after their early-morning summit trek, they could give the Hong Kong soldiers further practice in abseiling and ascending. Then the NCOs who had already taken part of their kit up the mountain would proceed over the Col into Easy Valley, while the other party returned to spend a third night at Gunting Lagadan and pick up the rest of their equipment. Neill's immediate concern was to make sure that he did not risk exhausting Chow again, and to give all the Hong Kong soldiers confidence in themselves for their descent into the Gully.

Back in the hut, he carried out an equipment check, partly to make sure that everyone had the right amount of rations, while there was still a chance to top up from the canteen. As an example, Brittan laid his kit out neatly on the floor for a photograph: ten days' rations, dive-sack, bivvy bag, spare clothes, rope, karabiners, parang and so on. Then Neill detailed the three men who had sorted out the Hong Kong soldiers' kit in Brunei to go through it again, for the last time – and very soon blasphemous muttering broke out, as the NCOs discovered that the Chinese did not have by any means all the food that they should have brought. They had enough for three or four days, but not for ten.

Neill, who had stood back and watched this going on, asked the NCOs why they had not all done what he had asked them to do in Kota Kinabalu – namely, to check the Hong Kong soldiers' kit properly. Belatedly he realised that what they had done was to lay out one day's worth of rations, and tell the Chinese, 'Right – make up ten days' worth like this, and put it in.' Now they demanded, 'Where's the food gone to?' – but suddenly language difficulties arose, and no straightforward answers were forthcoming.

One NCO rapidly jumped to conclusions. 'Christ!' he exclaimed. 'They must have thrown it away.' The truth was never firmly established. Kevin Cheung, for instance, later admitted that he had eaten several tins of sardines on his way up the mountain. (Later the Board of Inquiry spent a whole afternoon trying to establish what had happened with Kevin and his sardines and came to the conclusion that whatever else had happened the rations had not been thrown away: it was rather like Captain Queeg and the strawberry ice-cream in *The Caine Mutiny*.)

Neill now wrote down precisely what each of the Hong Kong soldiers should have to make his rations up: so many packs of noodles, so many tins of sardines or similar. He then told Kevin to go down with the other two to the small shop in the resthouse, and Foster gave them money from expedition funds to buy in enough sardines, chocolate and other things to make good the deficiencies. By the evening Neill was satisfied that everybody had proper rations – even though the experience of carrying heavy packs up the mountain had made the men pare their supplies to the bone – and he allocated Kevin the job of making sure that the party woke up in time for their trek to the summit.

* * *

At 0200 next morning, 23 February, everyone struggled up in pitch darkness. Leading from the front, Neill told the party to number off, one to ten, and detailed somebody to bring up the rear, so that no one got lost in the darkness. Then they set out wearing their head-lamps, which proved highly effective. The British NCOs, having already dumped some of their kit at the top, were carrying part-loads. The rest, who were due for one more night in the hut, took the opportunity of carrying half their kit up the mountain, as had the others the previous day. Both parties were therefore carrying about the same – a comfortable weight.

In some places the trail was extremely steep, with ropes slung on the inside for use as hand-rails. The team made good

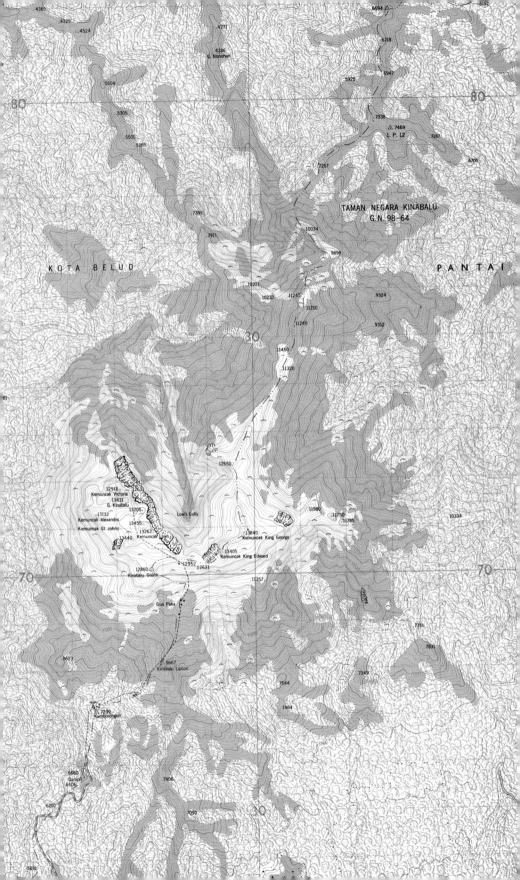

Previous page: Map (1:50000) of Kinabalu area

Above: Exercise Jungle Heights 3 – fighting the Penataran

Inset, right: Expedition members on the drive up to Kinabalu. Back (left to right): Foster, Mayfield, Neill, Shearer, Lam. Front (left to right): Brittan, Chow, Page, Mann, Cheung

Right: Aerial photograph of northern (lower) end of Gully taken by Mobray during search

Above: View northwards following the line of Low's Gully (1000 m below)

Right: Group shot on summit of Low's Peak. Back (left to right): Foster, Brittan, Mann, Mayfield, Neill. Front (left to right): Shearer, Chow, Lam, Cheung

Below: Neill's group trekking up to Easy Valley Col

Left: Victor, Kevin and Chow at Easy Valley Col

Below: Neill and Foster at Cauldron Gap

Above: Neill, Foster and Mann at Easy Valley Col

Right: Bivi spot in Easy Valley

Below: Late afternoon shot of Neill and Foster at Table Rock

Left: View of North Peak before the descent into the Gully

Below: Foster approaching the top of the first severe abseil

FACING PAGE:

Right: Stuck on the ledge – p.m. 27 February

Below left: Hong Kong soldiers halfway down the cliff – note the dry bed of the waterfall

Below right: The Gully bed from the top of the final waterfall abseil

Left: Neill at Owl Pinnacle

Below: New's Pools in tranquil mood

Above: The Gully in mild spate above New's Pools

Left: Foster descending on abseil in the Gully bed

Below left: Victor 'Chopper watching'

Below right: Kevin and Chow on 'Chopper watch' early days

progress, moving well together, and occasionally overtaking a party of tourists. Every so often they would stop in the dark, number off and continue. Neill was glad to see that the Chinese were keeping up well, and that Chow seemed to have no difficulty. After a passage through woods, they came out on to the rock face above Panar Laban and past the corrugated-iron huts at Sayat Sayat.

Some way short of the summit the party split in two, as Neill wanted his lot to drop their dive-sacks at a certain spot just off the trail, which by now was across bare rock marked with cairns, so that they would not have to lose height when they recovered them later on. (They were due to traverse high in order to reach the crags on which they were going to put the Hong Kong soldiers through their paces.) His aim, for the second part of the morning, was to explore the summit area, and in particular to take photographs of Easy Valley and the top of Low's Gully from above, while Mayfield recce'd a suitable spot for the abseiling.

The two parties reunited at the summit around 0615 – all except Page, who was overcome by altitude sickness and had to stop short of the peak. They had managed the climb in well under four hours, and the rest of them, including Victor, Kevin and Chow, were in fine fettle.

Still in the pre-dawn gloom, and in bitter cold, they huddled among the rocks, in the company, now, of a good many tourists. Gradually the eastern sky began to lighten: the horizon flushed pink, then orange, and suddenly the blazing rim of the sun came into view. As the light increased, the watchers realised that an immense area of Borneo lay beneath them – a crumpled black blanket of jungle which gradually took on its daytime colours of green and grey, laced with wreaths of white mist. The British NCOs, perhaps still disconcerted by their early start, thought it was no big deal, but to the Hong Kong soldiers it was the experience of a lifetime. Closer at hand, the party found a Kinabalu rat, which was heavily filmed and photographed as it crawled about among the boulders.

Among the other early-risers at the summit was David Powell, who asked whether Neill would like him to raise the alarm if the party failed to reappear on schedule in Kota Kinabalu on 8 March. Neill thanked him, but declined the offer because he preferred to put his faith in Park Headquarters, rather than rely on a casual acquaintance and fellow countryman: he was afraid that if Powell went into action in a private capacity, he might foul up any initiative that the Park authorities were launching. 'Thanks for the offer,' Neill said. 'But as you know, we've already left our itinerary with Park Headquarters. We'll look forward to seeing you in KK for a beer on the eighth.' Soon the tourists filtered away, except for one couple, who, the British felt certain, were hoping to join the three-mile-high club, and hung around looking purposeful.

Neill agreed with Mayfield that they would rendezvous at midday beneath the Donkey's Ears, the twin pinnacles of rock on the straight descent line between the summit and the Easy Valley Col. By then the corporal would have found a suitable crag and got his ropes organised for abseil training. The colonel's party spent the morning clambering round the peaks and looking down the hair-raising drops which plunged towards the top of Low's Gully. They tried to pick out the abseil point which New had used, and were disappointed not to be able to spot it.

Victor Lam stayed close to Neill and Foster, boldly peering down the most terrifying precipices, and taking photographs freely. But Kevin Cheung and Chow, apparently daunted by the immensity of the mountain, tended to lurk in the background. Neill told them to wait in the shadow of a rock, and to keep out of the sun. Mann also was none too keen on staring down into such vast depths, but he cheerfully overcame his fears. Back at the spot where they had cached their kit, Neill's group brewed up a hot drink and had breakfast of rolled oats.

At midday they rejoined the other party at the base of the Donkey's Ears, where the British NCOs had set up some ropes on a suitable rock face and were snoozing in the sun. By then the day had become very hot, but the Chinese insisted on continuing to wear their green Goretex waterproofs. They claimed to be afraid of catching cold, and Neill was unable to persuade them to take the jackets off; but by the time they reached the abseil area they had started to look thoroughly overheated – so much so that they did not feel like eating or drinking. It was obvious that they needed to be in the shade, and Neill got the other men to drape a flysheet over some bushes as a screen, so that Kevin, in particular, could have a rest out of the sun; and, after being persuaded to eat some chocolate and drink a brew of tea, they all felt better.

Mayfield then took them for a practice on an easy abseil designed to build their confidence, and afterwards Foster practised with his Petzl Shunt, and Neill and Mann with their jumars. The session was notably successful: at the end, all three Hong Kong soldiers were much more at home on the ropes – and, no less important, Mayfield expressed his confidence in their ability. At about 1500 they therefore rejoined the other NCOs at the bottom of the Donkey's Ears.

Mayfield, Brittan, Page and Shearer were planning to camp in Easy Valley for the night. The rest of the party would return to the hut to sleep and collect the second half of their kit. Next day, they would walk up to the Col and meet Mayfield there at 1400.

Neill was keenly aware of the fact that the Hong Kong soldiers had already suffered from lack of water, and that good water management was going to be a critical factor in maintaining their confidence once the party left Panar Laban, above which there was no reliable source. Thereafter, they would have to make do with the supplies they were carrying until they came down into Easy Valley, where Mayfield had been told to find them their next source. Neill reminded Mayfield that for the next couple of days, until they were lower down Easy Valley, water would be a vital consideration: the corporal's main task was to find a good camp site in Easy Valley, with a natural water supply adequate for the whole party, and then at 1400 to meet Neill's team on the Col so that he could guide them down.

Mayfield was itching to tackle some of the peaks that bristled all round him. 'Wish I'd brought my PAs [Pierre Alain climbing shoes]!' he said. Neill told him that if he had time on his hands, he could start compiling the first climbers' guide to the valley, and he should ensure that Brittan took suitable photographs to illustrate it.

With the words 'See you at 1400 hours tomorrow,' the two parties separated. The NCOs headed up the steep rock slabs for the Col and Easy Valley, while the rest hid their dive-sacks for collection next day, and walked down to the hut with packs empty. After a good supper in the canteen, the Hong Kong soldiers again expressed doubts about their ability to cope with what lay ahead. There followed a long discussion, in which Foster and Mann joined; by the end of it, Neill had managed to convince them that they were going to be properly looked after, and that he would not take them into any situation about which he himself had doubts. He emphasised that he had no intention of forcing them to continue, and eventually they seemed to be satisfied.

In the morning the party walked up with half-loads, and made reasonable time. The route to the Col lay well off any tourist trail, but earlier expeditions had erected cairns of stones up the rock-covered slope – and indeed on Neill's first expedition to the mountain his party had gone well into Easy Valley, building cairns on the way, and set out a large RAOC in stones on the slope opposite the peak. Now, because he was keen to maintain the Hong Kong soldiers' confidence, he did not want to take them up across the steep slabs and over the 3,870-metre ridge with full packs, in case they were overcome by a combination of weight, heat and altitude. So they all left their cached climbing equipment where it was for the time being, and as they went up, Mann pushed on ahead while Foster and Neill concentrated on bringing the Chinese crabwise across the open sheets of rock.

The party reached the Col shortly before 1330, planning to return for their remaining kit when they were established in camp and had refilled their water bottles. Once that last load had been collected, Neill reasoned, the heavy carrying uphill would be over, and afterwards everything would be downhill, as far as humping kit went.

When the Hong Kong soldiers reached the Col, and discovered the splendour of the view from the top, they were elated. A vast amphitheatre, perhaps a kilometre across, lay spread out below them. A 40-degree slope of naked, light-grey rock fell sharply

84

beneath their feet and swept away to their right. In the middle of the bowl gigantic boulders stuck up out of rough green scrub, and beyond them the ground rose again to perpendicular cliffs and the jagged, irregular peaks which bounded the valley on the far side. Perhaps because of the amount of bare rock, every noise sounded hollow: here they were on the threshold of a desolate, high-altitude wilderness, in which everything was still, and no living creature stirred.

Kevin and the others could see that the way down was within their capabilities – as Neill had promised it would be – and exulted in the fact that they were about to become the first Chinese ever to descend into Low's Gully. Only one small snag spoilt the team's enjoyment: there was no sign of Mayfield.

'Where the hell is he?' said Neill. Foster was equally puzzled. The lie of the land was such that they could have seen anyone coming up to meet them: from their vantage-point, they had a couple of hours' walking in view – and there was nobody in sight. Neill's primary concern now was water. He had been relying on the corporal to show them a good source, so that if the Hong Kong soldiers had been gasping, they could have been sure of getting a drink quickly. In fact they had enough water for the moment, but they would certainly need more that night, and it was more important to find a sure supply than to go back for the rest of the kit.

Neill waited half an hour, until nearly 1400, and then, since several routes down into Easy Valley were possible, sent Mann ahead to reconnoitre the best one. As they followed, Foster was surprised to see the sergeant heading out along a chain of cairns to their left: on earlier visits, they had descended through boulders to the right, and this (he thought) had been the intended route. But as it appeared that Mann had taken a good line, they followed him down, and inside a couple of hours they began to find signs of dampness on the rock. Then they came upon a tiny spring trickling out – enough for them to channel water into their bottles via biscuit-wrappers.

Already it was 1530. With Chinese morale still high, Neill decided to camp where they were. His only worry was Mayfield:

he could not tell why the corporal had not kept the rendezvous, or where he had gone. His failure to reappear rang alarm bells in Neill's mind; but, giving the NCO the benefit of the doubt, he felt there must be some good reason for it. Because the terrain was relatively easy – although punctuated by steep rock slabs – he was confident that nothing serious had happened to the recce group, and that they would all join up next day.

In fact Mayfield's party were a good way further down the valley, and were hacking their way through a belt of dense shrubs with the parangs – a slow and laborious task. Afterwards, they explained that they had lost track of the time and had been concentrating on finding a bivvy site.

The second group camped at 3,660 metres. Neill, Foster and Mann helped the Hong Kong lads wrench branches off rhododendron-type shrubs to make a sleeping platform on the steep slope. With camp established, and the Chinese tasked with making a fire, they set off downhill to see if they could find the others, Mann taking the left, Foster the right, with Neill in the centre behind, directing them from above.

Because there were numerous small ravines, they had to pick their way carefully. Soon Mann came on an old compo* packet, with a note written by Brittan: 'Hi, lads, you're on course. Follow the cairns', and signed with Parachute Regiment wings. After about 500 metres they spotted the recce group, much farther down – getting on for a kilometre away. Their red dive-sacks and a red-and-silver space blanket, spread out on a flat ledge of rock, were clearly visible. (This ledge became known to the first group as Alphabet Rock, because they played letter-games to pass the time while waiting on it, and to the second as Table Rock, because it was so flat.) Having discerned Mayfield's position, the three men climbed back to their own site, for it was already getting dark.

As evening came on, the sun went down behind the ramparts above them on their left, and the wide bowl was left in shadow, with the last of the sun's rays climbing its eastern wall. Straight down the centre of the valley, the dark scar of the Gully plunged

* 'Compo' is the unofficial army abbreviation for 'composite rations'.

86

away out of sight, and far beyond it to the north the lights of distant villages twinkled in the jungle. The air was still, and no sound broke the silence. Later, an immense full moon came up and filled Easy Valley with silvery light, but the Gully itself – their target – remained black and mysterious.

Neill's group lit a fire of dead brushwood, which made a cheerful blaze, kept them warm and saved their gas; but they could not see the other group's fire, which was hidden from them by the curvature of the valley floor, and they thought how spooky it would seem to anyone who looked down from the Col and saw sparks of light far out in the darkness, in spots that humans hardly ever visited, let alone slept in.

On the way up the mountain Neill had felt a sore throat coming on, and now it grew worse. During the night he kept waking up, troubled by an irritating cough, which he tried to suppress so that he did not disturb Foster, who was sharing his tent. To make him more comfortable, Foster gave him a piece of his own carry-mat, a lightweight foam underlay.

Neill was not the only one who had an uneasy night. Mann's tent had gone on down the mountain with the recce party (he was supposed to be sharing with Mayfield), so he slept out in his bivvy bag, near the fire. In the early hours he was woken by something crashing about among the rocks. At first he thought one of the Chinese was mucking around in the dark; but then he realised that the disturbance was not being created by any member of the party. Nor could the cause of it be rats, like the one they had seen on the summit: the rocks which were being moved were far too large.

'What the hell is this?' thought Mann, as he cautiously peered out through the opening of his sleeping bag. His neck crawled as he saw a shape which he took to be that of some large creature looking for food. Immediately his mind jumped to yetis, the alleged wild men of the Himalayas. Did such creatures exist in Borneo?

At that height above sea level the mysterious visitor could hardly be an orang-utan, which lives on fruit, for at an altitude of nearly 4,000 metres there was nothing whatever in the way of wild food. All the same, Mann did not like the look of it, and kept his head covered: the last thing he wanted to do was to attract the animal's attention. The rummaging noises continued for some minutes, and Foster also became aware of a sizeable dark shape on the move outside his tent in the glow of the moon; but he too chose not to investigate, so the identity of the nocturnal prowler was never established. In the morning Mann was still very scared, and there was much discussion of the incident. As the group went on down Easy Valley, several had the feeling that something was watching them.

By then Neill had started to lose his voice, and his face was starting to swell. Yet he was well enough to go ahead with his group's programme for that day, which was to go back to Sayat Sayat, pick up their dive-sacks, and return to Easy Valley, where they would join up with the recce party. Having got up and had breakfast, his group left their tents erected, in case they wanted to use them again that night; then they walked up to the Col with packs empty and down the other side to recover the rest of their equipment. The round trip took most of the day. On their way back to Easy Valley, they took the opportunity to recce Commando Cauldron, the topmost part of Low's Gully, to check for signs of water, in case this knowledge might be useful later on. As it was, they found they could not see into the bottom, because of convex rock hiding the depths below them. So it was not until 1530 that they were back at their bivvy site. The morale of the Hong Kong soldiers was still high; but, with only two hours of light left, Neill was not prepared to risk allowing his party to be caught out in a place where they could not easily camp: as he already had a good camp site, with plenty of water, it made sense to stay where they were for another night. There was still no sign of the recce group, and nothing to show that any of them had been back to the camp in his absence.

He, Foster and Mann decided that they must try to find out whether the recce group were still in the same place, and why they had failed to keep the rendezvous the previous day. As they were going to descend Easy Valley anyway, they took half-loads some way down towards Table Rock. On their way, they found that the first group had cut a good, clear passage through the forest of rhododendrons. Foster then led down a very steep rock slab, until they reached more vegetation.

Distances proved deceptive. As the light started to fail, Neill realised they were still a long way from Table Rock. Anxious not to be caught out in the dark, or to leave the Chinese on their own, not knowing where the others had gone, he decided they had better return to the bivvy site before night fell. They therefore dumped their dive-sacks at the edge of the vegetation.

Mann, who had been planning to move down to join the recce group if he could only find them, had brought all his kit with him, less his yellow video case, which he had left on a slab before the first patch of vegetation. Now he carried on down, getting lost in a dense rhododendron jungle and not reaching Table Rock until after dark. He found the others only by calling out at intervals: he had to be guided in by answering yells, and arrived very relieved. So he transferred to the first group, and rejoined his partner Mayfield. (He later said that he had become fed up with the slow progress which the back group was making.) Higher up, the second party again lit a good fire and settled down for the night. But Neill was feeling distinctly unwell, and Foster was worried that the split in the expedition had not closed. In his diary he noted: 'VERY important that we should regroup tomorrow.'

On the morning of Day Three, Saturday 26 February, Neill woke up feeling very weak and slow, and hardly able to speak. Foster had gone off to find water, but the colonel was pleased, if surprised, to find Mann heading back up the slope towards him. The sergeant – who could see that the colonel was unwell – explained that none of the first group had come up to the Col because it had taken them so long to cut their way through the rhododendron thicket. He asked for permission for the recce group to press on ahead, and Neill agreed.

The colonel, who was already feeling the effects of his illness, later had no recollection of this exchange.

Mann went down again, collecting his yellow case on the way, and rejoined the recce group. In view of the steepness of the ground, Mann and Brittan were both happy for Mayfield to assume leadership at the front – and Neill had always assumed that he would do so when his group came on to rock. Neill later accepted that he had failed to place anybody in command of the recce party. Mayfield had already decided that the second group was so close behind him that they would easily be able to follow the paths his party had cut for them. Knowing (from a recce) where he wanted to be that night, and set free by the permission which Mann had brought down, his group left Alphabet/Table Rock after breakfast.

The second party, having packed up camp, came down through the cut route and reached Table Rock at 1100, only to find that the recce group had again gone on. Foster expected Mann, a responsible senior rank, to have told the others about Neill's state of health; so when they reached the rock, and found the rest departed, he was perturbed. They were only about an hour ahead, but he was not to know that – and in any case, by then Neill, who had lost his voice completely and could barely walk, was so ill that for the time being he could go no further. All he wanted to do was lie down and sleep. Foster reckoned he had a viral infection: he made him a shelter under some bushes and brewed him a hot drink – whereupon Neill crawled into his sleeping bag and, except for the occasional excursion, lay there for the next twenty hours, all that day and all night.

The setback placed Foster in a dilemma. If the colonel was still ill next morning, they would have to get him back to civilisation – and that would mean retracing their steps, up over the Col and down to Panar Laban. Yet the other group had gone on ahead – heaven knew how far. If Neill was a real casualty, and had to be carried, it would need four men – the entire remaining rear group – to ferry him back; but this would mean deserting the reconnaissance party. If the recce group were left on their own, would they send anyone back? Would they wait? Or would they carry on down the Gully?

Foster felt that it was imperative to make contact with the others. He therefore decided to send Kevin and Victor forward to see if there was any sign of those ahead, and to look for any abseil-point that Mayfield might have set up by then. This would give the Hong Kong men a chance of making a positive contribution, rather than merely tagging along. The destination he gave them was the big rock which they could see from where they were, and had dubbed House Boulder, about an hour downhill: his plan was that they should take some of their kit down, to lighten their loads for the next day, and deliver a note to Mann, saying that the colonel was ill, and that they must all get together.

The route down to House Boulder looked comparatively easy and safe, and he sent the two men off without qualms, estimating that the round trip would take them between two and three hours. He himself decided to remain with Neill, partly because he was his partner, and partly because he had greater experience than Victor in mountain first aid. For a while he watched his two messengers start down towards House Boulder; but then, as Neill was sleeping quietly, he and Chow decided to retrace their route to the point where he and Neill had left their dive-sacks the previous evening and bring them down. They were away for about forty minutes, and returned to find Neill still comfortably asleep.

Victor and Kevin had instructions to deliver Foster's note to Mann, or, failing that, to leave it in a conspicuous place. If they found nobody, they were to look around for any abseil points that Mayfield might have set up. They were then to return, but on no account to attempt any abseils themselves. In the event, they could not find any of the recce group, or any abseil point, so they left the note on one of their own dive-sacks, which they dumped in the lee of House Boulder. The round trip took them longer than expected, but they eventually returned to their own camp site in good order.

That evening the Chinese found a spot under a tree on which to pitch their tent, with Foster on a ledge about ten metres away, and Neill nearby in the bushes. Foster cooked Neill some beef granules, but he could hardly eat, and during the night a rat came to help itself: Foster heard the mess tin rattle, and when he shone his torch at it, the rat merely blinked and carried on eating, with its pink skin showing through sparse brown fur. Once it had finished its meal, it scurried down the side of Foster's bivvy bag, between him and the rock, and made off.

On 27 February Foster was up early, as always, and at 0615 he set off for House Boulder, confident (from frequent checks) that Neill had had a good night, and leaving him to get as much sleep as he could. A great deal would depend on his state of health when he awoke.

Foster's urgent priority was to locate the others. He told the Hong Kong soldiers where he was going, and where he would be, so that Neill would know when he woke up. Hoping that Neill would have recovered by the time he got back, he took half his kit with him, planning to leave it at House Boulder with the dive-sacks already brought down by Kevin and Victor. The route was an easy clamber down and across a sloping rock shelf, which was steep, but not dangerous in the dry.

Arriving at House Boulder about forty-five minutes later, he found the dive-sacks, but was disappointed to discover that his note of the day before was also still there, evidently unread. He then went in search of an abseil point, and after twenty minutes spotted a blue sling looped around a prominent granite outcrop. There it was: he could see a fixed rope going down the face of the rock and out of sight. But he was puzzled to find a rope at that spot, for he knew that New and Pinfield had scrambled down the 50-metre drop, sliding between rocks and bushes, and had not bothered to abseil. (Later he realised that Mayfield had used the rope in preference to scrambling – which was reasonable enough, considering the weight of the men's packs.)

Still finding no sign of the others, he decided to leave them another note, in case they returned, and on a page torn from his notebook he wrote: 'Bob/Rich/Britt: RV 1100 27 FEB AT ABSEIL POINT. VITAL YOU COMPLY!' His sense of urgency was reflected in the way he wrote – abrupt phrases in large capital letters, straight to the point.

He planned that if Neill were still incapacitated, he himself would be at the rendezvous which he had called for 1100, together with Kevin, so that he could establish proper communication with Mayfield. If, on the other hand, Neill had recovered, the whole of the back group would go to the abseil point together.

When Neill awoke on Table Rock, he found – to his immense relief – that he felt back to normal: his face was still swollen, and his voice husky, but much of his strength had returned. The Hong Kong soldiers, who were making breakfast, told him what Foster was doing – and as he stood drinking coffee, he looked down the slope and heard two separate whistle blasts. Then he saw Mayfield coming up fast, wearing a T-shirt and shorts and almost running. He felt pleased and relieved that the corporal was going to tell him the form, so he greeted him warmly and gave him a cup of tea.

'Good to see you, Boss,' said the corporal. 'Sorry to hear you've been ill.' He was in a cheerful mood, and clearly excited by the ground ahead. He reported that from the point that they had reached he could see the riverbed in the Gully. His group had already gone down two abseils, one of 50 metres and one of 15, and he himself had recced two or three more below that. At the bottom of those drops, he reckoned, they would probably be on the bed of the Gully. One thing had become clear – that they would need two or three of the rear party's ropes; so he had come back up to collect some, to brief Neill on what lay ahead, and to obtain permission to go down the next set of abseils to the Gully bed.

He described the two fixed ropes which his team had descended already, and explained that because of the length of the abseils ahead, he would have to pull his ropes through. Once he had done that, he would not be able to get back up. He would, however, leave his belays in position, so that the second group could attach their own ropes to them when they made their way down. He also asked Neill to pull through any double ropes which he left, so that by the time they all met up again, each party would have about the same number of ropes.

Mayfield was in good spirits, but was clearly in a hurry. 'I can't stay long,' he said. 'I've left the guys in a dicey position. They can't move from where they are unless I'm with them.' Another reason for wanting to press on, he said, was that they had already used four out of the ten days' rations and he was concerned about the lack of progress given the increasingly serious food situation. Further, Bob Mann had cracked a tooth and was suffering from what seemed to be an abscess behind it, so they did not want to hang about.

Neill reckoned that if Mayfield needed only three more abseils to reach the start of the Gully, there was no problem. His recce group was doing what he intended they should – finding the way down – and he saw no reason to slow its progress now, given the fact that the expedition had lost a day through his being ill. So he said, 'OK. Crack on, and carry on laying the ropes out. RV with us at the bottom of the abseils. Wait for us there. How long do you think it will take?'

Mayfield thought that since it was less than an hour down to House Boulder, the second group should easily reach the bottom of all the abseils by that evening. Again Neill said, 'All right, then: but keep in contact, and remember I've got the Hong Kong soldiers with me.'

At the Inquiry there was a conflict of evidence when the Board asked about events on Table Rock on that morning. Neill had already explained how he had given Mayfield permission to carry on laying out ropes down the cliff, and had instructed him to wait for the second group at the bottom of the abseils. It then appeared that his and Mayfield's memories differed widely. The corporal told the Inquiry he had said to Neill on several occasions that he 'was not prepared to wait longer than the next morning.' Neill had no recollection of him saying this and he told the Board that he would not have tolerated such arrogance. But since there had been no witnesses to the crucial conversation between him and Mayfield, the two agreed to differ over what had been said. The Inquiry found that Mayfield's subsequent actions based on the remark he remembered making to Neill were justified.

Towards the end of this conversation, Foster arrived back from his early foray. On his way up he had heard someone blowing a whistle, and had immediately answered with a blast on his own. He also heard Neill shout, 'Mayfield's coming up behind you!' and knew that, with his voice returning, he must be feeling better.

94

Then he had seen Mayfield coming up below and to one side of him, perhaps 40 metres away, and called to him. The corporal asked where 'the Boss' was. Foster pointed to Table Rock, two or three hundred metres off, and shouted that the colonel had been ill the previous day; he called to Mayfield to wait for him, but the corporal, not hearing him, carried on out of sight below a long slab of bare rock.

As Foster reached the bivvy site on Table Rock, a hand came down to help him up – one of the Chinese. He found Neill and Mayfield already in conversation, and was delighted to see that Neill seemed fully himself again. The colonel told him that Mayfield had brought some good news, that he could see the bed of the Gully and that they would RV that evening. In conversation with Mayfield, Foster told him that he had extra rations which he would share out when they met up.

The corporal set off rapidly to rejoin his group taking three of the back party's ropes with him as well as some slings and karabiners. Soon afterwards, Neill's party packed up and set out for House Boulder, which they reached at 1030. They recognised the great rock from Robert New's photograph – an enormous lump, the size of a large building, with an overhang under which New and Pinfield had spent a night.

In front of them now was a view so dramatic that for a moment everything else was forgotten. Suddenly they could see right down into Low's Gully – and nothing they had read or heard quite prepared them for its impact. Far down in an immensely deep ravine, perhaps a kilometre away to the north, the boulder-strewn bed of the watercourse was lit up by the sun: on either side of it walls of granite climbed away at unbelievable angles, with pockets of scrub clinging to parts of the left-hand slope. Yet the aspect, though spectacular, was not forbidding, and the party's spirits lifted as they gazed at its sheer magnificence.

Soon they scrambled down through some boulders and reached Mayfield's first abseil: he had looped eight-foot blue tapes round two separate rocks, in a classic double belay, above a cliff about 50 metres deep. Foster picked up the note he had left earlier that morning, and found, scrawled on the back: 'NO CAN

95

DO. RETREAT.' The word RETREAT had been crossed out. He was struck by the ambiguity of this reply. What did it mean? Had Mayfield at one moment decided that Neill's party should go back, but then changed his mind? Mayfield had left the rope in place, and had told Neill that it could remain where it was – perhaps thinking that if the going became impossible lower down, it would give them an avenue of escape. At the bottom they found one of Brittan's chirpiest notes: 'FOLLOW THE M1 TO WHERE WE'RE SLEEPING.'

On this, the second group's first real abseil, Foster led, and Neill supervised the Hong Kong soldiers, rigging a safety rope to boost their confidence, and coming down last himself. The officers deliberately took things slowly, so as not to unnerve their less experienced companions, and gave them plenty of help. Kevin, Victor and Chow, for their part, moved carefully and did as they were told. Kevin went first, and shouted up instructions in Cantonese as his companions came down.

Leaving the fixed rope in position, the group crossed a patch of scrubby vegetation and came to another short abseil, where they followed the same procedure. But when Neill, the last man, threw the safety rope down, it snagged on a rock, so that he had to abseil down the main rope and manoeuvre it across the face of the cliff before he could jumar up and free the stuck one – an exhausting business which took some time and made him realise how much he had been weakened by his virus. Until that moment, he had thought that his strength was unimpaired.

Those first descents revealed how nervous Kevin was: now and then, as he swung out over a drop, he let fly a cry of alarm, which elicited ribald responses from his Cantonese comrades. When he was on the rope, he was often out of sight of Neill, who was playing out the safety rope as he went down; and the colonel found that the best method of giving him advice was to relay messages through another of the Chinese standing beside him, or to the third, who was already down and in sight at the bottom of the abseil.

Having descended through a short stretch of vegetation, they came on the other party's bivvy site, where one of them, ever humorous, had left his calling-card – a turd perched on top of a rock. Pressing on down the dry granite watercourse, Neill's group reached a dramatic drop, where wide, smooth sheets of rock vanished over a cliff, with mist swirling around and obscuring the bottom. After days of dry weather, there was only a trickle of water running down the middle, but it was clear from the lack of vegetation that if heavy rain came on, the whole fall-line would turn into a cataract and become lethally dangerous.

Now they were at the top of the abseils described by Robert New, their first serious obstacle: they recognised the place from a photograph which New himself had shown them. They had christened it 'Pinfield Edge'. As a belay Mayfield had left them a sling wrapped round a tree, with a karabiner through which ran a rope, joined to a second rope, with the knot one metre below the crab. Both ropes then ran down over the edge of the rock, and this showed them that there was a long abseil below – if the drop had been 25 metres or less, Mayfield would have needed only one rope doubled. The corporal had taken the quickest option of using the sling and crab, instead of taking time to search for a natural belay point.

To avoid leaving equipment behind, Neill re-rigged the system by passing the ropes round a tree, and carefully arranging the knot which joined the two so that it would not jam when the moment came to pull them down. All this took time.

Foster went over first, to discover what the difficulties were and guide the others down from the bottom. Then came the Chinese, secure on a safety rope, Neill having made sure that they were clipped on properly. He himself abseiled down last, after ensuring that the knot was clear of the tree and other obstructions.

The first major abseil was formidably steep: from the top, they could not see the bottom, so that they went over the edge blind, trusting that everything below them was in order. At the bottom of the 50-metre drop down the cliff face they came to rest on a ledge little more than a metre wide, and there they found another of Brittan's jaunty notes. This one told them that they were 'half way to getting wet', reminded them not to forget to pull the ropes through, and ended, 'See you at the bottom for tea and toast.' Far below them lay the Gully, in clear view now, and they thought that the wood which they could see, a couple of hundred metres down, was on or near the floor of the Gully itself. Beside them to the west an immensely steep face of rubble and dense vegetation soared away into Commando Cauldron.

In that exposed position they tried to pull down the abseil ropes – but after moving for half a metre, they jammed, and no amount of heaving or shaking could shift them, even when all five men exerted their full strength. Being dynamic, the ropes merely stretched, so that pulling did not put any great pressure on the obstruction, whatever it might be. Already the time was 1550. Neill, realising that he had not fully recovered from his virus, did not feel strong enough to jumar up 50 metres to free the blockage: he certainly could not send any of the Hong Kong men up, and he did not expect Foster – who was less agile than he – to go up either. Nor was he prepared to leave two precious ropes behind.

'I don't feel strong enough to do it safely now,' he announced, 'but I'll do it in the morning when I've got my strength back – unless Mayfield comes up first, of course.' He hoped that the corporal must be waiting for them only two abseils down, in the bed of the Gully proper. From where they were, they had a clear line of sight down to the woods, where they assumed Mayfield and his group were now pitching camp; and they thought that if they hung a red dive-sack over their ledge, Mayfield would spot it and realise they needed help. They would then lower a rope, up which he could climb to give them a hand. They hoped he would arrive before nightfall and meanwhile they put on a brew.

Leaving a lookout to keep watch, the rest of the party moved along the ledge to the point where it widened out into steeply sloping greenery, and Foster scouted for possible scrambling routes, to see if there was any way of getting up or down without using a rope, but without success.

When no one appeared from below, they prepared to bivvy down for the night. They had no means of knowing that the recce group, far from being close beneath them, was in fact eight long

98

abseils ahead: what Mayfield had understandably thought was the bed of the Gully was in fact only another false crest or rim, with hidden drops and cliffs below it. Having gone through the belt of scrub which he reckoned was at the start of the Gully proper, he had done six more abseils, pulling his ropes down each time, before he reached the real Gully bed. From this point it was physically impossible for him to climb back to where the second group had come to rest: arguably it could have been done from the wooded area, but not from the bottom, below all the big drops.

Strictly speaking, he had not exceeded his brief. Neill had told him to go on down as far as the start of the Gully, and to wait for the second group there. This he had done. The trouble was that both first and second groups had been deceived by the size and number of the drops ahead of them. Neill and Foster found it distressing that the team's specialist rock-climbing instructor was in a position from which he could not give assistance to those behind him. However the Board of Inquiry subsequently found that Mayfield had in fact acted quite properly.

In any event, the expedition was well and truly cut in two, and for the rest of their time in the Gully, the rear party never saw their climbing instructor, or any of their other colleagues, again.

Chapter 8

Problems

The night was clear and starry, and the second group slept well on their ledge, which widened out inside the wood, and offered them all fairly comfortable places in which to bed down. Normally they burned or buried rubbish, but on this site they left behind an empty sardine can, together with a green bag with the name NEILL on it. Over the years debris falling from above had built up a cushion of rotting vegetation and damp earth, in which scrub, orchids, pitcher plants and bamboo grass were growing. In case a sudden flood came down in the night, they tied themselves and their packs to trees and roots, but they felt safe enough. They just had to pray that no boulder decided to fall away from the cliff face above them while they slept.

Yet Neill was starting to worry that their progress was so slow. They had rations left for six days, and he knew that at their present rate of progress they would need at least one more day to reach the bed of the Gully. New and Pinfield, once down on the Gully floor, had done a day's boulder-hopping before they reached the point where they had broken out into the jungle – and from there it had taken them three more days to reach the nearest village. Neill reckoned that he was still just within New's time-frame, but had nothing to play with.

He and Foster spent hours discussing what Mayfield and company might or might not have done; but Neill was still convinced that the corporal would be back in the morning. The air in the ravine was still and quiet, and they considered shouting down, to see if they could raise any answer from below; but Neill told his people not to, for fear that a sudden noise might dislodge loose rocks from the cliff face towering above them.

They were up with the dawn at 0630 and began making breakfast. There was no sign of Mayfield, and by the time they had finished eating, Neill decided that he himself must jumar up the stuck ropes. Leaving his pack at the bottom, he went up in a slow, laborious ascent, to find that what had jammed the knot was a dislodged rock. Having cleared the obstruction, he descended again, and the others went to pull the ropes down. There were a few moments of suspense as they wondered whether they would move this time – but to everyone's relief they ran freely.

Glad as the men were to have recovered them, they knew that their act of pulling the ropes down had cut off their own retreat, and committed them to continue their descent of the Gully. On the other hand, if they had kept leaving ropes in position, they might well run out when they started their descent of the Gully proper. In fact Neill had little choice. Had his group retreated at that moment, and jumared back up the rope, he would have abandoned the recce group to their fate, for no reason, apart from concern about rations.

By 1030 they were ready to continue. Apart from their other worries, Neill and Foster were concerned that the recce party was poorly provided with essentials. They soon found another sling left round a conical rock in the middle of the watercourse. Foster removed it and put a rope round one tree, with a safety rope attached to another close by – an easy arrangement which would save leaving kit behind. 'First group have no aerial photographs or original maps,' Neill noted in his diary. 'Decreasing stocks of ropes, slings and crabs. They seem to be leaving equipment behind as if there were no tomorrow.'

By 1350 they had reached the bottom of the second major abseil. It ended on a very steep slab, and the rope was not long enough for them to pendulum across to safety. Foster, first down, set up a handrail to guide the others across, for their heavy packs were threatening to topple them over the next full pitch. On the third abseil, which they attempted in the afternoon, they found that Mayfield had left a belay in the form of a tape passed round a rock submerged in a pool, with a karabiner for the rope to slide through. Neill found a bush, well rooted but in a very precarious position, with room for only one person on the stance, which

101

they used as their third belay-point, and Foster attached their safety rope to Mayfield's belay. Another of Brittan's notes warned them that the drop was 15 metres longer than the rope. 'Go to right-hand side of ledge,' it said. 'Follow stream to river bed.' Foster, being last man down, detached the safety rope first, and brought the sling and crab with him.

On this abseil, of two 50-metre ropes joined together, there was a good deal of vegetation, and as Neill led, he could not help dislodging several large pitcher plants: they fell through the air to burst on the rocks below with sickening, juicy explosions which in his imagination sounded like human skulls popping. Guiltily he realised that they were of such a size that they would have been hailed as prize specimens on the tourist side of the mountain. At the bottom of the rope he had to pendulum across to an almost non-existent ledge and let go. He then slid down a steep incline through slippery undergrowth, to one side of a dry waterfall, using his own rope tied to shrubs, and making a handrail out of it to help the others down.

All this took time, and they did not reach the bottom until last light. In the entire day they had done only two abseils and descended no more than 120 metres. 'Bloody hell!' was Neill's verdict on their progress, which bore no relation to the swift advance made by New. 'Why are we using these very long abseils when New needed only two altogether?' Foster asked his diary. The short answer was that the army team was paying far greater attention to safety: the last thing that Neill wanted was an incident that would destroy the fragile confidence that was beginning to develop among the Hong Kong soldiers.

He and Foster decided that, with dusk coming on, they would do better to leave the last pair of ropes where they were for the night: if they tried to pull them down, and they jammed, it would be impossible to see what had happened. Instead, they made camp just before darkness descended, in a wooded area at the base of the waterfall, where a patch of begonias made an excellent bed. They got a good fire going and sat round it chatting; later they lay back in their sleeping bags looking up at a brilliant sky, with shooting stars hurtling across the Gully above them.

By now Neill was less confident about meeting Mayfield again in the near future. He still hoped that he would, but saw that he was perhaps being unrealistic. Yet he did not feel unduly worried about his own group's position, as each of them still had more than five days' worth of food. The party was also well equipped for making a fire. They had independent supplies of matches and gas-lighters, besides slow-burning matches which would light in a high wind. Now that they were beside the stream, there was abundant water, and, in dry weather, plenty of material for bonfires. Neill's biggest concern – about the ability of the Hong Kong soldiers on the exposed abseils – was receding as each day went by. He was pleased that he had persevered in encouraging the trio to remain on the expedition, and both he and Foster were quietly confident in their growing ability on the ropes. Foster, however, *was* still worried that the expedition was not all together, as it should have been, even though Brittan's notes seemed designed to help and encourage the back party. The situation reminded him of the carrot and the donkey.

On Day Six – Tuesday 1 March – they were up early. Neill and Kevin got their ropes down without too much difficulty. Foster washed and dressed a nasty leg wound, apparently inflicted by the end of a branch on the last abseil. Again the weather was fine, and by 0730 they were on their way, down through the jungly wood, following a tangled watercourse, clambering over mossy boulders along a rough trail paranged by the recce group. When they found that they were being followed by a mountain blackbird, Neill told the Chinese that it was flesh-eating. 'We've got to get a move on,' he warned them. 'It's just waiting for us to make a mistake before it devours us.' (The bird followed them for the whole of that day, clearly never having seen humans before.)

After half an hour they emerged from the wood and suddenly saw the bed of the Gully, very clear, and not at all far off below them – perhaps 500 metres in line of sight. This was a thrilling moment: at last to be within reach of the expedition's target. Vast boulders littered the bed of the watercourse, and above it granite cliffs rose sheer for 700-800 metres. The trouble was,

103

another huge waterfall-cum-cliff face fell away beneath them. At once, with a chill, Neill realised why Mayfield had not come back: the recce party would have needed all their ropes to abseil down it, and, having pulled them down, they would not have been able to return.

It turned out that Neill's party needed six separate abseils to descend that drop of perhaps 300 metres in all. Now, in the dry weather, only a trickle of water was going down it, but they could see that after heavy rain a torrent 10 metres wide would fill the whole channel. Foster, in the lead, found that water had eroded the rock into narrow channels or chutes, which were extremely smooth and slimy, but easy for a man wearing a pack to get stuck in. With sod's law being what it is, he became jammed: struggling to extricate himself, he moved out of the funnel, across to one side and picked out a route which avoided the sticking-point. Then, looking at the vegetation on the steep flanks of the dry waterfall, he decided to try the method which had been employed by New and Pinfield – sliding, and using packs as brakes.

This proved easy and effective, and he used it down the second abseil as well; but then Neill, who was leading down a third abseil, shouted up that Foster was heading for a precipice, and had better come back on the ropes: the slope was becoming just too steep.

The descent continued to be very tricky, and the officers spent much time reconnoitring the way down, deciding how best to tackle the next stretch, recovering the sling-and-karabiner belays which Mayfield had used, and finding trees or bushes strong enough to bear their weight. Foster kept thinking how much time they would have saved if the whole group had been together, and Mayfield had been able to show them what he himself had done.

Although still vaguely hoping to see the recce group, Neill sensed more and more strongly that the expedition was irrevocably split. All he could imagine was that one of the recce group had hurt himself, or that Mann's toothache had worsened. Yet there had been nothing in Brittan's occasional notes to suggest any such problem (and afterwards Mann confirmed that his toothache never became really serious). The messages had all been flippant comments on the route – 'You've got a wet one ahead. Enjoy your shower', and so on – but after this they ceased.

Perched above the final abseil, they could at last look straight into the Gully. Below them they saw the boulders spoken of by New, many as big as buildings, stretching away northwards for half a kilometre or more in a relatively straight run down, until they disappeared in mist round a shoulder of the mountain. From the fact that there was no greenery of any kind in the floor of the ravine, it was clear that after rain the boulders must be scoured by terrific flows of water cascading from the heights. Above to their left a colossal slope, covered in tangled vegetation and jumbles of fallen rock, soared up towards Commando Cauldron. Neill and Foster felt hemmed in and enclosed by the towering faces and peaks on every hand.

How New had reached this spot in two abseils, when their own party needed eleven, they could not imagine – but at least they were safely down. (Later they discovered from New himself that the two pioneers had slid down many of the drops on their bums, and had been exceedingly fortunate not to suffer serious injury.)

At 1730, as he unclipped himself from the final abseil, Neill found himself standing among gigantic boulders, light grey and mottled, in the bed of the Gully. Some of the rocks were rough-edged and brightly coloured, showing that they had fallen in comparatively recent times, but most were worn smooth by water. Neill's party could find no note, but the remains of a fire showed that the recce group had camped there – the obvious site, as it was level and open. Down there, deep in the ravine, darkness had fallen by the time Foster, the last man, reached safety. Because they were among so much rock, it was impossible to pitch a tent, and everyone had to doss down on granite in the open.

Towering above them to the east was the enormous wall of granite which plunged 600 metres sheer from the end of Easy Valley. Thirteen hundred metres above their heads, a ring of bare-rock ridges and peaks formed the valley rim, sharp against

105

the darkening sky. It was a thrilling spot, and everybody was exuberant at having reached it. 'Fantastic!' they exclaimed, shaking each other's hands. 'We've made it.'

The altimeter gave their height as 2,780 metres. They had abseiled 250 metres during the day. By then the Chinese were full of confidence: their morale was high, and they felt fully integrated into the party. 'You're the first people from Hong Kong ever to have stood in this place,' Neill told them. 'Well done!' Their chests puffed out visibly – they had conquered their fears and accomplished feats which they had imagined would be far beyond them.

After another good night – in spite of rock beds – it took Foster and Neill two hours to pull down the ropes, mainly because they had to climb a considerable distance, and their route of the previous afternoon had taken them round an elbow, making the recovery awkward. By now the ropes seemed to have minds of their own, twisting and tangling, and once again a knot had jammed – this time in a branch bleached white and smooth by the passage of time and water. While Foster and Neill battled with the ropes, the others spent a few minutes making a large RLC out of stones, on a flat slab. (This later became known to the Royal Air Force mountain rescue team as 'RLC Slab'.)

At 1000 on the morning of 2 March the group was at last on its way. The omens seemed propitious. The weather was still fine. They had reached the Gully and begun the rock-hopping stage of the trip, à la Robert New. Three, four, five metres high, the boulders demanded the greatest care. Sometimes it was possible to step from one to another; in other places the men had to slide down the smooth sides and rely on becoming wedged when the gap between that rock and its neighbour narrowed towards the bottom. On other boulders they took off their packs and lowered them to colleagues below, who helped them down, after which they struggled back into their straps. To their right was an almost vertical wall of bare granite; to their left, a steep concave slope covered with rough vegetation gave way to a vertical rock face which soared up towards Low's Peak.

Slowly and laboriously they made their way down, with a few

minor falls, but no serious injury. At one point they found another huge watercourse coming down off the mountain from their right, and made a note of its position, at 2,630 metres. Already they had established that the contours marked on their maps were pure speculation on the part of the cartographers, so they were hoping to help produce a more accurate record of the Gully. A brilliant turquoise kingfisher darted by, surprising the two officers, who did not expect there to be any fish at this level. They also wondered what the mountain blackbird, which continued to follow them, could be living on.

Then at 1500, in the middle of this steady progress, the weather suddenly changed. Mist swept up from below, rain began to fall, and within ten seconds the surface of the boulders changed from smooth but negotiable to as slippery as if they had been coated in grease, and the chances of breaking a leg or ankle immediately tripled. All at once it was dangerous to move at all, and progress dwindled almost to nothing.

With rain now falling heavily, the group was going to need shelter for the night. The onset of darkness, at about 1830, would end any chance of further movement; but again there was no chance of pitching a tent, so well before nightfall they began to look for a boulder with an overhang under which they could take refuge. In fact they bivvied under two adjacent overhangs.

By now Neill was seriously concerned: he had expected to lose height much faster. Officially, as from next morning, they had three days' rations left. During that day they had lost only 200 metres of height. They had at least another 1,300 metres to go down before they reached the Penataran river. The problem was beginning to look very difficult.

The morning of 3 March was fine, but the rocks were still wet and treacherous, so progress was again slow. Inevitably, Kevin slipped and sprained an ankle: after Neill had checked the joint to make sure that nothing was broken, Victor strapped it up for him – but thereafter he was limping all the way. At 1100 the sun cleared the wall of the ravine, to shine on them, and soon after midday they reached a high, lone tower of granite which Foster dubbed Owl Pinnacle. Neill stared at it for some time, finding it hard to discern the shape of a bird – but Owl Pinnacle it became.

Chow was proving, if not exactly the joker in the pack, at least accident-prone: he was very thin – gangly, almost – and his movements were rather uncoordinated, so that he tended to stumble about. Yet the one who hurt himself was Victor, who, when he was leading, slipped on a rock chute, landed on his back and hurtled down into a pool. He was able to haul himself out, and the others, who had hastened down to his aid, helped him out of his pack and checked him over. After a few minutes, although in pain, he was able to proceed.

If the boulders became too big to climb down, or were so tightly packed that there was no way between them, small abseils became necessary. Every so often the group discovered a sling and a karabiner, and occasionally a cut-off rope, which the recce party had left behind. This gave them the impression that the kit had been left in place for the second group to use, causing Kevin to ask, 'If Richard knows we're following him down, why doesn't he wait for us?' At the time nobody could answer that question. Later the recce party expressed their clear belief that the second group had turned back. When they looked back up the Gully and saw a lone figure on a rope, they got the impression that Neill's party was retreating.

In any event, whenever it was possible, the second team gathered everything up for future use. Wet rope is heavy, awkward to coil and time-consuming to pack, so Neill and Foster alternately carried a coil and threw it down or over obstacles, to recover it later, or used it for occasional abseils.

After a quick lunchtime snack, the party did two short abseils. Here and there the Gully widened out, and lush vegetation clung to the lower slopes, before the cliffs reared away above. Suddenly the stunted palm trees, rising out of the mist, reminded Neill strongly of Conan Doyle's Lost World.

At about 1700 huge drops of rain began splatting down. As the party turned a corner of the Gully, they found an immense overhanging crag – a whole cliff, in fact, a vast buttress protruding from the left-hand face of the ravine. To Neill it was the shape and size of the prow of an old-fashioned battleship, and he named it Battleship Cave. To escape the rain, they clambered into it, and then had to abseil about 10 metres to reach a level area at the back. There they found enough dry wood to make a fire: the timber had obviously been swept down by a flood and stranded when the water subsided. Inside the cave lay an old red sling, held down by a rock: Neill suspected (and later confirmed) that New had also taken shelter in the cave, but what gave him pause was the fact that the nylon was frayed and faded. This showed that in times of flood the water in the Gully must rise dramatically.

It was now the evening of Day Eight. Battleship Cave was at 2,280 metres, which meant they had descended only 230 vertical metres during the day; and as the group sat huddled round the fire for warmth, Neill pointed out that their problems were fast becoming acute. With food supplies dwindling, he asked everyone to turn out their packs and see what they had left, so that he could make an accurate assessment of their stocks. As he expected, each of them had roughly the equivalent of two full days' rations, with a few extra bits and pieces which they had saved, and some reserves which Foster had intended to offer to the first group when they met up. The Chinese still had relatively good supplies of dried noodles (their favourite food) and biscuits, as well as some of the sardines and chocolate they had bought at the Panar Laban kiosk.

Neill announced that they must all plan to stretch what they had left over six days. He reasoned that, at best, it would take one day to reach New's Pools, and then, if the worst came to the worst, at least three more to climb out along his escape route – four days, plus two for unforeseen contingencies. The mere fact that they were in trouble seemed to reduce their appetites, and a small meal that evening was enough to stanch their hunger. Luckily they were all still well supplied with sachets of tea, coffee, orange and lemon powder and Bovril. After they had eaten, they went into their by now familiar routine of changing into dry clothes for the night – pulling on tracksuits, fleeces and so on before the never-ending drizzle, drifting into the cave, made them damp, and then wriggling into sleeping bags.

On Friday 4 March, after an indifferent night on lumps of

granite, they set off early. During the day they did three short abseils, and on two of them they used short ropes cut off and left behind by the recce party. In the absence of any further notes, Neill assumed that all was well up front – and again the scatter of equipment encouraged Foster to think that the recce group was expecting the others to follow. 'They're using up valuable rope and cutting it,' he noted. 'At some stage they're going to want the ropes, slings and crabs which we've been left to collect.' By now Neill had dispensed with safety ropes for the Hong Kong soldiers, who relied solely on prussik loops attached to their chest harnesses to prevent themselves being turned upside-down by the weight of their packs whenever their boots slipped on the greasy rock.

At the bottom of a controlled slide down a short waterfall, Foster landed awkwardly on gravel and fell over on to his chest on a protruding rock, with the full weight of his pack on top of him, and water splattering down all round. 'Fierce pain,' he recorded in his diary that night. 'Thought I'd broken a rib.' He remembered the occasion on which he had cracked two ribs in a skiing accident on Cairngorm, and likened this mishap to the earlier one. There was nothing the others could do for him; but Victor, looking worried, said comfortingly, 'If you've broken your rib, you could die!' The remark may have sounded melodramatic, but he was not far wrong: a broken rib could easily puncture a lung, and everyone watched Foster anxiously for signs of blood frothing out of his mouth. None appeared, however, and later it turned out that the rib was only cracked. In half an hour the patient judged himself fit enough to carry on.

Almost immediately after this mishap, they stopped for the night, above a short but not particularly difficult waterfall. Since there was no obvious belay point in sight, Neill considered it prudent to let Foster nurse his injuries before tackling this next abseil. Evening saw them at 2,025 metres – a vertical loss during the day of only 255 metres.

Because of the disposition of the boulders, they had to split into two groups to find shelter. The Hong Kong soldiers had first choice of a good overhang, in which they soon had a brew going, and the two Britons scouted back upstream for a few metres until they came to the waterfall on which Foster had had his accident. Close by they found another small overhang, where they devoted the last hour of daylight to the task of trying to make a bed out of stones and gravel; Foster could not use his left arm to lift, as it was causing him severe pain, but he did his best to help level out a sleeping area. When they had finished, their beds looked like two gravestones surrounded by the green, slimy algae of the small grotto.

In the last minutes of daylight Neill went forward and found a suitable tree, around which he looped a rope, ready for the first abseil of the morning.

That was the end of Day Nine. When they had their evening brew, Neill announced that their remaining rations – about one and two-thirds days' worth – would have to be spun out indefinitely. He himself proposed to cut down to one biscuit or its equivalent a day, which was all he thought he could afford. 'Don't worry, though,' he added, lying through his teeth for the benefit of the Hong Kong soldiers. 'This isn't an emergency. We just need to be sensible and conserve our food.' He could see that Kevin and the others were not convinced, so he jokingly pointed out that they all had plenty of flesh on them, and that – best of all – nobody was seriously injured. Foster had stove in his ribs, Victor was still muttering about his back, and Kevin had twisted an ankle; but all were mobile, and the expedition as a whole was still going forward. More ominously, they had noticed an appreciable increase in the level of water in the Gully. That night, for the first time, the roar of the waterfall made conversation difficult. Nobody needed reminding that this was the day on which they should have reported back to Park Headquarters.

Later that evening, in the warmth of their sleeping bags, Neill and Foster discussed their worsening situation. Neill was particularly worried by their slow progress: they were taking far too long, and there was nothing they could do to accelerate. Minor injuries, and the difficulty of obtaining a footing on the glass-like surface of the rock, had slowed their progress

111

drastically. Already it was clear that they would have to make stringent economies with their remaining rations.

The morning of Day Ten, Saturday 5 March, dawned cloudy, but at least it was dry. The group was up at first light, and after an early brew and a couple of spoonfuls of rolled oats, they abseiled from the tree and pulled the rope down behind them. Hardly had they completed that operation when rain came on once more. Neill was wondering where the hell New's Pools could be: his party had now been in the Gully for three days, and should have reached those two small obstacles long ago. All they could do was carry on down, over rocks made dangerously slick by the rain; but when, after one more short abseil, he came round a slight bend and over a lip, he suddenly knew beyond any doubt that he had reached the critical point.

Recognising the place from New's slides, he saw at once why the two earlier explorers had decided not to go on. In an instant the nature of the Gully changed from negotiable to almost impossible. The next section looked lethally dangerous, and brought New's words vividly to mind: once a man committed himself to the waterfalls proper, he would never be able to get back up again.

Chapter 9

Trapped

The Gully, already extremely steep on either side, narrowed dramatically to a V-shaped channel scarcely more than a metre wide at its base, with smooth rock faces rising sheer from the water, black and glistening for the first 10 metres, then cloaked with vegetation above. Below their feet two slender pools, about 20 metres long and three or four wide, lay in line – ahead along the bed of the ravine, steel grey under the cloudy sky, the second on a level lower than the first. At the near end, above the start of the first pool, a single boulder or chock-stone was wedged in the foot of the rock V, with water pouring under, round and over it. The far end of the little lake was blocked by a second chock-stone – and beyond that the Gully simply vanished. As Neill put it, 'We were looking at air.' It was clear that beyond the pools the ravine turned sharply to the left, and dropped precipitously, with all the water from the northern face of the mountain plunging through the one tiny gap.

No wonder New and Pinfield had decided that to go on would be madness: after a look round, they had retreated perhaps 50 metres, climbed 150 metres up the fragile foliage on the eastern wall of the Gully, and gingerly traversed along it until they could look down and get a better view of the bottleneck – a series of narrow channels with water boiling down them. Liking the look of it even less, Pinfield – experienced rock-climber as he was – decided not to chance it, but to escape from the Gully altogether. He and his partner somehow managed to claw their way hundreds of metres up to the ridge and break out through the jungle to the north – but they had done it in dry weather.

Now Neill and his party were faced by the same obstacle. Looking down at the pools, they saw a blue sling looped round a rock, with a karabiner attached, half a metre under water, and so knew that the recce group had passed through the gorge. Going down on one rope to examine the karabiner closely, Neill glanced across to his right and saw another rope dangling down a steep slab of rock and cut off at the bottom, where it entered the first pool. It seemed that Mayfield had devised some system designed to prevent his team from having to abseil straight into the pool, and Neill spent half an hour scrambling about on the end of his own rope, trying to pendulum across the fall-line to a slightly easier area on the other side, in an attempt to find the way down.

The surface of the wet rock was like a skating rink. Eventually, frustrated by the difficulty of manoeuvring with his pack on, he took it off and managed to wedge it behind an exposed root. Five frenzied minutes later, fast running out of strength, he admitted defeat, and hauled himself back up to the others, leaving his pack where it was for the time being, to recover it later. The rest of them, meanwhile, had been scouting around to see if there was any way to bypass the pools through the undergrowth, and had come to the same conclusion as New – there was none.

To cap their difficulties, heavy rain had started again. All this time, the water level had been steadily rising, the power of the current increasing, and the noise swelling to a roar that began to make normal conversation difficult. Neill and Foster saw that they were now in serious trouble: it was an awful feeling, and their optimism, which had carried them that far, suddenly evaporated. All at once the Gully had declared its true nature, and they felt its menace crowding in on them. They still thought that the recce group had probably gone down past that point: at low water, it might have been possible. But the puzzle of the dangling rope made Neill wonder if they had broken out.

'They can't have more than two and a half rope-lengths left for whatever's ahead,' Foster shouted, above the noise of the water. 'Why the hell did they leave all this stuff strewn about the mountain?'

Whatever they had done, Neill did not feel confident about leading his own party over the falls ahead, especially now that the flow of water was so much greater. To have done so would have been pure recklessness. More than ever, he needed the expertise of Mayfield: this was precisely the sort of situation for which a JSRCI had been included in the party. His group also badly needed one of the parangs, both of which were with Mayfield's group: without a heavy, slashing blade of that kind, they would make little impression on the jungle if they tried to break out.

Foster, equally, did not like the look of the swollen pools and the dark, forbidding terrain beyond, which seemed to him 'bloody lethal'. Now, he felt, it was no longer a case of a carrot and a donkey: more like lemmings going over a cliff. The fact that the NCOs had not waited seemed to them then to be more incomprehensible than ever – especially as this was obviously the start of what they had identified from aerial photographs as the gorge section of the Gully. In Kota Kinabalu Mayfield, Shearer and Page had missed the late-night briefing at which Foster had shown a video version of New's slides; but Mann and Brittan had seen it, and must surely have recognised New's Pools – the beginning of the most difficult passage.

While Neill recovered his strength, with the water level rising by the minute, he and Foster discussed their predicament. Water splashing down on their climbing helmets, and finding its way into their clothes, increased their misery. Both feared that if they abseiled into the first long pool, to recce the way ahead, they might not be able to get back up against the formidable weight of the current. When the heavy rain turned into a downpour, compounding their worries, they made the decision to abort the expedition: a good command decision, short, sharp and to the point. They would not proceed any further down the Gully. Not only did it seem physically impossible: the menace of the place was amazingly strong. Foster reckoned that he could actually smell the danger. The officers knew they had made the right decision when the Hong Kong soldiers said that they too were most unhappy about the idea of going on down. Kevin stated categorically that they were not up to it, and that the Gully had become far too dangerous.

'Right, lads. It looks as though we're in a mess,' said Neill. 'We can't go down, so we'll adopt Plan B and find the escape route out. Up there – where New went.' He pointed at the jungle above them to the right.

They retreated 50 metres to a point where the wall of the ravine was not quite so steep. By then rain was hammering down, and the water in the Gully was rising visibly. They started trying to find a route up through the jungle on the right, the eastern flank of the ravine. The face was desperately steep, about 70 or 80 degrees, and covered in vegetation rooted in shallow, slimy black mud. Time and again, as the man leading put his weight on the mat of greenery, it would come away from the rock beneath, sending him flat on his face, or falling backwards, to knock off the man behind him. Whenever they did fall and start to slide down the cliff, they were eventually stopped by vegetation; but soon they were soaked to the skin, plastered in black mud, and losing strength as they fought the mountain.

Wide bands of smooth, vertical granite kept forcing them to their right – opposite to the way they wanted to go. In efforts to gain height they threw ropes round the more substantial trees – which were growing on such poor soil that they were only about three metres high – and pulled each other up; but most of the vegetation was as sappy and brittle as cucumbers, and broke off at the slightest pressure. With less than half an hour of light left, they had gained little more than 15 metres up the side of the Gully. Beneath them, the roar of the stream, surging over the boulders, grew ever louder.

Now they urgently needed shelter from the elements. Neill, taking his turn in the lead, shouted back to Foster, 'This is bloody useless! Let's pack it in before it gets dark.' So they reversed their steps, with Kevin Cheung now leading, sliding and slurping their way through the sodden undergrowth, about 100 metres upstream of the pools, still among dense foliage. By then it was almost dark, so Neill sent Kevin down a rope to the riverbed in a last, desperate attempt to find shelter. At the edge of the jungle Kevin suddenly came upon a large rock overhang and shouted back the good news to the others. Descending the rope and crawling in by the light of their head-torches, they found there was room for the whole party – and this refuge, soon named Kevin's Cave, became their home for the next three weeks.

116

They believed that they had come to rest at about 1,950 metres above sea level, but they could not tell precisely, as Neill's altimeter had started to fog up in the constant damp. Water was dripping from the underside of the overhang, but this seemed immaterial: they were out of the main downpour, and perhaps a metre and a half above the level of the torrent. After a look round the natural shelter, Neill put the Hong Kong men in the highest and driest area at the back, where the roof slanted down to meet the floor and there was barely half a metre of headroom. Neill decided to sleep at the other end, where a mass of rocks protruded from the floor of the cave. Foster was left with a sloping, shallow depression full of gravel, with granite lumps coming through it: to fit into it at all, he had to slide his legs right under a boulder nearly two metres high. (Had this fallen during the night, his legs would certainly have been crushed.)

A hot drink helped raise morale. There was no chance of drying the sodden clothes they were wearing, so Neill told everyone to concentrate on the task of protecting the rest of their kit from water, and in particular to make sure they kept their sleeping bags dry. Once out of their wet gear, into dry clothes and sleeping bags, the Hong Kong soldiers were reasonably comfortable, since they had space to stretch out, even if they did not have headroom. Neill and Foster could only lie doubled up among the boulders on the wet, muddy outer floor of the overhang. The roar of the torrent kept increasing outside, and they could hear water gurgling in fissures at the back of the cave, only a metre or so from their feet. Neill warned them all to be prepared to make an emergency exit in the middle of the night, should the water suddenly rise to a dangerous height.

Heavy rain continued throughout the hours of darkness: they could hear it beating on the leaves of the undergrowth. In the morning of Day Eleven – Sunday, 6 March – Neill wrote in his diary, 'Rescue situation now?' The seriousness of their position had hit him the previous night, when he and Foster realised that they were already one day overdue at Park Headquarters: now they could not go down, and they could not go up. He knew that the downpour had further reduced their chances of finding a way

117

out of the Gully. New and Pinfield had only just managed it when the ground was dry – so what hope had they after this deluge?

By first light the rain had eased off: peering out of the cave, they could see down the gorge – and the sight appalled them. Its bed was a raging mass of white water, with the odd boulder protruding from it. As Neill put it, 'you didn't need the brains of a bishop to realise that there was now no possibility of descending the Gully'. A man would have been washed away instantly and dashed to pieces over the falls.

In his journal Foster summed up the reasons for staying put, for the time being at least:

a. *Water level too dangerous to carry on.*
b. *Hong Kong soldiers need rest.*
c. *Several minor injuries.*
d. *Any escape bid must be planned properly, in view of our failed attempt yesterday.*
e. *Conserve energy and rations.*
f. *We are by water.*
g. *We have shelter.*
h. *Liew said helicopters available.*
i. *We can be seen from the air.*
j. *This is the most suitable spot in this part of the gully for a helicopter to get in.* *

Victor, Kevin and Chow did not stir all that day. Very tired, and perhaps in a state of shock, they simply slept – and the two officers were happy that they should, because none of the party was eating much, and conservation of energy had suddenly become a priority. At least, in their bags, the Hong Kong men were warm, dry, and recovering from the exertions of the day before; rest would also help heal injuries.

---

* Although Neill and Foster had been told there was no official rescue service, they knew that helicopters could fly as high as the summit area. They had seen one flying over Easy Valley as they were descending the rock face on 1 March. Foster recalled his conversation with Francis Liew the previous year, when Liew told him that he could hire a helicopter to reconnoitre his proposed route. They also knew that there was a helipad just below Panar Laban, at 3,344 metres.

When they eventually emerged, the officers explained that things were now looking very serious, and that whatever food remained would have to last indefinitely. The only way to survive, they said, was to stay dry, to avoid exposure, and, even more important, to conserve energy. The more energy they burnt up through nervousness or physical exertion, or trying to dry out when wet, the less they would have left, and the quicker they would lose weight.

Neill told them that he and Foster would look around, but that, with so much water in the stream, there was little they could do for the moment. Pulling on their wet clothes, they went out into the open. With only light rain now falling, the water level gradually dropped enough to allow limited exploration. Hopping from boulder to boulder, they examined the mountainside above the cave, to search for escape routes.

At that point the bed of the Gully was about 20 metres wide, with slabs of fern-studded rock rising almost vertically on either side. To continue down it was out of the question. To climb back up the falls above was equally impossible, because they had pulled their ropes down: even if they had managed to climb back some of the way, they would have been confronted by the immense cliff down which it had taken them three days to abseil. To stay where they were was their only realistic option. Higher upstream, the watercourse was overhung by trees, which would have hidden them from any helicopter on a rescue mission. They drew some comfort from the fact that it was already two days beyond the date – 4 March – on which they had said they would return to Park Headquarters. They suspected that the Malaysians would take little action on a Sunday, but there seemed a good chance that they would launch some form of search next morning. Neill remembered with remarkable clarity the joking remark made by the clerk in the office: 'Ha ha!' he had said. 'If you don't turn up, we'll come looking for you.' Now he kicked himself for not making firmer arrangements with Hong Kong in case of emergency.

Another line of hope lay with Robert New: they had arranged to meet him for a drink on the evening of Tuesday, 8 March – and if they failed to appear, he would surely raise the alarm. Further, they had left some of Foster's equipment with David Powell, and if no one came back for the kit, he, too, would sooner or later realise that they were in difficulties. So would their military contacts in Hong Kong and the United Kingdom, to say nothing of their families.

Neill found that the harsh reality of being stopped in his tracks bore down on him: he hated the 'awful feeling of being totally dependent on other people', but became all the more determined to look after his group, and not put them into still greater danger by doing anything foolish. His aims on that day were reduced to pure survival – making what food they had last, conserving energy, and trying to keep dry. Neill several times brought out one of his favourite adages: 'You know the saying,' he told Foster: '"If you're stuck, stay where you are, and you'll eventually be found."' So they decided to make Kevin's Cave their permanent base.

The most valuable task the trapped men could perform was to put out distress signals on the tops of those boulders which rose well above water level in the centre of the Gully, where they would be visible to any aircraft flying over. Foster began gathering stones and setting them out in the form of an SOS three metres long and over a metre high, and Neill joined in the work: for an hour or so Foster threw suitable stones up to him, on top of a large boulder with a fairly flat top. The stones – pieces of washed granite – were predominantly light grey, and stood out well on the carpet of thick green moss that covered the boulder. Foster also brought out his emergency space blanket – a two by one-and-a-half metre rectangle of aluminium sheeting, designed to contain heat when wrapped round a person, but also useful as a reflector to flash in the sun. Neill deployed his red dive-sack, which also stood out well, and later replaced it with a pair of red waterproof trousers. Foster made a figure '5' of stones, to represent five people. While working, they noticed that there was a good deal of bright, freshly broken granite in the bed of the river, but did not immediately recognise its significance. Only later did they realise that it must have come from recent rockfalls: in other words, the sides of the ravine were by no means stable.

Yet again the Gully was drenched by heavy rain, which persisted for the rest of the day, and the officers spent the time improving their area of the cave by excavating offensive boulders. Neill had been so uncomfortable the previous night that he decided to crowd into Foster's depression – but clearing it was real neolithic endeavour: Neill pounding away with a stone to loosen an embedded rock, Foster using a mess tin and tent-pole to scrape away surplus earth and grit. At the back of the overhang, little more than an arm's length away, they could see water glistening as it gurgled past, and realised that this showed the level in the main torrent, which for the moment was falling again.

A small meal of reconstituted egg mixed into a few noodles, together with a hot drink, completed their intake of nourishment for the day, but hunger seemed to have been killed by the danger of their position, and they felt little need for food. Neill, who had never been in a rescue situation before, felt 'gutted' by the fact that he was responsible for the party's predicament. Their aim was to conserve energy, recover strength and wait for the weather to improve – when they would try again to make a breakout. In his diary Neill asked the simple question: 'How many days can somebody survive on water?' and added: 'I have clearly been over-ambitious.' Foster recorded in his diary: 'Not a good night. Painful rib, and cramped conditions.'

On the morning of Monday, 7 March they found to their joy that the rain had stopped. The current in the watercourse was still very strong, and they were relieved that they had not tried to carry on beyond New's Pools. With the sun coming out occasionally, they seized the opportunity to dry their sodden clothes, which they spread out over the tops of big stones. Neill and Foster stripped off, glad to feel the sun on their bare skins, and the Hong Kong men wore their green Goretex anoraks, with nothing underneath them. They also made many unsuccessful attempts to light a fire: their matches were still working, but there was no dry material to be found. Little wood of any kind had survived among the boulders: the force of water had swept almost everything away. Nevertheless, they took elaborate precautions to keep their fire-making equipment dry, by religiously wrapping matches and flints in numerous layers of polythene, and, whenever they took out a single match, stowing the box again before tackling the fire.

There was one dead tree wedged among the rocks in the middle of the Gully, on which they could hang their clothes; its wood had been bleached white by innumerable floods and by the tropical sun, but even when they shaved slivers off it with their penknives, and sacrificed some precious blank pages from Neill's notebook as kindling, they could not get a blaze going. Here again, a parang would have been invaluable: with it, they could have hacked deep into the tree and perhaps excavated some drier wood from inside.

Because of the mountain walls towering on either hand, the sun was on them for only five hours, from 1000 to 1500, and intermittently at that; almost always mist shortened the day prematurely, and in mid-afternoon, inexorably, the light began to fade. The damp, the gloom and the constant sound of water reminded Neill of rivers on Dartmoor, and the temperature was not unlike that of Devon in autumn: only six or seven degrees Celsius at night, but pleasantly warm by day if the sun was on them.

Having little else to distract them, they watched the sun creep across the Gully, turned their clothes constantly to catch any gleam of warmth, and noticed once again the phenomenon of the mist coming in. One moment the air was clear; the next, cloud had billowed into the ravine, closing in on them from above and below simultaneously.

The two officers discussed every possible permutation of events at Park Headquarters, in Kota Kinabalu, in Hong Kong and in the United Kingdom, noting down dates on which people in each place might start to worry and take action. Whatever Park Headquarters might do, it was bound to be some days before anyone in Hong Kong or the United Kingdom became sufficiently worried to initiate a rescue operation. Neill and

Foster planned to go out on reconnaissance the following day in search of an escape route, one on either side of the Gully, each accompanied by a Hong Kong soldier. The fifth man would stay on the site, in case a rescue helicopter appeared.

With the sun gone, they worked again at improving their lair, and slung their tents and flysheets at an angle to intercept drips falling from the overhang. This proved successful, and greatly reduced the amount of water landing on them at night. They also broke large, fleshy leaves from undergrowth such as rubber plants and used them to carpet their sleeping area, slightly softening the impact of the underlying granite and keeping their bivvy bags clean. Neill was especially concerned that they should all stay dry: he knew that if they got wet, their chances of holding out would diminish, because they would gradually lose body warmth: hypothermia would set in, and their lives would fade away. One feature which gave Neill some relief was the absence of wind in the Gully: for almost all the time they were in still air, and therefore less prone to heat loss.

For supper they ate a small amount of beef granules and noodles – their only meal of the day, amounting to only 150 calories apiece, and played their first game of chess on a tiny plastic board which Neill had brought along. Throughout their enforced starvation, Neill and Foster were well aware of the debilitating effects of undernourishment. They were not experts in nutrition by any means, but they knew the truth of the simple equation, calories in equal calories out, and realised that they must have a minimum intake to keep their bodies functioning.

'We all wonder what has happened to the first group,' Neill wrote. 'Are they stuck, like us? Or are they cutting their way through the jungle?' He was haunted by the thought that, with the torrent in spate, they might have been swept down the Gully to their deaths. If they *were* dead, to what extent would he be to blame? How could he explain to their families that they had brought their fate on their own heads by pressing on? Had he not allowed for the exuberance of youth, and given them too much rope – enough to hang themselves with?

Chapter 10

Over the Falls

From the moment the two groups parted, Mayfield's team had made rapid but hazardous progress. Due to the difficult nature of the ground, they had had no choice but to spend the night of the 26th in a dry stream-bed on a slope of bare rock, which would obviously become treacherous when wet, and as a safety precaution they slept in harnesses or slings clipped to a rope which Mayfield had fastened between trees. On the morning of the 27th the corporal made his way back up to the second group, and obtained Neill's permission to proceed down to the bed of the Gully, which he thought was at the bottom of the next three abseils. This would be the rendezvous for the two groups that evening.

He was already anxious about the speed with which his group was eating into their stocks of food and fuel, and they had all become impatient, waiting for the rear party to catch up. Yet none of them was yet worried enough about rations to cut down on their daily intake – and in fact their optimism about progress was such that Shearer, for example, ran out of food promptly on Day Eleven.

Mayfield hurried back down to where Brittan, Page, Shearer and Mann were waiting for him, and immediately 'went over the edge' on the first pitch of what turned out to be a 600-metre cliff face, down ropes which he had placed in position the day before. As he admitted later, 'it was quite scary in places. If you'd slipped, you'd have gone all the way.' This was the place which (according to Page) Mayfield later called the 'point of no return': as he was about to start he said, 'This is it, lads: we go down there, we're not going back.'

After descending the three rope-lengths, they hit the patch of jungle which they had thought marked the start of the Gully; but after they had scrambled over moss-covered boulders and cut their way through the trees, they found themselves perched above 300 metres of slippery waterfalls, and were unpleasantly surprised by the number of abseils, some of them very difficult, they would need to go down that treacherous stretch. Before he went down, Brittan spent twenty minutes making his way back through the strip of jungle to the base of the last abseil, a 160-metre waterfall, in order to leave a note for those behind saying, 'MORE ABSEILS AHEAD – MORE LATER.'

This spot was the place which Mayfield had described to Neill as being the bed of the Gully, and thus their evening rendezvous. But because he had been cleared to proceed until he was indeed on the Gully floor, he took the recce group on down. At one stage Shearer's pack slipped off a narrow, grassy ledge, where he was resting between abseils. The 30-kilo bergen went hurtling down and smashed into the rocks below, a few feet from Brittan. Had he been hit, he would almost certainly have been killed: the pack and its contents were badly damaged, the most serious casualty being Shearer's last canister of gas, which was punctured. Kevin, his partner, was carrying the pair's only remaining canister, in the second group.

Altogether, the descent was far more dangerous and demanding than New's descriptions had led them to expect; but there was a lot of mountain experience in the group, and under the direction of Mayfield, whom one of the others described as 'razor sharp with his rock-climbing knowledge', they kept out of trouble.

At 1800 that same evening the recce group safely reached the bed of the Gully, where they built a big fire and were 'in really high spirits'. Above the belt of jungle, right at the top of the cliff, they had left two ropes in place for the second party, but on the waterfalls they had pulled their ropes down behind them. This meant that they had cut off their own retreat, and were committed to going on.

In the morning they waited until about 1000 in the hope that the rear party was catching up. The young men decided to press on in view of the urgency of their dwindling rations. After a

125

couple of hours, just before the Gully changed direction, they came to a place which gave them a clear view to the top of the cliff face. Checking with binoculars, they saw a single man, without a pack, apparently descending on a rope (in fact this was Neill, abseiling down after he freed the rope which had jammed the previous afternoon). The figure was too far away for them to identify it, or to be sure what it was doing: the man could have been descending on a reconnaissance, without a pack, or (as the recce group decided) retreating. Either way, this proved to be their last glimpse of the main party.

The recce group carried on boulder-hopping for the whole of that day. At 1400 on 1 March, having spent one night among the boulders, and made quick progress in the dry conditions, they reached two little lozenge-shaped stretches of water which they correctly identified as New's Pools. Luckily for them, only a trickle was going down the watercourse, but Mayfield sensed that the place was highly dangerous, and the others agreed with him. Page added later that 'Colonel Neill might have been more sensible, and he might have said, "We're not going down there."' Brittan was of the same opinion, and added that, when they eventually reached civilisation, he fully expected to find the two officers, together with the Hong Kong soldiers, waiting for them at the village, tapping their watches and saying, 'Where the hell have you lot been to?' having escaped from the Gully at that point and made their way out through the jungle.

The almost vertical walls of the ravine were so steep and smooth that there was no question of climbing them: if the group committed itself to the gorge, it would have to carry on down, whatever happened; the men would have to take the chance that if heavy rain came on, the trickle of water would soon turn into a flood, which might sweep them away. Even at low water the rocks were covered with treacherous slime, and there was practically nothing from which to belay. In spite of the obvious dangers, the group took a collective decision to go for it.

Later, they all gave vivid accounts of their passage through the pools, down a rock-chute and over countless falls. Sliding, jumping into water, swimming, abseiling, they were sometimes

126

under control, sometimes not, and, as they themselves were the first to admit, they were fortunate to come through without being seriously injured.

Above the first of New's Pools they stripped to their shorts, and some of them exchanged their boots for training shoes. Then they sealed their packs inside dive-sacks and bivvy bags, tied off to keep the contents dry and provide buoyancy. As they stood on a slippery slab, with mist closing in on them, Shearer reflected that they 'were going into the unknown, where probably no one had gone before'. The drop into the first pool was between five and six metres, but since there could well be boulders beneath the surface, Mayfield decided that it was not worth the risk of jumping. Having looped a sling round the chock-stone, he thought better of it, and put up a fixed rope on the right-hand side of the pool.

Shearer was the first to abseil. At the bottom he deliberately allowed his pack to fall into the water, and swam with it to the top of the next fall. Then he and Mayfield fixed up a similar arrangement for the second pool. As he put it, 'for the rest of the afternoon it was waterfall after waterfall, pool after pool and constant slippery rock'. In Brittan's recollection, 'we swam, slid, jumped, dived and did some pretty outrageous things'. When they tackled the rock-chute, which grew progressively narrower towards the bottom, Brittan, without thought to life or limb, was the first to go. According to Mayfield:

> *He threw his bergen in and just went* 'Waaaaagh!' *until his feet went. Then it was* thump *on his back, and he went* wosh *until he was literally missing the rock by inches at the bottom. Myself and Sergeant Mann were at the back. I was trying to hold back as much as I could at that stage, and all I could hear was, 'Fuckin' hell! Did you see what Britt just did?' I thought, 'This is starting to get a bit silly, now.' But we all went down in, and we all eventually did it.*

The only things that could stop them were rock and water: if they hit a pool, all well and good. If they had been unlucky, they would have been dashed to pieces. The three cardinal principles of adventurous training – Safety, Enjoyment, Learning – had gone by the board. Because of the increasing severity of the gorge, it was no longer adventurous training: it was survival.

At about 1800 they ended up on the right-hand side of a long fall whose base they could not see: the tumbling water simply disappeared – possibly into a sump, a tunnel or a cave. By then they had been in and out of the water for eight hours, and Mann was shivering uncontrollably. They had left behind so many ropes that they had less than two full lengths left, and one of these was in Shearer's pack, which had gone over the fall and was floating in the pool below. Evidently the pack was too big to be sucked down into whatever lay below. Standing on a ledge the size of a desk-top, they took a communal decision not to try to carry on down that night: the big fall looked too dangerous, and might easily kill them. Yet it was absolutely essential to recover the pack and the rope.

Mayfield decided the watercourse was impassable at that point, and that he must climb out into the jungle to find somewhere for them to bivvy down for the night; but first he needed to cross the top of the waterfall. Surrounded as they were by smooth rock, they had nothing to which they could belay him; so he got his four companions to sit in a huddle against the back of the ledge, and made what he called a 'big body belay', passing a rope right round them. Anchored by this safety line, he walked very gingerly across the top of the fall, and climbed 20 metres into the jungle, where he found some small but fairly flat ledges, on which they could spend the night. Even Mayfield, with all his strength and ability, was stretched to his limits, so dreadful was the going.

Their bivvy bags were torn – Mann's so badly that he threw it away – and three of their packs were saturated. Shearer's pack had yet to be recovered. It was nearly dark, but Mayfield told him to abseil down 'because he had dropped it', and he went over the fall on the short rope. Because the cliff was overhanging, communication between the top and bottom was extremely difficult; down there the gloom was intense, and the rope was only just long enough. But Shearer managed to reach his floating pack, and clipped it on to his harness.

Then came the herculean task of getting him back. His pack was so wet and heavy that he had to be hoisted, and Mayfield could not manage the lift alone. He called to the others 'to put some power behind the belay', and when they all pulled together, they raised Shearer three or four metres. But then he stuck, dangling cold and scared above the lower pool; and only when Mayfield put an extra loop into his hoist were they able to heave him on to the ledge, after half an hour of all-out effort, which left them all exhausted. The contents of his pack were saturated, and the diary which he had been keeping was ruined, the ink all smeared. Later he made an attempt to dry out his sleeping bag beside a fire which Brittan and Page had lit, and hung the rest of his clothes on trees. The group as a whole were feeling 'pissed off, wet, cold, miserable'. When rain set in, Page felt that it 'added insult to injury'.

On the morning of 3 March, after reveille at first light, they were all, in Mayfield's words, 'a bit scared'. They felt that their situation was becoming desperate, and debated whether to leave the Gully altogether and strike off through the jungle, or whether simply to make a detour to bypass the waterfall. They settled for the detour, and Mayfield decided that they should try to traverse along the face above the fall. With great difficulty he climbed three or four pitches up a near-vertical, scrub-dotted face, made more treacherous by the fact that the vegetation kept giving way. Every now and then he found a good tree, to which he could fasten a belay, and he set up ropes for the rest to ascend – a slow, exhausting business, which they had to repeat several times. So severe was the slope that they could not manage it wearing their packs, but had to haul them up on ropes, the packs constantly getting stuck and tangled in the bushes. Without a rock-climber as skilled as Mayfield, they would have been lost. Again and again he went up solo for a rope-length, and next brought up Mann and one of the others, to haul the packs; then one of them would belay him as he went on to the next pitch and fixed another rope.

For the rest of the day they followed a ridge through dense jungle, up what Shearer described as 'an unrelenting slope'. Trying all the time to head right-handed – northwards, towards safety – they constantly met crags which deflected them from their preferred direction, and they were further confused by what Mayfield described as 'false peaks on the ridge', with the ground dropping away very steeply on either side. In the end their spur gave out altogether at a point where the ground seemed to have collapsed in a landslide. The morning had been fine, but cloud, coming in during the afternoon, reduced visibility to a few metres and robbed them of any chance to get their bearings. Mayfield had a compass, but his altimeter was out of action, smashed during the dramas of the previous day, and the group's two photocopied maps had been soaked, so that they could no longer be read and were useless.

That night he and Mann slept in the base of a tree whose roots had been exposed by rainwater washing off the ridge, and the rest on a small ledge, under a shelter made of tents. They could not light a fire, since everything had been drenched by the heavy afternoon rain; morale had revived somewhat, because they were farther downstream than Robert New had managed to go, but Mayfield was finding it difficult to think clearly about what route they should take, so utterly confusing was the terrain.

In the morning they held a 'great debate' about what to do, and decided they must head back into the Gully, because they had no water. Mayfield was in favour of traversing southwards, back towards the mountain – and if the group had done this they would have ended up opposite Kevin's Cave, where the rear party were soon to be marooned. In the end, however, the consensus was for abseiling straight down from the spot in which they had spent the night. For as long as they had been on rock, Mayfield had taken charge of the group; but now, as he became exhausted, Brittan began to emerge as the natural leader. From that point he and Mayfield 'did things hand in hand', taking turns to lead.

Their hope was that when they regained the gorge it would be less dangerous, and more like the course of a normal river. So, on the morning of 4 March, having abseiled down off one spur, with razor-sharp thorns slashing them as they went past, they landed in a re-entrant with a stream in the bottom, and hoped it would bring them back to the river. Then they did another very difficult two-pitch abseil down a bare rock face. At the bottom of the first pitch Mayfield pendulumed across, trying to find another belay point; the only one he could see was a small tree just out of reach; he had to unclip himself from the rope and go down almost vertical rock to reach it.

The first four managed the transition safely, but as Shearer stood on a ledge, holding on to the small tree, its roots suddenly gave way, and all he could do was cover his face and head with his arms as he went somersaulting and bouncing down the rock face. He tried to grab hold, but the rock was so smooth that he simply gathered speed. As usual, he was not wearing his climbing helmet. Mayfield, watching from below, saw him drop:

He was a good sixty feet up, and initially all I heard was 'Ugghhh!' He started to fall, and he was in an upright position. Then his feet caught on some vines, and he landed about half-way down on his back, and I thought, 'That's good. The Bergen will have saved his back and his head.' But he bounced about ten feet and he did two good somersaults, and I thought, 'Jesus, he's going to die!' But he landed about five feet away from me, face-first on a boulder.

I thought, 'Shit – he's dead.' So I screamed 'CASUALTY!' at the top of my voice, ditched my Bergen and went to him, expecting bones poking out and brains everywhere. But by this stage he was bringing himself round. He was obviously concussed. He had a gash in his head, he was having difficulty breathing, and his legs were quite badly bruised. But there weren't any bits sticking out that shouldn't have been.

Mayfield was so shocked that for a few moments he 'wasn't functioning properly'. He went up to Shearer and got his pack off, but when he spoke to him, the injured man did not answer.

131

His face was covered with blood, running from a gash on his head. Then Brittan pushed past him and started to administer first aid. Mayfield turned his back and began coiling his ropes – the only way he could cope with the stress of the moment. By the time he had finished, Brittan had Shearer back on his feet. Clearly the casualty was in a lot of pain: the cut on his head bled profusely, but proved not to be serious, and a crepe bandage stanched the flow. He had also lost half a tooth, banged his left leg below the knee, and suffered a sharp impact on the base of the spine. He had pains in his back and chest, and was badly shaken, and his eyes were dilated. It seemed a miracle that he had not been seriously injured or even killed; but after going over him carefully, and checking for signs of internal injuries, Brittan decided that the best thing to do was to get him moving. So he gave him a drink and they went on slowly.

With Shearer limping along as best he could, and Mann and Page leading, they hacked their way through dense vegetation around another spur. Mayfield was still trying to return to the Gully, but could not manage it, and was becoming annoyed. Brittan then took over the lead, climbing, abseiling, but 'getting nowhere fast'. Sometimes, from the noise of the falls, they thought they were close to the water, but it never came into sight, and they stopped for the night harnessed on to a flat ledge in the jungle, perhaps 100 metres above the bed of the Gully. By now they were all in a state of some anxiety.

On 5 March they were up at first light. After a quick reconnaissance, Mayfield found that the drop into the Gully was too long for their surviving ropes, and that even if they did go down, they would come to the top of a huge waterfall, which was best avoided. After a group discussion, they decided to maintain their height, continue their traverse, and try to return to the Gully lower down. From one high point they got their first, thrilling glimpse of civilisation: in the far distance beyond the ridges they could see roads, buildings and cars.

After cutting their way through the jungle for a couple of hours, they began to descend, and went down a rock chimney by means of an abseil which Shearer described as 'a classic'. For this they tied both ropes together, swung out, passed the knot,* and dropped to a wet landing near the river. Another abseil, a swim through a pool, and they looked back up a huge double waterfall, which they felt they had done well to avoid. Back in the Gully, they went boulder-hopping again for a short distance until they reached a fall which Mayfield reckoned was nearly 150 metres deep.

Again they were forced into a change of plan. Remembering that New and Pinfield had found a hunters' lodge somewhere east of the river, only one day from civilisation, they decided to search for that, and climbed out of the Gully to the east. Almost at once their spirits leapt when they discovered a trail, which led up from the right-hand bank on to a knife-edge ridge. Weathered parang cuts on the bushes showed that the track was man-made, and Brittan found a bag of nails and some polythene, which gave further proof that the track was being used by humans. He felt sure that the path had been made by local hunters, because he knew that animals tended to move around on the ridges.

Since the trail seemed to lead in the right direction, they followed it; but then it turned east and later south, back towards the mountain. During the afternoon, Brittan brought up the rear with Shearer, who was in a bad way: he was showing signs of concussion, and needed rest. Then he had another bad fall, landing on his chest on a tree-stump, and this slowed him down so much that he and Brittan began to lose contact with the three in front. Brittan sprinted after them and told them to wait until Shearer caught up.

The path went on and on along the ridge, under the jungle canopy, and at nightfall, in very heavy rain, they found a clear spot beside the track with enough space for three of them to sleep. Mann and Mayfield bivvied slightly farther back, but within shouting distance. Shearer ate the last of his own rations – a packet of beef granules and half a packet of dried peas – but Page gave him a packet of dried mashed potato, and he borrowed

* To do this – a dangerous but essential manoeuvre – each man had to use a jumar or prussik loop to take his weight while he unclipped from the rope above the knot, and then clipped on again below it.

some spices from Brittan, who also made him a cup of sweet tea before he went to sleep. Mann and Mayfield had already run out of food, but Brittan and Page gave them something as well.

Brittan still did not reckon that there was any great cause for concern, despite Shearer's injuries: he thought they were so close to civilisation that they must reach a village next day. Nevertheless, he later admitted that the accident accentuated the split which had been opening up within the team. Mayfield and Mann, coming from the same Commando background, had a natural affinity with each other; but to Brittan they were 'always on the periphery', and the increasing severity of the going drove them still closer together into their own little clique. Brittan and Page had been paired off throughout the expedition, but, as Brittan later said he had never felt close to any of the others. Shearer should have been paired with one of the Chinese, but since the separation of the parties, he had been on his own; and now that he was injured, Brittan and Page had to look after him. The recce group was thus divided internally into two smaller units of two and three.

On the morning of the 6th Mayfield and Mann, who by then were sharing Mayfield's sleeping bag – Mann having abandoned his, after it had disintegrated in the constant wet – got up early, wet, cold and hungry: unable to stand the sight of the others eating breakfast, and not wanting to ask for any more of the scanty rations that remained, they left the bivvy site on their own at 0800, walking off along the trail up the ridge. As they passed Brittan, he reminded them that if they came to a junction of any sort, they must stop before branching off.

What happened next remains a matter of debate. Mayfield later described how for some time he and Mann could hear the others close behind them; after an hour he shouted back to see if they were following, and got a reply. Soon after that they came to a stick with a can on it that had contained Malay stargazer mackerel – another indication that they were close to civilisation.

Some time during the day they felt so weak, and realised they were in such severe trouble, that they 'lightened their load' by taking out training shoes, T-shirts, shirts, flysheets and other by now unnecessary things, which they dumped on the path. (Mann, however, kept his precious video camera.) At that stage Mann was leading, and when he reached the top of the ridge he found a small depression, the size of a table, which someone had dug out and in which a fire had been lit.* But there the trail came to an end, and he was left staring at an impenetrable wall of undergrowth. After a wait of five or ten minutes, and a good look round, they returned down the trail, blowing a whistle and expecting to see the others at any moment. After about ninety minutes and no contact, Mayfield decided that for some reason the three must have turned round and gone off in the opposite direction. By then he was 'quite angry', because he thought they had done it deliberately. So he and Mann were now on their own.

Neither wanted to go back to the Gully, having seen how difficult and dangerous it was. Being already on the east side of it – the side on which New had escaped – and having found the ridges easier going than the valleys, they decided to try to cross on to the next spur and escape in that direction. At about 1400 they broke from their track, cutting their way northwards through dense jungle, but soon after that Mann, who had been in the lead, slipped and fell about 15 metres on rough ground. He was holding a parang in his right hand, and as he fell the big knife hit a root or a rock; the half-metre blade slid through his fingers, cutting them badly. Mayfield could see at once that the wounds needed stitching, but as he had no suitable materials, all he could do was to put Betadine on the cuts and immobilise the fingers with bandages. The iodine preparation made Mann 'hit the roof'.

They then fought their way down to another river, but it proved just as difficult as the Gully itself. Here Mayfield had a narrow escape. Trying to climb out up a waterfall, he was on a vertical slab of rock, clasping his hands over a tree, with a drop of 50 or 60 metres beneath him. He was feeling so shattered that he had just said to Mann, 'Bob – let's sleep here', when suddenly the

---

* Research by Mann established that when the two climbers went missing a few years earlier, rangers were lowered by helicopter on to that ridge, where they cut and burnt a circular area so that they could be picked up again. Having cut a track down to the Penataran, but found nothing, they returned to the ridge and were lifted out.

vegetation under his feet gave way, and he felt the tree which he was clutching begin to move. Had it not been for Mann, who quickly passed him a rope, he would have fallen and died. But he managed to clip his harness to the rope and slowly climb out. At the top of the waterfall he crawled away exhausted and fell asleep in the jungle.

He and Mann had no food left. By now their cooker had been damaged, so they could no longer boil water, and their water-sterilisation kit had long since been ruined in a fall. That evening Mann found what he thought was a fruit, about the size of plum: he peeled it, 'looked at it, smelled it and made the mistake of eating it'. In the night, sleeping out in the open, and trying to shelter from the pelting rain, he was assailed by violent cramps, stomach pains, vomiting and diarrhoea.

* * *

Brittan was equally baffled by the separation. He too called and whistled repeatedly, and at first got an occasional answer. Then silence fell. The grazes on Shearer's legs had become infected, making movement painful for him, and he was generally lethargic, which slowed the party down. Later in the morning Brittan saw foliage moving in front of him, and thought the others were only a short distance ahead. But a shout of 'We're just behind you' brought no answer.

With Mayfield and Mann had gone the only remaining compass (Shearer's having been smashed in his fall), so that when mist came down, as usual, in the middle of the day, Brittan nearly lost his bearings. He came to what looked like a crossroads on the ridge track, with an empty Fanta soft-drink can lying by it. Had Mann and Mayfield waited at any junction they came to, they would have been there. The fact that they were not convinced him that they had somehow taken a different track, and he decided to camp for the night where he was. All he, Page and Shearer had for supper was curry powder and boiled water.

That evening, as he put up his tent, Brittan could not decide whether his companions had simply got lost, or whether they had decided to make a run for it and leave Shearer in his charge. Either way, he felt 'not particularly chuffed'. Page felt that the others had deliberately cleared off.

The Board of Inquiry later concluded that both groups had become separated by the exceptionally confusing terrain, and attached no blame to either. Nevertheless, by the evening of 6 March, Exercise Gully Heights had disintegrated into three, with one party stuck in the gorge and two others lost in the jungle, all without food, all thinking that the others had 'done a runner'.

Chapter 11

In the Gully

Tuesday 8 March was dry – the first dry day for some time – but it began badly for Foster, who slipped off a boulder and fell into the water, soaking himself from head to foot. Apart from that, the party was in good spirits: they had recouped some of their strength and no longer felt so weak. Neill and Foster were determined to go for it. They had asked the Hong Kong soldiers if they wanted to join in, but – perhaps daunted by the instructions to conserve energy – the Chinese preferred to stay put.

After a breakfast of a few spoonfuls of rolled oats and a hot orange drink, the officers set off on their planned reconnaissance in search of escape routes, one on the left or north-west flank, the other on the right, the side up which New had managed to find a way.

Neill, feeling strong, chose what appeared to be the steeper side, on the left, and had a fascinating but utterly exhausting day, during which he gained more than 150 metres of height up the western wall of the gorge. A few minutes after leaving the overhang, he was elated, for the slimy slabs gave way to more secure vegetation, and he began to make real progress, gaining height rapidly. Having left his heavy gear behind, he set out wearing the two side-pouches from his pack put together as a light day-sack, with water bottles and other essentials. Although bereft of a parang, he had a very good knife with a five-inch blade, which he had borrowed from Chow, and every few yards, whenever he found a decent-sized tree, he cut blazes on both sides of the trunk by slicing off strips of bark until shiny white wood showed. He also snapped off branches – anything to indicate his trail. The undergrowth had a remarkable habit of closing in behind him, but soon, as he looked back, he began to be able to pick up his own trail, at least for a few metres behind him, thanks to the slashes on the trees. For most of the time he was fighting his way through a hideous tangle of creepers and wait-a-while thorns, whose barbs dug deep into clothes or flesh whenever he tried to pull back.

The further up he went, the higher his elation and confidence rose: he was making good progress, climbing well, and on the drier ground from which the water had drained, everything seemed much easier. Suddenly, after passing through an avalanche zone where a cliff had given way above him, to his intense excitement he came on definite traces of human activity – freshly broken twigs, trampled leaves and smears of mud. The tracks could hardly have been those of native hunters, so utterly remote was this spot – and soon he realised that they might have been made by his own recce party.

The trail, by now on a knife edge, led him to a vertical granite cliff 15 metres high. A ledge, formed by decayed vegetation which had fallen from higher up the face, led along the bottom of it to his left, so he looked for signs that the party had gone out that way – only to find that the ledge petered out in a vertical drop. The same happened when he tried to the right: another sheer drop. The most baffling part of it was that he could not find any more signs of passage, or work out where the party had gone. When he looked down through the mist, which had sneaked up while he was on the ledge, he realised he was on the lip of a huge, rounded bowl, surrounded by cliffs, with jagged limestone crags sticking up in the middle through what appeared to be the jungle canopy.

When the ledge petered out, he was left hanging on to the rock, overlooking a huge amphitheatre, at least a kilometre across, with an immense waterfall thundering down somewhere into the mist. Whenever he hesitated, as now, a small voice kept whispering to him, 'Go on – go for it. Avoid the ignominy of having to be rescued, and the military nausea which is bound to follow.' But the terrain was so impossible that he kept his head, and looked round carefully to see if he could deduce how many days had passed since his men had been there.

Then he retreated. On his way back along the ridge he noticed a hollowed-out area beneath the roots of a tree, and there inside it was clear evidence that the recce group had spent a night under its shelter: ration wrappers, discarded clothes, and the remains of a tattered sleeping bag. His spirits leapt when he realised that the men were alive – or had been a day or two earlier – and had managed to climb out of the Gully.

As the mist cleared again, he caught a glimpse of the terrain all round him. Sheer cliff faces, ravines, ridges leading in all directions, dense green jungle everywhere – all this amounted to an 'appalling prospect', and he knew that there was no hope of his own group escaping through it, especially as they were already more or less out of food. He reckoned that to attempt it would be a death sentence. 'Desperate terrain and obstacles,' he noted afterwards in his diary.

Aiming now to return to base, he began following tracks which he thought were his own, back down the knife-edge ridge. With mist swirling around, he suddenly became aware that he could not tell which direction he was facing, and he did not remember coming up such a steep climb at that point. He began to suspect that the signs he was following – broken branches, roots and so on – were those of the recce party. Which way had they been going? He could not tell. His sense of direction was faltering. Then came one of his worst moments of the entire expedition. A branch on which he was relying gave way: he slipped and fell, hitting his head and leaving himself so disorientated that he did not know which direction to take, to pick up his route back to the Gully. When he stood up, his compass had disappeared. Mist cloaked the mountain. Rain was pouring down. The noise of falling water seemed to come from all around. Never had he felt so defeated: for twenty minutes he was totally lost, bewildered by the multiplicity of ridges, and on the verge of panic, particularly as he could not see any of his own blaze marks or identify his trail. Suddenly he thought of 'the poor sods in the Burma campaign who were lost in the jungle – how they must have felt, and how they realised that if you panic in deep forest, you are lost'. He recalled how they had sat down until equilibrium

140

returned, and reminded himself that being lost is often largely a state of mind.

To regain a grip of himself, he sat down and tried to reason things through. The time was already 1600, and he knew that even if he found his own route, it would take at least two hours to pick his way back to the Gully. With his mind clearer, he started to see, further up the slope, marks which could have been his own. Eventually, after floundering around, he found fine, clear, white blazes – and a more welcome sight he had never seen. He soon retraced his steps to the bivouac site under the tree, and after a couple more hours' sliding and battling with the thorns, following his own slashes on the undergrowth, he was mightily relieved to see his own SOS showing up through the gloom, alongside the space blanket. His hands were severely lacerated and punctured by thorns, many of which he had to dig out over the next few days as they threatened to turn septic. He had been climbing and scrabbling about for seven and a half hours, but he was elated by his discovery of evidence that the recce group appeared to have escaped from the Gully: that was the only interpretation he could put on the signs he had seen (in fact they had had to climb that high in order to find a piece of ground flat enough to bivouac on, and had gone down again the next morning, getting into severe difficulties almost immediately).

Crawling into the cave at last light, he found Foster putting a brew on, and told him what he had seen. Although there *was* a possible escape route in that direction, he said, they would kill themselves if they tried to take it. The better option was to sit tight, conserve energy and wait for rescue.

Foster had had equally little luck. He began by following the watercourse through the vegetation to the point where he had cracked his rib; then he scrambled up a stream-bed out of the floor of the Gully. He made some progress, but he was soon cursing his lack of a parang for hacking through the wait-a-while thorns and rattan creepers, which were thin but immensely strong. With his pocket knife he cut a stick, and bush-whacked his way through the jungle, partly by hitting it, partly by throwing himself at it. At times he felt convinced that he was on a track, but again and again this proved an illusion. All the while he was mentally noting sources of water – because the higher he went, the scarcer they became.

After one hour he passed a small cascade, but from then on found nothing. Occasional rock bands pushed him away to the south-east, the direction he did not want to take. When at last he saw a ridge above him, he was elated – until he reached it, and again found himself looking over into the Gully. After he had been climbing for three and a half hours, rain came on, making the going treacherous, and he stopped for a piece of Kendal mint cake and a couple of Dextrosol tablets, frustrated by the impossibility of heading north, towards the kampongs, the native settlements on the plain. He put his chance of reaching the east ridge no higher than fifty-fifty. Would it be worth a try? He had come to a point at which he would have to squirm for several metres up a steep slab of rock coated in rotten leaves, with almost nothing to get hold of – an obstacle better tackled by two people than by one.

Wanting to be back in the cave before dark, he started down. The descent proved much quicker, and he was able to follow the marks which he had left on trees to guide him. He reached base at 1600, filthy, soaked, and dejected by his conclusion that the group would not all be able to climb out wearing their packs: going up with very little on his back had been bad enough, but to tackle that terrain with a full weight would have been impossible. The stark truth was that the whole group was unlikely to be strong enough. An hour later, with no sign of Neill, he started to feel anxious – yet there was nothing he could do except wait, and he was greatly relieved when a bedraggled figure at last loomed up out of the twilight.

Supper that night consisted of chicken soup, one brown biscuit and tea. Victor brewed up a handful of noodles and soup on his cooker for himself, Chow and Kevin. As they ate, they talked about how Robert New might react when they failed to show up – although in his heart of hearts Neill knew that it would be too much to hope that chance acquaintances like New and David Powell would start playing detective to find out where the missing

142

men were. Both officers were exhausted, and Neill had been shaken by his experience. He realised how highly he valued the companionship of Foster and the Chinese: after his ordeal by jungle, the Gully and the dripping overhang seemed as welcoming as home. 'I am now content to stay in my sleeping bag, awaiting events,' he wrote in his diary. 'I will never go alone into the jungle again.' The Chinese felt the same. 'Wait for rescue,' said Kevin, speaking for them all. Filling in his diary, Foster wrote:

> *Robert and I have hope – are convinced – someone is doing something to rescue us. We feel that now we are four days late getting to Park HQ someone MUST spark. We don't know what has happened to the other group. . . . Why did they leave us behind, and why didn't they leave a parang?*

As night fell, cicadas gave out their dusk chorus, loud enough even to compete with the noise of the river. Then they fell silent, and during the long, uncomfortable night the five men lay listening to the incessant roar of the water thrashing its way over the rocks scarcely two metres away from their shelter. In the dark they could no longer see the wall of rock and vegetation which bounded their world three metres in the other direction, but outside the cave brilliant white fireflies floated like gently moving stars, glowing for a few seconds and then vanishing. If only, thought Foster, we could harness a few hundred of them and put them together to form a lamp. . . .

Neill slept better that night, secure in the knowledge that the recce group had broken out from the Gully. Day Fourteen – 9 March – was the day on which the party had booked to fly back from Kota Kinabalu to Hong Kong on Malaysia Airlines. They awoke to find the cloud down, and rain falling. Obviously helicopters – if there were any – could not fly, so there was no point in anyone getting up early. Instead, they conserved energy and food by remaining in their sleeping bags until 1000, by which time some of Foster's clothes had dried on him, and he was pleased to find that he had a pair of dry socks for the following night. At just under 2,000 metres above sea level, the nights became distinctly cold – probably down to five or six degrees Celsius – and the air was permanently damp. The best way of keeping warm, they knew, was to wear as many thin layers of clothes as possible – two or three T-shirts, shirt, light jersey and anorak – with air trapped between the layers for insulation.

Short spells of sunshine were not enough to dry anything properly, so the bedding and clothes remained damp. After a clear spell, the mist swept in from above and below, earlier than usual. Neill and Foster put in much time removing boulders from their bed-space. Now they began to regret not bringing flares: if a helicopter came over, a distress signal would have increased their chances of being spotted. Neill's diary recorded a variety of thoughts and emotions, crowding in on one another:

Last night we should have been meeting Robert New and David Powell. So we hope they will spark today and make enquiries. We were also booked into the Travellers' Rest. So the clues are there. Impossible to dry anything. Everything is wet to the touch. Dry sleeping-bags are critical to survival.

We wonder whether the other group has been able to make it over the hills to safety. The ground I saw was horrific. I can also feel my ribs easily. I am warm at night in the black track suit you gave your menfolk for Christmas [Fiona had given identical presents to all the men in the family]. The weather will affect flying operations ... I hope Hong Kong will involve Brunei and Seria [the British garrison in Brunei] in the rescue operation, if and when it gets going. Supper was one packet of beef granules between two of us, and one biscuit (brown) each.

Kevin, Victor and Chow again ate a handful of noodles each and some soup. Foster had begun to wonder how long they could all hold out. His own loss of weight was obvious, and his beard seemed to be growing thicker: he thought he must be looking more and more like his bearded younger brother Bernard, another experienced climber and hill-walker. The gash in his leg which he had sustained ten days earlier had still not healed: it was clean enough, and free from infection, but the bandages with which he covered it were continuously being soaked, and he could not keep the wound dry enough for the skin to knit together.

Thursday, 10 March dawned dry and fine. Neill felt rather weak; but his clothes had become so filthy during his struggles in the jungle that he decided he could not put off washing them any longer. This led to an interesting discovery – the water in the Gully was wonderfully soft and it was easy to work up a lather, so that garments washed perfectly. The problem was to dry the clothes afterwards, but he laid them out on the rocks, and at least began the process (he once calculated that it took him ten days to dry a shirt – and he managed that only because he wore it damp). Brunch consisted of one biscuit and liver pâté, together with a hot drink. By now Neill had convinced himself that rescue must be imminent; but when no helicopter appeared, in spite of the fine weather, he and Foster renewed their determination to discover New's escape route. It was amazing how, with a bit of rest and companionship, their latent desire to escape kept reviving: their instinct, which persistently flared up, was to save themselves by their own efforts, rather than rely on the problematic reaction of other people.

Foster, in particular, felt that he could not rot in the Gully while he had energy to make another attempt. They decided that their best chance was to leave the Hong Kong soldiers where they were, and when they put the matter up for discussion, the Chinese agreed. Kevin's ankle was still sore, as was Victor's back. Chow was intact, but he had never been very robust, and now he had started to complain of feeling weak. Clearly, the presence of any of the Chinese soldiers would only slow progress – and besides, somebody had to remain in the Gully to man the SOS, and, if rescuers arrived, give word of where the others had gone to. The officers emphasised that the Chinese were not being deserted: rather, it was essential that they should remain in the Gully, as a base, while the British went in search of rescue. 'They seem quite hopeful,' Foster recorded, 'and we are positive.'

Having stripped their kit to essentials, and taken the side-pouches off their packs, they set aside three days' survival rations, and spent the afternoon in their sleeping bags, planning their route as exactly as they could, with all distances and compass bearings recorded. Their idea was to use Foster's recce route, and leave a copy of it, together with a duplicate map and a letter of explanation with the Chinese, so that if rescuers did suddenly arrive, they would know where the officers had gone. Once on the east ridge they would set off on a bearing of 6,000 mils to the nearest river, a tributary of the Penataran, and then steer on a bearing of 5,400 mils to the village of Melangkap Kappa. On the map it looked as though the distance as the crow flies was less than ten kilometres – but they knew it would be a great deal farther on the ground.

On Friday, 11 March the weather was fine. Neill and Foster set off at 0845, feeling optimistic once more. With them they took £900 of expedition money in sterling, plus their Visa cards!, in case they had to pay cash for a rescue, and they left the Hong Kong soldiers with 100 Malaysian dollars, to supplement what they already had, in case they were rescued and had to buy food. Kevin was formally placed in charge of the base party.

Foster led, taking a line which he had seen and thought looked promising during his earlier foray. His aim was to gain as much height as possible before traversing and going on to the ridge, which would take them out in the right direction. They paused to gain their breath on the false ridge that Foster had found during his recce; and as they looked back up the Gully, they had an unrestricted view of the ramparts of rock to their right. In the distance a vertical split in the skyline denoted Cauldron Gap, and the rock faces glowed a splendid reflected pink in the early sunlight.

After three hours' climbing they were stopped by a rock slab rising almost vertically ahead. Each of them explored to one side of it; Neill carried out a one-hour probing reconnaissance on the left, before he was driven back by an impassable vertical cliff; but in due course Foster found a possible route on the right. This was extremely gruelling; the two pushed on all afternoon, only to find

146

themselves being channelled southwards, into a waterfall and away from the direction they wanted to take.

In the evening Neill found a good site for a bivouac – apparently the only flat patch on the whole flank of the mountain – and they settled down for the night. The sound of a small brown bird, ticking away like a wren, brought a moment of relief in such forbidding terrain, and after a brief search they found its nest – an untidy sphere made out of strips of bamboo. Putting a finger in, Neill could feel some baby chicks inside, and remarked, 'I'll have to be a damned sight hungrier before I even think of eating little birds like that.' Instead they ate a few beef granules and some powdered potato.

On the morning of 12 March they continued upwards, but the ground grew ever more treacherous. Foster had woken up feeling rather lethargic. Neill, on the other hand, felt stronger than for some days past, and carried out a three-hour reconnaissance, leaving his pack behind. In fine, dry weather, he found a good line and made such excellent progress that he returned to Foster saying he thought he had found a way out. They spent the rest of the day climbing that route. Neill led, using a short length of rope at times; but the face became progressively steeper and eventually impossible. 'Very steep and precarious route,' wrote Foster:

> *Hanging on to bushes, orchids and grass. Underfoot was dodgy: two to three inches of loose, wet moss over rock. Continued climbing, but impeded by packs up some hairy gullies and crevices. Clung to roots, branches and anything else we could. Robert slipped once in a narrow chute, but the greenery saved his fall. At times we put ourselves in extreme danger to overcome an obstacle, and we were always conscious of the fact that there was no one but us there.*

It was all too clear that if one of them injured himself, he would have to rely totally on the other person to get him back to the Gully: every action had to be weighed carefully, every risk assessed, and nothing hurried. In the end Neill, who had been

147

leading all day and had never in his life climbed at such a high standard, declared that if they went on, they would fall and kill themselves. He was all for retreating. 'Look,' he said, 'we've spent two days fighting our way up this bloody ridge. We're probably not half-way up yet. We aren't going to make it. Far better to go back while we're still in one piece and wait for rescue, which must turn up sooner or later.'

'No,' said Foster. 'We've got to push a bit harder. Let's go for it.' So he took the lead, off to the right again, and at one point his spirits rose because he had come out on to open scrub dotted with a few larger bushes, and thought he could see the top of the ridge ahead; but then, some 300 metres straight above Kevin's Cave, they were stopped by a vertical bank of soil and mud. Foster took hold of some ornamental grass that hung over the edge, but could not gain enough purchase to pull himself up. There were no decent roots in the bank, and it offered no secure foothold, as its face kept giving way. Nor was there any substantial shrub or tree on to which they could belay themselves – and below them 150 metres of clear ground fell sharply away. Had they slipped, nothing would have stopped them.

Neill, visibly tiring (according to Foster), was secretly pleased that the ground had decided matters for them. Apart from anything else, they were seriously adrift from the route which they had written down for the Hong Kong soldiers, and any rescue party might well have missed them. So they made their way back to a place where he had noticed water dripping on their way up.

This was the spot on which Neill had slipped into a rock chute on the previous day – and now it nearly claimed another victim. Foster fed a doubled safety rope through some tree roots, and was half-way across the chute when his foot slipped and he began to slide. Immediately he thought, 'I'm going all the way!' He clung on fiercely, but the impetus of his fall dragged the wet rope through his gloved fingers, and only at the very end of it did his grip pull him up.

By then Neill was filling his water bottle a short way below, and Foster, with his feet scrabbling desperately on wet rock, yelled, 'Will I be OK if I let go?'

148

'You'll slide a bit,' Neill shouted back, 'but the bushes'll stop you. Hang on and I'll try and get to you.'

At that moment, one of the rope-ends slipped out of Foster's grasp and ran up towards the root, causing him to accelerate down the chute, until his feet hit a pile of dead leaves and twigs, and brought him safely to a halt. His heart was pounding, but he grinned as he said to Neill, 'I thought I was a goner then.'

Soon after that they found a place to bivouac, among the tall, dead, matted ornamental grass on a narrow ledge at the base of a cliff. After a brew, Neill found to his delight that the dead grass was readily inflammable, so they lit a fire, only to realise that the whole platform on which they had perched consisted of nothing more than vegetable detritus: if the blaze became too hot, they might set fire to their own platform and incinerate themselves. Unfortunately their fire was no use as a beacon, since the surrounding ground cover shielded it so effectively that it could not have been seen from any habitation to the north of the mountain.

Their minds kept harking back to the fact that at 1330 they had heard the engine of a helicopter or light aircraft for about thirty seconds. Later analysis showed that this was nothing to do with any rescue operation, but at the time they naturally took it as a hopeful sign. They had gained a good deal of height, but had not achieved their aim and had exhausted all the possibilities of that particular route.

That night they slept well, relieved not to be lying on naked rock. On the morning of Day Eighteen – Sunday, 13 March – there seemed to be no hurry. They were weary from the exertions of the previous two days, and all they could do was go down: they had told Kevin and the others that they would be away for three days, and that the next time they saw them, it would be with a helicopter.

At 0753 they got a jolt. Foster had begun a letter to Jeanette, but he never finished it, for he heard the unmistakable thudding beat of a helicopter, and saw a small, white aircraft circling far out to the north, probably over the River Penataran. Quickly he woke Neill, and they watched the helicopter pass in the distance across the V-shaped opening of the Gully. With hearts racing, they stuffed belongings back into their packs and hurried down to the nearest open area, where they deployed a red dive-sack, mess tins and other shiny objects. Foster suddenly had the idea of trying to attract attention by firing the flashgun of his camera, and he rapidly loaded some new batteries into it. He could not give the international distress signal of six consecutive flashes, because the camera mechanism took several seconds to recharge itself, but was prepared to fire a single flash if the pilot headed in their direction.

For over an hour they watched eagerly for the helicopter to reappear, full of hope, as it had appeared to be searching methodically. From where they sat they had a clear view of New's Pools and the narrow gorge beyond – from this distance no more than a vertical slit in the rock. For the hundredth time they wondered aloud what had happened to their recce party, and were relieved that they themselves had stopped when they did. They realised, of course, that the helicopter might have had nothing to do with them: it could have contained a logging magnate, checking some new area of jungle that he was about to clear. But would such a man have been flying early on a Sunday morning? And in a national park?

The songs of birds, coming from all round them, made a welcome contrast with days in the Gully, where the only noise was the roar of water. The men were jerked back to reality, and their hopes soared briefly a second time, when the aircraft reappeared way out over the jungle, but still it did not fly over the Gully, and was much too far off for them to attract the occupants' attention. At 1030 mist swirled in, and soon rain was falling once more. Nevertheless, the men were elated, and decided that if a search had indeed begun, they had better return to base with all possible speed.

After the exertions of the day before, exacerbated by the lack of food, Neill felt weak as a kitten, so Foster led the way down, and it took them all day to retrace their route, even though for some of the time they were sliding on their backsides and using their packs as brakes. This was less of a risk than it sounds, for they were constantly impeded by wait-a-while thorns and rattan, which caught in their packs and slowed them down; but they had to keep a watchful eye out for their own marks (such as knots tied in the grass), otherwise they might have slid over precipices.

By the time they reached the Gully, rain had begun falling again, so that they were sodden and filthy, as well as exhausted. It was already late, and they were reluctant to disappoint the Hong Kong soldiers that evening by revealing that they had failed in their mission. They also wanted to get a better night's sleep than they would have on the lumpy rock floor of Kevin's Cave, so they returned to the site they had used on the night of 4-5 March – a reasonably flat patch in the Gully bed. They spent the last half-hour of daylight scraping at the sandy gravel to make a platform, which they covered with a layer of leaves. They pitched their tent and after a brew, they went to bed, but had a hideously uncomfortable night: the gravel compacted and turned into something akin to concrete, which was almost worse than the granite in the cave. At last light, heavier rain set in, and it continued all night; for some time they lay awake, wondering whether they were going to be flooded, but the tent and bivvy bags proved more or less waterproof, and the level of the river never rose as high as their site.

Next day they were awake before daylight, convinced that with the dawn would come the helicopter they had seen the day before. They knew by now that the weather was normally clear in the morning, and that clouds came in about midday: everything seemed to point to a morning rescue. By standing on a prominent boulder, Foster found that he could see his own reflective space blanket, set out as a distress signal, and so knew that they were only 150 metres upstream of base. At 0745, after a brew of orange, they had packed up and were almost ready to move back to the cave. It seemed a good moment to do some filming, and for the benefit of Foster's video camera Neill described how their clothes were rotting on them, and how he was disturbed to notice that one of his boots was falling apart. Then suddenly they heard voices and were astonished to see three familiar figures in green anoraks heading up towards them.

151

When asked what they were doing, Kevin said they wanted to make their own escape bid, and were following the British officers' route. But since they too had heard a helicopter, their decision to decamp struck Neill and Foster as thoroughly illogical – for, once in the jungle, they would never have been seen from the air. Neill was appalled, and had to make a conscious effort to suppress his irritation: had he and Foster not intercepted the Hong Kong soldiers, they would have had little chance of finding them again. The party would have been spread all over the place and there would have been no one left in the Gully to attract the attention of any aircraft that came over. But to have given them a dressing down would have achieved nothing: the officers realised how disconsolate and deserted they must have felt.

It turned out that the Chinese themselves had had disagreements about what to do. On 12 March Kevin had told the others that he wanted to try the British officers' escape route; Victor and Chow were both in favour of waiting for a while to see what happened, but by the 13th they had changed their minds, and sorted through the kit which Neill and Foster had left behind, extracting anything they thought might be of use. They also tore Foster's aluminium sheet in two, taking half with them and leaving half on the rock.

When they saw a white helicopter in the morning, they thought it was a tourist aircraft: all the same, they waved clothes and blue slings in an effort to attract its attention, but it was too far away. They then packed for departure the following day, and studied the map and route that the British had left them. Kevin also wrote an explanatory message for potential rescuers and left it in a plastic bag held down by a rock.

On the 14th they were up at 0600, made hot drinks, and set off at 0700. After only half an hour on Neill and Foster's route, they saw two figures just below a waterfall – and thought they were a rescue party. Back in the cave, all except Foster changed into dry clothes and took refuge in their sleeping bags. The day was noticeably cooler, with a wind for the first time, and clouds were moving fast across the sky: clearly some new weather system was coming in, but whether it would be for better or for worse, they could not tell. Yet it was still warmer outside than under the dank overhang, and Neill, very tired, spent most of the day in the open, lying in his bivvy bag, soaking up the warmth. Foster, on the other hand, was all action, as his diary records:

On return scrubbed pack and washed gloves, boots and socks. Trousers I will not keep anyway (with no arse in!) Robert looking really gaunt and is in sleeping bag to keep warm. I suppose I should be too, but I'm too much of a fidget. Mustn't think of food – have a drink of water instead. Constant reminder is the incessant rushing of water past us.

Wonder if Jeanette is worried in UK. My thoughts are forever with her and my family. I miss them all, and wonder if I will ever see them again. I also wonder if we have made the news yet. I cannot believe that now, with us missing for ten days, not one helicopter has been into the Gully for a look. They would have seen us first time. We are in a widish point, and a helicopter could rescue us, if only by winch from twenty to thirty metres.

There are no tears, though. Robert and I are carrying on with things as normal. Hunger pangs are not there – surprisingly – and we seem sustained so far. Funny that the motto adopted by The RLC is the one previously used by the ACC [Army Catering Corps]: 'We Sustain'.

At 1400 light rain set in. Foster moved into the cave, but because Neill felt comfortable and dry in his Goretex bivvy bag he elected to stay where he was. Then suddenly the rain became much heavier, and he was trapped in a dilemma. If he remained *in situ*, the rain would probably penetrate the bivvy bag in the end, and if he emerged from it he would get his precious dry clothes soaked. Eventually, with the deluge unrelenting, he steeled himself to undress down to pants, left all his other dry kit inside the bivvy bag, and with that slung over his back, made a dash for shelter, mercifully not slipping. Safely back under the overhang, he realised that he had left his pack out on the rocks.

No problem, he thought. There was nothing in the pack that he needed for the night. Their meal that evening consisted of half a packet of potato powder, half a packet of dried peas, and some tea. After that, they had six days' starvation rations left. Then, as Neill tried to settle down, his blood suddenly ran cold as he realised that among his stranded belongings was one proper day's ration for him and Foster, kept intact all that time. This was their final store, which they planned to stretch out for six days. His passport and £300 in cash were also out there – but those seemed relatively unimportant. To have left the food behind was criminally careless. Even Foster was shocked into silence. For hour after hour he was racked by the thought of how irresponsible he had been, in failing to bring the pack back with him – but in the dark there was nothing he could do about it. He noticed that his Goretex bivvy bag, which had performed faultlessly so far, was at last beginning to feel damp inside. When Foster went outside for a pee, getting soaked in the process, he returned with the news that the water in the Gully had risen so high that they were cut off from the rock on which the pack was marooned.

Then, at 2245, with astonishing abruptness, the cave was flooded. The Hong Kong lads were asleep. A Cyalume chemical light-stick was glowing green under the roof. Foster also had drifted off, but Neill, who was lying with his eyes open in what he called 'the pit', the lowest part of the whole overhang, could hear the noise of the water rising steadily. Soon he also detected the sound of stones tumbling in the current, and suddenly he felt water moving under his bivvy bag. As he looked up, a horrifying sight caught his eyes: jets of water were spurting from the rock around Chow, hurtling out on either side of him.

'Ron!' he yelled. 'The water's coming in!'

Both men struggled from their bags, shouting at the Chinese to wake up. Chow came to, bewildered, and sat in a huddle on a rock next to his bed-space, already soaked, with water pouring past on either side of him. His two companions were still more or less dry, but as they watched, one of Chow's flip-flops floated out of the cave on the torrent and disappeared. Neill had seen it moving gradually down, and was preparing to grab it, but at the last moment it was swept out of the overhang by a surge of water.

The fugitives spent a miserable and highly alarming night. It seemed that a catastrophic surge of water might flood the cave at any moment: the noise of water and tumbling rocks rose to a continuous roar. By yelling at the tops of their voices, Neill and Foster were just able to communicate with the Chinese, a couple of metres away. '*Be prepared to evacuate!*' they bellowed, and they themselves took up perching positions, ready to scramble out into the jungle if things became any worse.

Luckily, their light-stick continued to give out its comforting green glow right through the night.* This meant that, apart from being able to watch what the water was doing, they could also see the way out of the overhang, round and over various boulders, which they would have to take if an emergency exit became necessary. After a while the flood abated, only for another surge to spurt through the fissures round Chow's sleeping position at three in the morning, and for the whole drama to be repeated.

Watching the water flash in the green glow, Foster remembered reading how, after a plane crash in the Andes in 1972, survivors had improvised hammocks out of seat-harnesses, and slung them from the roof of the fuselage, to make room for others below. He thought of his own recently acquired hammock, and wondered whether he should have brought it along; but even without it his pack had been too heavy – and there was nothing in the roof of the cave from which he could have slung it.

* * *

In England, Fiona had been looking forward to 9 March, the first day on which Robert could be back in Hong Kong (as one of his postcards had told her). But she had thought this estimate optimistic, and was not too worried when no word came. Then on Saturday 12 March she went to a tree sale at Castle Howard, where two other army wives asked if she had heard from her husband. When she said, 'No', and they asked where he was, she

* Advertised to function for twelve hours, it went on – incredibly – for more than 250.

replied, 'I haven't the faintest idea.' They laughed, and remarked how calm she seemed – whereupon she said that she was confident that the Army would 'switch on' if anything had happened.

On Sunday 13 March she had lunch with Major David Bentley, Robert's second-in-command and an old friend, and his wife Fay, at their home about fifteen miles away. She thought it strange that David kept asking if she had any news; afterwards, she realised that he had been very tense, and had already thought that something was wrong.

On the Tuesday – 15 March – she went out into the paddock to start planting the trees she had bought; but although she took a pickaxe and began to set out the trees in their places, she suddenly came to a halt. She could not dig the holes or decide what to do: for an hour she wandered about, gripped by an odd feeling. Then she went back into the kitchen, and was making a cup of coffee when the telephone rang. It was Fay Bentley, asking if she had any news, but also (as she later admitted) ringing to make sure she was in: a few minutes later, David appeared on the doorstep with three grey canvas travelling bags, saying, 'I've brought some of Robert's things.' With a wild surge of hope Fiona assumed the party was back, and thought that her husband had somehow sent some clothes on ahead. In fact the bags contained the uniform out of which he had changed at Colchester just before leaving for Heathrow.

But instead of dumping the luggage and going, David asked if he could stay for coffee. As she put the kettle on, he said, in a sombre voice, 'Fi – we've had some news of the expedition.'

'What?' she cried. She felt herself go hot and cold, immediately suspecting the worst because the tone of his voice was so peculiar. 'Is he dead?'

'No, no. Don't get alarmed. But the news isn't very good. Five of the team have come out. But Robert and Ron and the three Chinese soldiers are missing.'

A strange jolt hit Fiona's feet, and worked its way up to the top of her head, like an electric shock. Automatically she went on making coffee, instantly thinking up reasons for the delay. 'Well, of course,' she said. 'The Chinese soldiers will have held them up.' But David said, 'No – it's worse than that. The others have come out half-starved – and Robert's lot are already more than a week overdue.'

Her premonitions of disaster were reinforced when Mabel, Robert's black Labrador, sat by the bags in the hall, refusing to move for hours on end. When she shifted them into the drawing-room, the dog continued to sit by the door, and her mistress kept wondering, 'Does she know something that I don't?'

Chapter 12

Breakout

On 7 March Brittan woke to clear skies and found that from their high position he could see a good deal, including some villages in the distance. Better visibility also revealed that the track they were on headed up the mountain, back towards North Peak, and that there was bare rock not far above them – but, given the state they were in, he did not think seriously about attempting to go back over the top and down to Panar Laban. The best option seemed to be to retrace their steps to the Gully and try their luck along it.

The track led straight to the river and Brittan and his two companions walked down to the water comfortably enough. Emerging on to the bank below a waterfall, they thought that they were on the Penataran, and had left the Gully behind. Things seemed to be looking up, especially when they enjoyed a stretch of relatively easy boulder-hopping; but Page realised that it had taken them two and a half days to make a net gain of about 200 metres to the north. For the rest of that day their advance was straightforward, if laborious, and they crossed the river just below a confluence, where another stream joined it. That evening they made camp on a flat spot beside the water, and because they had so few rations left, they decided to eat on alternate days. For that night they made do with curry powder and hot water, and saved the bulk of their provisions, which consisted of a packet of creamed rice and some soup.

* * *

Mayfield and Mann had a rough night, sharing a single sleeping bag, which was soaking wet and full of holes. When they woke at first light, Mayfield was feeling better than on the previous day.

158

But Mann's hand was festering, and he was soon in such pain that he 'thought he was in a film' and told Mayfield to go on alone: 'Leave me,' he said. 'Save yourself, Richard.' Mayfield's response was positive: 'I assaulted him then – got behind him, gave him a swift kick up the arse, dragged him to his feet, and said, "We're not in the films now," and pushed him forwards.'

Once again they hoped to emerge from the jungle that day; but at one stage Mann felt so exhausted that he left his pack behind at the bottom of a small crag. Mayfield went back and retrieved his passport, money and video camera, but the rest of his kit was abandoned. Their plan now was to head as nearly due north as they could, terrain permitting, so they carried on beside a river, cutting their way through the jungle, until they found a place where they could go down to the water itself.

By now Mayfield was so debilitated that individual events began to blur in his memory. The hills seemed to be growing smaller: he could climb to the top of one within two or three hours, and down again in the same time. Later he thought that he and Mann had been going over spurs, but he could not be sure. Things seemed to him 'quite desperate', with 'lots of leeches everywhere'. Mann also became confused about the sequence of events, and he was increasingly concerned about his fingers: they had started to stink, and he feared that gangrene was setting in. Mayfield kept treating the wounds with Betadine, but he knew that the cuts urgently needed stitches and a surgical dressing.

* * *

On 8 March, still beside the river, Brittan's group had what he described as 'a bit of a nightmare'. They had walked only 100 metres from their overnight camp when, on their right, they found a cave, which 'looked quite organised – neat and tidy, with a fire, and an oven'. Somebody had also left some fresh rice, newspapers only four days old and clothes hanging on a washing line. The survivors' spirits went soaring: now, they thought, they really *must* be close to civilisation. With no mean self-control they left the rice alone, reckoning that whoever had left it must

159

need it. After a reconnaissance of various tracks leading off into the jungle, they chose one that followed the river – only to find that it soon gave out. Then they were back in the bed of the river, crossing from side to side on the boulders.

When they came to more waterfalls, which they could not avoid, they resorted once again to jumping – throwing their packs over and leaping after them – and on two of the falls Page had terrifying experiences. Standing at the top of the first, he could not see the bottom, but by then he had reached the stage at which he 'couldn't care less'. As he recalled afterwards, 'there was only one way down, and we were prepared to take that chance'. So he threw his pack over and waited for it to bob out below. When it failed to appear, he climbed a rock so that he could see down – and spotted one of the pack's straps stationary in a patch of white water, with the torrent foaming around it. Trying to jump right on to the bergen, he aimed perfectly and landed so that he was spreadeagled on top of it, with water hurtling over his head and shoulders, pressing him downwards.

The force of the current was wedging the pack down between two rocks, and heave as he might, he could not shift it. He decided that the only way of saving his kit was to open the top and pull things out one by one. Lying over his rucksack, holding his breath beneath the torrent, he struggled with the straps and had just got one undone when the weight of water overbalanced him. He did a somersault, still clinging to a strap, but he could not hold on to it, and the current swept him away. 'So that', as he remarked afterwards, 'was my bergen gone' – and with it his passport and all his money.

The next waterfall was even worse. It nearly killed him. Brittan had gone on ahead and thrown his kit down a fall about five metres deep, with steep rock walls on either hand. He was disconcerted to see that his pack did not surface in the pool below – but when he himself jumped, he soon found out why: immediately he was sucked under the wall on the right by a fierce undertow. Surfacing, he was dragged under the wall on the left, and came up in 'the land that time forgot' – a dark cave with a small opening at one end, above water level, and his pack

160

floating in front of him. A few moments later, treading water furiously, he managed to throw his pack through the opening, and scrambled out to rejoin the main river.

Shearer's pack, meanwhile, had also gone under and vanished. As it contained their remaining rations and only rope, this was a potentially disastrous loss, and in Brittan's characteristic understatement, 'he was not particularly happy'. Standing on top of the fall, Shearer shouted to Page, 'Ah, fuck it! We've got to go.' Over he went, and was sucked into the cave as Brittan had been. Page described the pool at the bottom as 'like a whirlpool in the middle. You jumped in, and it spun you around three times, and away you went over the top.' As Brittan said, it was like a 'killer washing machine'.

Having waited a couple of minutes, and seen no sign of Shearer emerging below, Page began to panic and shouted out, 'Pete! Pete!' He was thinking, oh, fucking hell – he's dead. Where is he? Then he looked round and thought, well, I'm not staying *here* on my own, and jumped over.

Plunging deep under water, he 'swam like hell', but felt he was making no progress. When he opened his eyes, all he could see was bubbles. He began to panic and swallow water. Unable to breathe, struggling desperately, he suddenly felt his hands close round a rock, and managed to drag himself up so that his head was clear of the water. He was left gasping, vomiting, 'shaking and horrible'. Then he heard Shearer calling, 'Steve, Steve!' He opened his eyes, found he was in pitch darkness, and thought, bloody hell! Coming to his senses, he realised that he was in the cave, and that Shearer was with him. The cave was a stagnant pool, 'full of all kinds of shit'. Together they battled to tread water and lift Shearer's sodden pack up through the exit hole, but could not manage it. Page decided the only thing to do was to empty the pack and pass items up one at a time: this they did, but by the time they had finished, darkness had fallen, and Shearer repacked his belongings more or less by feel.

Brittan, who had been anxiously watching for the others from the bank a short way downstream, came back, to find both of them still struggling in the water, so he climbed through the opening again to give them a hand, then led them to an area that was fairly level, but alive with leeches and frogs. All round them on the ground they could see leeches standing on end like upright worms, alerted by the vibrations of their arrival, with their heads waving around in the quest for targets. Every now and then one would start towards them, doubling its body down, end over end, in purposeful little advances.

When Shearer checked through his belongings, he found that his passport and money had gone – a tribute exacted by the river. But he reckoned it was a fair exchange: their lives in exchange for his passport and cash. All they had for supper was a cup of hot Diarolyte (a powdered replacement for minerals and salts lost by the body, usually after diarrhoea).

Torrential rain persisted all night, making them wonder what state the river would be in next day. Page could not stop talking about his narrow escape from drowning: the others complained that he kept them awake all night. In the early hours of the morning Shearer awoke to find something sticking to his eyelid: not sure what it was, he pulled it off and threw it away – but in the morning his whole head was covered in blood, and on the flysheet they found the biggest leech any of them had ever seen, bloated with Shearer's blood. Kicking it out of the tent, he had the pleasure of squashing it between two rocks with a sickening squelch – but he was left with a nasty bruise and an inky-looking mark like a love-bite on his eyelid, in which the jaws of the leech were still embedded. Later they worked out that it must have been a king leech, the most fearsome species. (The best way of removing leeches is to touch them with a lighted cigarette or some brands of insect repellent, which makes them withdraw their jaws.)

That morning – 9 March – they found they were just short of some very dangerous-looking waterfalls. The river seemed to have turned itself back into the Gully, or an extension of it, and once again the sides were steep and smooth. Forced back into the jungle on the right-hand side, they climbed up, and were driven higher and higher. Though not on a track, they made quite good progress, crawling through the vegetation as they moved from

162

one spur to another, from knife edge to knife edge. At one stage Shearer suggested that the others should leave him behind, in a place where rescuers would be likely to find him – but of course they ignored his request. He was in a very poor way, starting to hallucinate, and only by willpower had he kept going. Not only did his companions think they were close to civilisation: they also imagined that Neill had long since got out and raised the alarm – so they expected rescue helicopters to appear above them at any moment.

By then huge butterflies were much in evidence, and brilliant yellow hornbills lolloped from tree to tree with their characteristic dipping flight. Brittan had also begun to have hallucinations: he heard car radios, whistles, children playing – and he blew his own whistle frantically in response. Even this modest activity now taxed him severely, and he had to give himself long breaks. That night they camped in the jungle, fairly high up. Page observed that they only got into trouble when they left the river, so they resolved to return to the watercourse, and stick with it.

Wondering what had happened to Neill's group, Brittan felt convinced that they had taken New's route and broken out of the jungle, and he fully expected to find them waiting for him – probably not in any of the villages, but back at the Park Headquarters or in Kota Kinabalu. Page's feelings towards the officers' group were not charitable. *They* were perfectly all right, he was sure: they were 'out and gone' – and yet they had done nothing to organise rescue for the others.

*   *   *

Of 9 March Mayfield remembered very little, except that he had 'walked up and down hills trying to take bearings', and had had an argument with Mann, who wanted to go directly north, against his own preference for north-north-west. In the end they compromised, and at some stages, as Mann stumbled ahead, Mayfield steered him with his compass – 'Left . . . right' – so that they kept more or less to their bearing. Leeches and mosquitoes

163

tormented them all day, and they passed through several distinct types of vegetation. By now, having lost their sterilisation tablets, they were drinking untreated water. In one area all the trees were dead, and covered in moss. Their loads were by now much reduced, and they had jettisoned everything except their money and passports. Mann was in such a state that he dumped his precious video camera, films and all, which earlier he had guarded with his life. But still he reckoned their loads felt as heavy as the packs they had carried at the outset of the expedition. He began hunting obsessively for banana trees, determined to cut one down with his parang. He did not see any, but because Mayfield had said, 'Oh, well – we'll keep alive on bananas', Mann thought every tree he came to was going to be full of them. They spend a very uncomfortable, wet night on top of a hill.

* * *

On 10 March Brittan and his group made a final effort to regain the river. They faced a horrendous climb down without ropes, and went in an almost straight line, jinking to left and right to avoid sheer drops. When they came to a 10-metre vertical cliff, they threw their bergens down first, and Page and Shearer managed to slither down one side. Brittan found a tree like a telegraph pole about six feet out from the cliff, sprang into it, and shinned down. So they returned to the river, boulder-hopping again, although the boulders were noticeably smaller and the watercourse was widening. They were frustrated by the need to keep crossing the stream, for the water was deep, the current strong and the rocks slippery. Leeches were a constant menace. The group camped on a beach of grey sand studded with rocks, some of which they managed to dig out with their parang; but even so they had a wretched night. Inevitably, morale was sinking: battered, bruised, half-starved and exhausted, they were all growing weaker and battling to survive.

* * *

Mann and Mayfield were also far gone. That same day, 10 March, also following a river, they found a lean-to shelter – the first real sign of civilisation. That night they came on a cave, with some empty noodle packets, Japanese or Chinese, but very old. The cave was full of bats, so they dossed down for the night in the entrance. Mayfield said to Mann, 'Listen to the river – it sounds like the aircraft on the way home.' By now he had convinced himself that Neill's group had never committed themselves to the large abseil, and had retreated up Easy Valley. He too was wondering if wives and families had been told that his team was missing, and hoped that search parties were out looking for them.

*   *   *

For breakfast on 11 March Brittan and his two companions had a little cod-liver oil and some vitamin tablets, and set off again downriver, zigzagging between interlocking spurs and walking from one side of the stream to the other, depending on how clear the beaches were. In some places the water was waist- or chest-deep, and flowing strongly, and at others only up to their ankles. On the spurs they kept finding tracks, some wide enough to drive a car down, and they covered a good deal of ground by using them. Signs of civilisation steadily increased: graffiti in big red letters on a prominent rock, improvised bridges, sardine cans, parang cuts. After passing through scrub and secondary vegetation, they were now into some form of pine forest and lush, primary jungle, full of birds and insects.

During their day's march they saw signs of logging with chainsaws, and at 1800 they noticed a large concrete hydro intake, with a metal grille across it. A track led off to the left, with a large rubbish dump beside it. Excited enough to scream and shout, Brittan and Page tried to convince Shearer, who was dragging himself along some distance behind, that their troubles were over; but he was so far gone that he showed little interest.

Now they did find a banana plantation, and were strongly tempted to nip off and help themselves to the growing fruit. But, starving though they were, they were put off when Page reminded them that in Muslim countries hands are cut off for theft: they were in a bad enough state already, without having any extremities lopped off.

At a junction they came to a building, where – miracle of miracles – they saw another human being, 'a wiry old chap' who was sitting on his tractor. Toothless, and speaking no English, he offered them a rolled bamboo cigarette, which 'looked like the sort the police confiscate', and gave them directions. Following the track he indicated, they eventually reached, at about 1700, a village of thatched huts on stilts, and asked a woman who was hanging out washing in her vegetable patch where they could get transport. When she saw Shearer's face with dried blood all over it, she realised that he needed medical help, and gestured them on towards the middle of the settlement, which turned out to be Melangkap Tamis.

There they found a big football field where children were playing. One of the players politely offered them a game, but they declined, hardly having the strength to put one foot in front of the other. According to Brittan, 'we dumped our packs there, took our shirts off and collapsed'. The local schoolteacher, Mr Yapis Juriba, appeared, and began to question them in excellent English. Other people also appeared and gawped at these amazing creatures that had crawled out of the jungle.

Brittan asked Mr Juriba if he could take them to civilisation, or at least point them in the right direction – but he refused, saying that they needed immediate treatment and food. Seeing the state they were in, he refused to allow them to move, and insisted that they stay that night in his house, promising that he would take them to Kota Kinabalu in the morning. He had not heard that anyone was missing, and when Brittan said they had come down from the summit of Kinabalu, via Low's Gully, the teacher's jaw dropped. Clearly he thought they were pulling his leg – so they abandoned that claim for the moment. But they explained that some people were still lost in the jungle, and that they themselves must get back and raise the alarm as soon as possible. (Brittan was thinking only of Mann and Mayfield, assuming that Neill's group had already come out.)

166

At Mr Juriba's house they attracted a good deal of attention. People came up to shake their hands and prod them. By then Shearer's legs were badly swollen, his grazes 'a nice shade of green with a red surround'. Brittan made enquiries about a telephone, but learned that the nearest one was in the next village, some distance off.

Their host regaled them with a feast of fish, rice and seaweed-like vegetables. They ate so much that their shrunken stomachs could not stand the sudden onslaught, and during the night Brittan and Page were 'rolling around in agony' with pains in the belly. On the morning of 12 March, by now eight days overdue, they were helped into the back of a truck at 0800 and set off for Kota Kinabalu, with Mr Juriba and his neighbour, Andrew Sualan. It was a fantastic relief to be back to civilisation, travelling in a vehicle again – but their minds were whirling with the problem of what they were going to say to Neill when they saw him again in Kota Kinabalu.

They reached the Travellers' Rest before midday, and were shocked to find that none of the others had reappeared. A check showed that all the baggage was where they had left it. Suddenly they realised that something was badly wrong. Their own appearance was so awful that other inmates of the hostel stared at them in horror – and Shearer was so weak that he subsided then and there while Brittan and Page made urgent enquiries at the Sabah Parks head office, in the block next to the hostel. When no information was forthcoming, Page demanded a meeting with Francis Liew, the Assistant Director. The idea was that Page should go in 'and jump up and down on his desk and find out the score'. Brittan, meanwhile, had gone to the travel agents, to make sure that Neill's party had not taken flights out: he hardly thought they could have, but he wanted to tie off that loose end.

In the Parks office Page managed to force his way past the secretary who dealt with normal tourist enquiries, and explained to Liew that things had gone seriously wrong. The expedition should have reported back to Park Headquarters, on the mountain, on 4 March, and it was already the 12th. Seven people were lost, and a rescue operation was needed. Liew was clearly alarmed, but began by saying that it would be difficult to mount a search, as the national holidays began next day, and everybody had made arrangements to do other things. Page insisted that help was essential, so Liew telephoned Eric Wong, the Chief Warden of the Kinabalu National Park, whom Neill had tried in vain to meet on his way up the mountain. By evening it had been agreed that a helicopter would be made available for a reconnaissance flight next morning, and that Liew would collect Brittan and Page from the Travellers' Rest at 0600.

Later that evening Brittan telephoned Major Ramsden in Hong Kong. Since this was Saturday, he knew that he would be lucky to get through, and sure enough, he found that Ramsden had gone off on leave to – of all places – Borneo. Brittan spoke to a warrant officer, giving him a brief outline of what had happened: he took care not to spread panic, and left a fairly low-key message, alerting Hong Kong to the fact that there was a problem, and giving a contact number. He himself felt confident that the helicopter would soon find the missing men in the morning.

* * *

Throughout 11 March, as Brittan correctly imagined, Mann and Mayfield had been having a dire struggle, and were rapidly growing weaker. After every few steps, Mann would have to stop for a whole minute, and Mayfield naturally found their lack of progress frustrating. He himself then had a severe fall: tumbling about 10 metres he bounced off a rock slab and landed 'like a sack of spuds' in the water, soaking all his kit, including his sleeping bag.

In the evening they reached what they thought was an abandoned orchard: a patch of jungle had been cleared, and trees were growing in semi-straight lines. Seeing fruit in the branches, Mayfield climbed up, only to find that most of them were rotten and mouldy – small, yellow, melon-like gourds, with orange flesh and white seeds. They tried to eat one, but it was very dry and tasted like wood. With his last match Mayfield managed to light a fire, which was enough to dry them and start drying the sleeping bag. They built a small shelter, and spent another uncomfortable night on the ground, squashed into the damp bag and slowly drying it out with the warmth of their bodies. Even though they were down in the tropical jungle, with the temperature about 20 degrees Celsius at night, they had lost all their body fat and desperately needed all the warmth they could get.

By now Mann was in a very poor state, weak, stumbling, continually falling over. In Mayfield's memorable phrase, it was as if 'the lights were on but nobody was at home'. Mann could see that gangrene was setting into his wounded hand: he greatly feared he was going to lose his fingers, and that the infection had spread up his arm, which was starting to throb painfully.

On the morning of 12 March they tottered through the plantation in search of a track, but could not find one, and set off along the river instead. After only twenty minutes they came to a fork and decided to go right, over a bridge made of wood and chicken wire, which crossed the river. A forty-five minute climb took them to the top of a hill, where they found a derelict hut; it fell about them when they sat down in it. Following the track further, they found another makeshift hut, in which was a plastic shopping bag containing the desiccated remains of a dead fish. Mayfield's hunger was so desperate that he ate some of it, but he spat it out in disgust, describing it as 'bloody awful'. They also found the old skin of a melon, which Mann chewed at; but Mayfield – by then wary of all fruit – declined to touch it.

An hour's trek later Mann looked to his left and saw what he took to be a television aerial rising through the jungle canopy, but he ignored it because he 'thought it was bloody stupid'. Fifteen minutes later, however, he saw more of the same things and said to his companion, 'Rich – can you see what I see?' 'Yes,' Mayfield answered, 'TV aerials.' They sank to the ground with relief and the knowledge that they were safe. Then they dragged themselves to their feet again and staggered on.

Over one more ridge at 1000 they at last hit a village of about fifty wooden houses, which turned out to be Melangkap Kappa, the settlement neighbouring Melangkap Tamis, where Brittan and the others had emerged. Mann was heading for the centre of the settlement when Mayfield heaved himself up the steps of one of the big huts. Waiting for him, Mann then collapsed beside a fence. When some children came over and began to prod and poke him, he tried to explain that he needed to speak to an adult. They could hear singing, and it seemed that most of the population had gathered for a religious service in the village hall (it was Ramadan, the Muslim month of daily fasting). One of the children sprinted across with the news that strange white men in rags had arrived.

Suddenly people poured out and began talking to Mann: he could not understand a word, but a village elder gave him a drink of water, helped him to his feet and led him to the hut which Mayfield had already entered. Inside, he found the corporal 'sat on a table with a bloody great amount of food around him'. There were also 'about six girls', one of whom was feeding him and another dressing his wounds. They sat Mann down and gave him a plate of food as well, but he was 'totally lost'. Finding he could not eat, the Malays gave him hot, sweet milk and began to dress his wounds. They also ushered in a woman skilled in local medicine (later inaccurately described by the British press as 'a witch doctor').

He was scared stiff that she was 'bent on cutting bits off him' when she began to work at the cuts on his legs. He drew her attention to his festering hand, which by then looked and smelt so revolting that one of the girls who had been feeding Mayfield recoiled with horror and ran off. The woman's response was to plunge the hand 'in this jar of dead things, literally' – a glass jar with a lid, full of herbs and floating objects, which he learnt was a concoction of snake venom and bones, bear bile and crushed poisonous centipede. The impact of the potion was agonising – far worse than iodine. Mann yelled aloud, feeling that his hand was on fire. After twenty minutes' immersion it looked rubbery, as though it had been soaked in water; the vile brew cleaned up his wounds immediately, removing all the pus and killing the infection. When the woman had dressed his wounds, Mann at last had something to eat, but was immediately stricken by diarrhoea. Mayfield also got stomach cramps – whereupon the old woman rubbed his stomach with the same potent concoction, and the cramps subsided.

By then the villagers had dug out some clean shorts and T-shirts, and the survivors lay down on quilts, with the entire population crammed into the hut, staring at them with friendly fascination. After an hour or so, there appeared a man who could speak some English. He told them that three other white men had come out of the jungle at a neighbouring village the previous evening – and the survivors slumped back on their makeshift beds, overcome by relief and exhaustion. The village elder told them that he had transport, and could take them to Kota Kinabalu; so they collected what was left of their kit, walked to a pick-up truck, were photographed like exhibits in a zoo, and set off for the capital, with quite a few stops for Mann 'to nip into the hedge'.

Lurching into the Travellers' Rest, they found Brittan, looking gaunt but alert, and at once asked if anyone had seen the colonel's group. The answer was no. Brittan countered with, 'Where the bloody hell did you lot get to?' but then made them a cup of tea. As Mann sat out on a veranda, having his first smoke for days, a female tourist, who was a doctor, took one look at his hand and his general condition, and told him he needed immediate hospital treatment. She went with him, Mayfield and Shearer in a taxi to the local infirmary, where, after an inspection in the casualty department, Shearer and Mann were admitted straight away. Mayfield, not liking the look of the place, was determined not to stay there, and reckoned he could look after himself better elsewhere.

On the morning of Sunday, 13 March, Liew collected Page and Brittan at 0600 and drove them to Sabah Old Airport, from which some private airline operated. With them they took a day-sack full of tins of sardines and Mars bars, with which to bombard any survivors they might see: they knew that the missing five, if still alive, would be exceedingly hungry, and it was almost certain that the helicopter would be unable to touch down anywhere in the jungle. In Brittan's view, the park authorities were embarrassed by the fact that they had not raised the alarm, and laid on the helicopter as a means of making amends.

Wong met them at the airport, looking worried, and they took off in a white, two-engined Bell Huey 212, whose pilot flew them round the mountain to the area of Melangkap Kappa, and then back and forth above the Penataran river. Visibility was excellent. After a while they touched down for forty-five minutes in a kampong to give the survivors time to put up a signal (perhaps with smoke); then they went up again and searched some more, but saw nothing. In all they flew for more than three hours: they did not go up over the Gully, but concentrated on the river and the spurs flanking it. Brittan formed the impression that although the helicopter had the power to go higher up the Gully, the pilot was a commercial one, and not used to that sort of flying. He never flew quite as low over the jungle canopy as Brittan would have liked, but they got a good view of the riverbed, and would certainly have seen anyone out on it. He recognised the hydro installation he had seen, and Page's waterfall and cave. Yet, as he remarked later, 'once you're up in the air, there's rivers all over the place', and the flight brought home to him the indescribable confusion of the terrain.

Back in Kota Kinabalu, Wong told them that on Monday, even though it was a public holiday (which would last till Wednesday), he would send in a foot-party of Park rangers from one of the kampongs upriver, and on to the ridge. Brittan found that a telephone call had come in from Hong Kong while he was out; so he rang back and spoke to the Commanding Officer, explaining what had happened and what had been done so far. He also called England and spoke to his girlfriend, Sadie Gray, who worked in the Regimental Headquarters of The RLC at Deepcut: he told her that the expedition had run into difficulties, so he would be late back. At his request, at 0900 on Monday, 14 March she told the officer in charge of the Mobile Display Team, Captain Steve McMahon; he told Brittan's Officer Commanding, Major Bob Corbey, who made several calls to Neill's headquarters in York. Until then no one there had heard of any problem, but a member of Neill's staff passed the news to David Bentley. He in fact had already sensed that something was wrong, and on his own initiative had sent a signal to Hong Kong asking what the form was. Rumours were thus flying in the United Kingdom before any official notification had come from Kuala Lumpur that the expedition was in trouble. When Mayfield telephoned his wife that evening, he asked her not to tell anyone yet, as the missing men would probably pop out of the jungle at any moment (he was so ill with stomach cramps, after his excessive eating in the village, that he could hardly walk).

That evening Mann discharged himself from hospital, after a day on a saline drip. Thinking he would be better off in the hostel, he waited till 2000 that evening, announced to the staff that he was going home, and walked off. Shearer endured one more night, and then also discharged himself.

On Monday 14 March, Robert New and Mike Scott – the Honorary Consul in Kota Kinabalu, and manager of the local branch of the Hong Kong Bank – appeared at the Travellers' Rest, alerted by a tourist who had asked them what was happening. Brittan brought them up to date, and Scott said that he would inform the British High Commission in Kuala Lumpur. Brittan told them that Page and Shearer had lost their passports. From then on he or one of his colleagues manned a telephone all day, and Mayfield was startled when a Malaysian general came on the line to ask, 'How many regiments do you want for the search?'

The corporal coolly answered, 'Hang on a moment', and with his hand over the mouthpiece said to Mann, beside him, 'We've got some general on the phone, asking how many regiments we want to search up the river.'

'How many men in a regiment?' asked Mann.

'About six hundred,' Mayfield answered.

'Give us two, then.'

So Mayfield went back on the line, and said, 'I'll have two, please.' When the general said, 'OK', and rang off, Mann was flabbergasted – but two regiments were what they got.

173

Chapter 13

Living on Water

The dawn of Day Twenty, Tuesday 15 March, found Neill's party wretched and bedraggled. The officers were particularly worried about Chow, who was drenched, and liable to hypothermia. Neill's other special concern was for his pack, last seen out on the boulder in midstream. He had spent much of the night cursing his stupidity in leaving it there – but when daylight came he saw to his unbounded relief that it was still where he had left it, high and dry in the middle of a raging torrent. Not so several items of climbing kit and Foster's only pair of trousers, which had been washed away. All he had left to wear on his lower half was a pair of long-johns.

Given that the pack contained one day's food – which represented maybe ten days' survival – Neill could not stand by and watch the water hurtle past it. With rain still falling, but with the water level dropping slightly he stripped off to his own shorts and Foster's boots and tottered across from boulder to boulder, clambering on all fours to reach his precious pack, with one end of a climbing-rope tied round his waist, in case he slipped and was washed away, while Foster clung to the other end, and got soaked for his pains. Safely back in the overhang, Neill felt pathetically grateful to Providence that he had recovered his belongings without further dramas.

Because of the cloud and rain, it was obvious that helicopters could not fly, so they reluctantly abandoned all hope of rescue that day. Neill's primary concern was to make sure that Chow did not succumb to hypothermia. Kevin and Victor still had dry sleeping bags, so Neill told them to take turns, lending Chow one of their bags, and occupying his to dry it out.

The Hong Kong lads were now openly worried about ending their lives in that wretched place. 'We're going to die here,'

174

Chow said to Foster in a matter-of-fact voice. But Foster told him and his colleagues that they must be positive about being rescued. To cheer them up, Neill jokingly said, 'You don't need to worry. I'll tell you when you're going to die.'

In private, the officers had briefly mentioned the question of cannibalism, but had not dwelt on it: yet inevitably their minds turned to the Andes air crash, when the survivors had stayed alive for seventy-one days by eating the bodies of the dead. They justified their action by claiming that the souls had left the bodies which they ate, and all that was left was meat and bones. (The reason they survived so long was that the corpses were preserved in the ice and snow surrounding the crashed aircraft.) Foster reckoned that cannibalism, as a means of survival, might be physically justifiable in such circumstances. Whether or not it could ever be morally justifiable he saw as a matter for individuals, who would have to make up their own minds.

He and Neill reckoned that they were still a long way from any such enormity, and did not mention it to the Hong Kong soldiers. Apart from other considerations, they all had so little flesh on them by that time that they would hardly have been worth eating.

Again they spent the daylight hours working to improve their sleeping quarters. One particular boulder, which had defied earlier attempts at eviction, occupied their attention: using penknives, mess tins, spoons and a tent-pole, they scrabbled away to excavate the gravel round the base of the most annoying rocks, not knowing whether they were loose or part of the underlying formation. Since the trench which Neill had been occupying was liable to flood again, he was keen to move up higher if he could make enough room. By the end of that day there was space for only one person – Foster – to sleep in the new area: Neill tried it, but later moved back into what they called 'the pit', under the lee of the boulder.

By now Foster had decided to adopt a daily routine of packing his kit for rescue, and he encouraged Kevin, Victor and Chow to do the same. 'If a helicopter comes,' he told them, 'it won't be able to wait – we've got to be ready.' His drill was to fill his dive-sack – which was already inside his rucksack – with essential

175

items such as dry clothes, money, passport and video camera, leaving room for his sleeping bag and bivvy bag to go in at the last moment. He was confident that in the event of rescue, he would be ready first. He would then be able to help the others over the boulders with their kit, to the middle of the river, which he and Neill had calculated would be the natural winch-point nearest to the cave.

As the days wore on, they found it increasingly important to make regular entries in their diaries. Foster felt that, to capture the truth as he saw it, notes should be written as events and thoughts occurred, and not later, so that important details would not be left out or distorted through stress and haste. He almost always used a pencil – the most reliable instrument; he also enjoyed the further benefit of being able to talk into his video camera – and he had all the time in the world to do it. (During the whole expedition he used less than two whole ninety-minute films, and was carrying eight more in reserve.) He began to realise how rarely in his life he had had the conditions or the solitude in which he could concentrate totally on a subject and follow an idea through to its conclusions. His previous work had taught him to think logically, and now he was able to transmit thoughts on to paper without interruption – except from the rain.

This concentration frequently blocked out the gravity of their plight for a while, and he felt mentally stimulated by its effect. During such moments of introspection he reviewed his own life, not least his schooldays in Barton-upon-Humber. He particularly remembered Mr Goddard, the headmaster, and Henry Treece, the novelist who was his English master: the first wrote the music, and the second the words, of a song which embodied the school motto, 'Keep Faith' – and now the chorus from it ran persistently through his head:

Keep faith in all you do.
These words will stand as true
On future morrows as they do
Here today.

Every member of the party was aware of physical deterioration.

Kevin's Cave and Chow the day before the rock-fall

Neill and Foster's end of the overhang

Scrabbling for the rations

Above: Aerial view of
the southern side of
Kinabalu

Left: Helicopter shot of
the top end of the Gully
taken from 1000 m
above the river bed

Right: Foul weather on
the northern flank –
dangerous flying
conditions

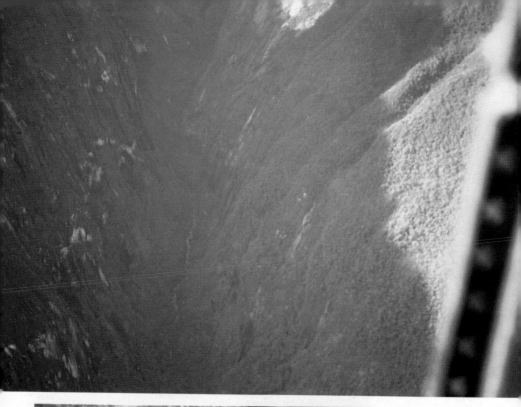

Above: Somewhere down there were the trapped group

Left: GOT EM! Shot from the Sikorski – 25 March (Neill's red anorak can just be seen at the bottom of the photo)

The Alouette about to lower the medic

Above: The most welcome sight in the world – the Sikorski coming in to the rescue

Right: RESCUE! Crewmen coming down

0:51:42

Above: Welcoming smiles inside the Sikorski (taken from Ron's video)

Right: Neill with rescue cup of fortified tea in Kampong

Below: Foster with rescue cup of fortified tea in Kampong

Above: The last ones out of the Gully – 26 March 1994

Right: Neill, none the worse for wear, the day after rescue

Below: Robert New visiting Foster in the Sabah Medical Centre

Left: Recce group recovering at base of severe waterfall

Below: **All's well that ends well. A beer in the Providence Inn in Yedingham**

Only a few days after the failure of the officers' seventy-two-hour attempt at escape did Neill realise how much he had been weakened by the effort. With hindsight, he saw that he had used his remaining energy reserves, and he never regained the strength he had maintained until the breakout. From then on he found it a struggle even to keep warm.

The survivors could not check their own appearance, for they had no mirror, and their mess tins – which they might have polished up – were too scratched and blackened to act as a substitute. Further, there was no water still enough to give a clear reflection. Foster remained relatively well covered, but Neill, who had carried very little spare flesh when the expedition started, could tell by a simple check how fast he was losing weight and condition. At the outset, when he placed both hands round one thigh, the tips of his thumbs and middle fingers would just meet immediately above the knee, but no higher. Now, when he did the same, he could easily run the circle of his fingers half-way up his emaciated leg. He still felt warm internally, but was 'a bit tottery' and weak in his movements. All members of the party except Foster were finding it more difficult to retain their upper-body heat and keep warm at night. Inevitably, the less flesh they had on them, and the wetter (and thus colder) they became, the greater the chance of hypothermia setting in.

They worried that the low temperature of the water they were drinking must be cooling their inner cores. In an attempt to balance his body heat, Foster had taken to drinking small amounts frequently during the early part of the day. Whether or not this had any effect he could not tell, but he felt better psychologically for doing it. He also wondered how much nutrition, if any, he could expect to get from a clear mountain stream.

He and Neill spent much time playing chess. The light under the overhang was so dim that it was often difficult to discern the difference between pawns and bishops, but by that evening the score in matches was two all.

There was a major calamity when one of the pieces fell down between their sleeping bags, and they became entirely preoccupied by this catastrophic loss – until, by groping about in the half-dark, they found the missing castle. They sought to raise the morale of the Chinese by talking about families, friends and background, about the Army, China and the Cold War. They were disappointed to discover that both Chow and Kevin were due to take redundancy from the Army later that year, and would probably be out in six months. Although Neill had talked to them at length about their careers, both before they went up the mountain and when they were camped in their various overnight bivouacs, they had never thought to mention their imminent release. Neill wondered why the hell Hong Kong had sent him two men who could not possibly gain military benefit from adventurous training.

Victor, the most articulate of the three, talked about his training as a swimming instructor, and how he hoped to teach civilians when he left the Army in two years' time. He asked Neill for his help in becoming a member of the Open University, and showed him snapshots of his girlfriend, Pansie, together with notes they had written to each other. A good rapport was developing; but because of the constant noise of the water, which exacerbated communication difficulties, it was hard to hold extended conversations inside the cave. Only when they were sitting in the open, drying themselves or their clothes, was it easy to have a proper talk. In general, the Chinese seemed to have an enviable ability to put themselves into limbo; Neill had explained to them that the more inactive they could remain, the longer they would be able to last – but even without this advice they were usually content to lie in their sleeping bags, keeping warm. Unlike the British, who were intermittently hounded by the feeling that they must take active steps to end the stalemate, the men from Hong Kong seemed to be sustained by a form of Oriental fatalism.

At about this time Chow discovered a single small berry, brown on the outside and red within, which had fallen from somewhere above. After sniffing and licking cautiously, he ate it, and pronounced it good – but alas, no more could be found.

Heavy rain continued all through Day Twenty, but the water

level did not rise any higher; it was as if the Gully could cope with anything that the weather might now dump on it. Neill noticed that this was the day on which the group should have reported for CNFP flights from Hong Kong to London: their failure to appear would surely raise the alarm, even if nothing else had. (In fact this was the day on which the Royal Air Force mountain rescue teams were mobilised.)

As always, he and Foster endlessly speculated on the fate of the recce party. They also spent hours discussing their own failure to find an escape route from the Gully. If New had managed it, why had they not been able to do the same? By now Neill acknowledged that he did not have the strength to make another attempt; already it was taking him longer and longer to do simple things, like climbing out of his sleeping bag. Then he began to wonder what would happen when he grew too weak to get out at all, and wanted to go for a pee. Already, to leave the cave at night was a major operation, and far from safe: with co-ordination faltering, there was always a danger of falling down between rocks. Rather than risk it, Neill and Foster reduced their fluid intake in the afternoons, and made do with one hot drink as late as possible before settling down for the night. They found that by this method they could last through until daylight, when they could again inspect their urine for signs of discolouration due to dehydration.

Foster had given up trying to use his two long-life candles, or nightlights. Whenever he lit one, hundreds of tiny insects hurled themselves at the burning wick, snuffing all life out of it. Attempts to relight it led nowhere, so he came to rely on the chemical light-stick, and on rare occasions his head-torch – although, to conserve batteries, he and Neill always took to their beds by dark.

They were all finding it difficult to sleep at night. Because they were resting so much during the day, the officers were not tired when dark fell, and their minds would start to wander uncontrollably: they began to think about dying, and wondered what would happen to their families. Whenever their thoughts did turn to death, they felt a need to talk about them, and for a while Neill gave in to what he considered a weakness. Then he told himself that he was being wet, and resolved to keep quiet on the subject in future: whenever someone else raised the matter, he would talk about it for a while, but then end the discussion by declaring jauntily, 'This is ridiculous: we're going to be found, and that's all there is to it.' Foster tried to shut out thoughts of death, believing them to be counter-productive.

Neill had one terrifying dream which, once established, kept returning night after night to torment him. He was climbing out of the Gully. He would reach up for a handhold, but it would give way, and he would find himself falling. Because he was attached to a rope, he would finish upside-down. Water was trickling everywhere, so that he was getting soaked, hanging, totally trapped, unable to move, looking up into the sky. At that moment he would wake up, to find himself struggling to climb, upside-down and stuck fast – in his sleeping bag. It was appalling to come round and find how exactly the dream reflected the reality of his position: caught, unable to move, growing weaker, with the first group gone and possibly dead.

When he saw the friendly green nightlight – already three times past its claimed span – he could at least tell which way up he was, and sort himself out. Then he would drift off to sleep again – and the whole nightmare would repeat itself. So the night would pass, with new versions of the dream following hard on each other's heels. Sometimes his nightmares were so bad that he had to wake Foster up and talk to him to regain some form of sanity – but his companion was having dreams of his own, of a similar nature, if not quite so violent.

On 16 March Foster was up first, as usual, and at first light he stood on a rock outside the cave, staring down the valley under a clear sky, willing a helicopter to arrive. 'Twelve days missing,' he entered in his journal. 'Thinking a great deal about Jeanette and the family at home – of their anxieties. WE know WE feel fine, and I'm trying to concentrate on Jeanette's mind and let her know we're OK.' Then at 0715:

Heard a whistling noise uphill through undergrowth. Big

spray of water. Thought, 'Oh my God, the water's coming into our cave!' Worse than that, a big rock was hurtling towards me. I jumped for cover behind a boulder. As I did so, I heard whistling again and saw more rocks crashing their way down through the vegetation at tremendous speed, heading for our shelter. Five big rocks crashed into the cave. I thought someone must have been killed.

Somehow he had time to register that boulders one or two metres across were cannoning into static rocks and dislodging them, as if on a gigantic snooker table, so that the rocks which had been struck also came careering downhill, from several directions simultaneously. Neill had just awoken to find himself back in the trench under the big boulder. Lying there semi-conscious, he felt the ground start to vibrate, as if in an earthquake, and even though he had his head tucked inside his bivvy bag for warmth, he became aware of thunderous crashes outside. Instinctively he doubled himself down inside the bag to squeeze himself as far under the boulder as he could go. The next thing he knew, he was hit by two heavy impacts in the small of the back, and forced forward against the rock so that his nose was jammed into his sleeping bag. He could hardly breathe. His shoulder felt as if it had been scraped raw by a fierce blow, and it too was being compressed into the rock. Nor could he move: a huge weight of rock was pressing into his back. More thudding and knocking sounded close at hand. Then he heard Chow crying out, as if he had been seriously hurt.

After his soaking during the previous night, Chow had shifted position and decided to sleep on the boulder just under the edge of the overhang. When he felt the first rock crash alongside him, he hurled himself downwards, towards Neill's position, out of the way. As he went, three more rocks smashed in immediately behind him and ricocheted off to pin him against another large boulder, bringing down the tent which they had rigged against drips. Foster leapt into the cave, pulled the first two rocks away and threw them aside: he also dragged away the tent, but could not shift a third rock until Kevin helped him. Under the landslide

181

lay Neill and Chow, and Foster fully expected to find them both dead.

Neill knew that he was not injured, but he was running out of air, so he began giving muffled shouts for help. It seemed to him that the others were taking an interminable time to galvanise themselves. Then he heard Foster yell at Victor to get a move on, and he felt rocks being lifted off his back. Struggling out of his bivvy bag, he found that a cliff face above them had given way in the heavy rain. Jagged lumps of fresh granite, full of bright quartz, had ricocheted off other rocks, vaulted clean over the big boulders at the edge of their shelter, and bounced into the overhang.

Chow was hurt: he had blood on his cheek and hand, and was clearly in shock. He was lying on his right side, still in his sleeping bag, with his nose pressed against the flat rock which formed the back of the trench. To Foster, looking down on the heap of debris, it looked as though he had been chopped in two – yet the fact that he was moaning, and could complain, was a good sign, and when they got him out they were astonished to find nothing seriously wrong. Victor, who was trained in first aid, checked him all over to establish that nothing was broken, or damaged internally. Chow's only visible injuries were abrasions on one hand and on his cheek, which they promptly treated.

Because Kevin was lasting better than his compatriots, Neill told him to swap sleeping bags with Chow, whose bag was wet, and who now needed maximum support. So Chow was helped into the warm bag and spent the day there recovering, cheered by some Chinese tea and by the fact that his glasses had been found intact: they had been knocked off by the impact of the rocks, and without them he was helpless. But Foster recorded that he was complaining of a bad back, and appeared to be hallucinating. Victor kept a close eye on him all day.

When Neill inspected his own sleeping area, he realised how lucky he had been. It looked as though the flysheet brought down by the rocks might have contributed to his escape by fractionally retarding the fall; but the tough skin of his bivvy bag had been punctured in several places at the top end, where his head would have been if he had not ducked. The rock that hit it must have weighed 50 kilos, and would certainly have killed him in a direct impact.

Oddly enough, the incident did much for Victor's morale. He had strong religious beliefs, and saw this as a sign that God was on their side. 'It's a miracle we're alive,' he said. 'If we were going to die, we would have died just then. We'll be all right now.' Foster felt much the same. 'Is there a "force" trying to get us out of this Gully?' he wrote. 'I decided in my own mind that as we had escaped serious injury – a miracle – we *must* be rescued before too long.'

Some of his optimism brushed off on Neill, who agreed that his own time did not seem to be up. Nevertheless, the landslide made him even more wary of the Gully: to be trapped and starving to death was bad enough, but the long streak of devastation down the cliff above them, where the avalanche had snapped trees off like matchsticks and left a straggle of shattered, yellow-white trunks, reminded them that they were in perpetual danger of physical destruction. 'What the hell else has this bloody mountain got to throw at us?' he muttered to Foster – and immediately found that the rocks had crushed Chow's gas cooker, leaving them one only, and reducing their capacity to brew up hot drinks. For the rest of the expedition, to conserve gas, they had to be content with warm brews – but the officers were extremely glad of the extra gas canister which Kevin had been carrying.

Later in the morning there was a gleam of sun, so they washed some clothes and laid them out. Neill managed to dry his anorak for the first time, and tried to catch tadpoles; but as his fishing hook was bigger than his quarry, he had no luck. Nor did he manage to coax any tadpoles into his mess tin, and he made a mental note to include netting in any future survival kit. At 1500 rain again drove them into their shelter. 'Chow appears recovered,' Neill recorded,

but even if he isn't, we can't do much about it. There is a permanent air of crisis in this Gully – keeping stuff dry, and

*the physical danger of the mountain. No luck trying to light a
fire. How long will our gas refill last with five people using it?*

That evening he and Foster each had one biscuit and a
mouthful of chicken soup. With great reluctance, but acting on
the principle that lightning never strikes the same place twice, he
went back into his trench to sleep: there was really not enough
room for him and Foster on the platform above it. His reserves of
energy and body heat had sunk so low that he had taken to
wearing all his clothes, including the anorak, inside his sleeping
bag – anything to keep heat in. The small piece of sleeping mat,
together with his dive-sack, helped to prevent cold rising from
the floor.

The night was beautifully clear, with the stars shining bright
above the ominous deep V of the Gully; but at first light on
Thursday, 17 March heavy rain set in, so they remained in their
sleeping bags. It was thirty-four years to the day since Foster had
joined the Army. 'Played chess,' he recorded. 'There was
nothing else to do, it was so dark.' Neill wrote:

*Hunger is not an obvious difficulty for us. Keeping warm and
dry and comfortable if possible is more important. Having
dried out my anorak yesterday, I wore it all night
successfully: no condensation, and I kept warmer. Non-flying
weather today should add pressure to rescue action when
weather clears. Continue to be concerned about the fate of the
other party, over whose actions I have no control.*

Foster wrote:

*They all look very thin. I suppose I do too. Always wanted a
thirty-two inch waist. Now I've got a twenty-eighter! Kevin is
in Chow's bag to try and dry it, and Chow is in Kevin's to
keep warm.*

At 1500 they were hit by another flood, more serious than the
first, and just as unexpected; they all took another soaking, Chow

184

worst of all. This time a waterfall cascaded off the roof of the cave, from the previously dry area where Kevin and Victor had been lying. Even more ominously, outside, a new torrent began to pour down the bare track which the avalanche had smashed through the jungle. Now there seemed a real chance that half the mountainside would crash down on them, and for nearly four hours they remained in a state of crisis. Again the flood seemed to take advantage of Chow's untidiness: this time it seized one of his jungle boots and bore it away. At last, around 1900, the downpour abated and the rush of water slackened, and this enabled Neill and Foster to make a brew, which they passed up to the Chinese, so that at least they had something warm inside them.

That night was dry, but Neill, struggling to find a comfortable position, was assailed by repetitions of his climbing nightmare. In his dreams he was constantly clambering up the sides of the Gully, falling, becoming twisted in ropes. Rain would start to pour down, and he would feel water landing on him – this was in fact drips falling from the roof of the cave. After violent convulsions he would wake up not knowing where he was. Even after all their work on his new bed area, he was still doubled up in a V-shape. Whenever he woke, he was comforted by the green glow of the light-stick, which gave him his bearings and reminded him where he was.

* * *

In England friends had begun to rally to Fiona's support. But on Thursday she got a severe shock when an army spokesman telephoned and advised her to move out of her house, as a statement about a rescue operation was about to be released to the press. If she remained there, he said, she would be besieged by reporters. With characteristic resilience she thought: no, to hell with it. She had always acted as the family's sheet-anchor and communications centre, and now, if she disappeared, Robert himself would not be able to contact her, should he reach a telephone.

The news that the five men were missing hit television screens at lunchtime, filling Fiona with 'absolute horror'. Suddenly she felt that Robert no longer belonged to her: he had somehow been snatched away and had become public property. It was almost as if he had been physically taken away. From that moment she involuntarily began to refer to him in the past tense, as if he were dead.

She had already asked two neighbours, Mrs Andrew and Mrs Dunwell, to look after her ducks and geese, if she had to go away suddenly; and now she asked them to take over the feeding, as she proposed to remain indoors. They were also to tell reporters that she had gone away to stay with relatives. Within an hour cars started to pull up in the park of the pub across the road, and television crews began setting up cameras. She closed all the shutters and moved around in artificial twilight. The telephone rang continuously, until a neighbour brought round a spare answerphone, and set it up so that she could either ignore calls or answer them.

She had already made arrangements for her younger son, James, who was at Sherborne School in Dorset, to be told what was happening, but not until the news was about to break. Now, when the boy was urgently summoned by his housemaster, Patrick Haigh, he immediately thought he must have committed some fearful crime – but when he heard what the problem was, his reaction was typically positive. 'Oh,' he said, '*he'll* be all right. For goodness sake! You don't need to worry about him.' Nevertheless, he decided to come home on the Saturday.

Fiona had also tried to contact her elder son, Alexander, who was reading Mandarin at the School of Oriental and African Studies (part of London University), and about to take his important end-of-term exam. She left a message, asking him to ring home, but before he got it, he heard the news from a friend, who had seen it on television, and was furious that his mother had not told him first. He was supposed to be taking his exam the next day, but said he would skip it and come home. Roger and Thelma Scruton, close family friends, collected him from the station in York, and smuggled him in after dark.

The farmhouse was under siege by the media. The reporters camped in the pub car park sensed that Fiona was in the house and pushed note after note through the door, expressing sympathy, but also requesting interviews. Unable to eat, or to face cooking, she told the boys to look after themselves, and not to bother her. Family morale was greatly strengthened by the arrival of her father, Hugh, a former captain in the Royal Marines, and her stepmother Alison. So that nobody should become muddled about time differences, she set a clock to Sabah time and stationed it prominently above the refrigerator. She also banned outward telephone calls between 2300 and 0600, in case any news came in during Sabah daylight hours. Each evening, as 2300 London time drew near, and the family knew that dawn was breaking over the jungle, tension in the house would rise.

* * *

Jeanette Foster was able, for a short time, to escape the worst assaults of the media. Believing that she and Ron lived somewhere near his Territorial Army headquarters in Grantham, reporters went looking for her in Lincolnshire. But on Friday, 18 March they zeroed in on the Fosters' home in Tewkesbury – and at one point the answerphone logged fifteen calls in seventeen minutes, all from press or television representatives.

Jeanette was well used to Ron being away: he had done three unaccompanied tours of service abroad – that is, without wife or family – and had often been overseas for shorter periods on expeditions and exercises. Most recently, he had spent the early part of the year working as a ski instructor in Bavaria. Nevertheless, in the past few days Jeanette had had plenty of cause to worry. Before Ron left, he had agreed that she would fly out to Hong Kong on about 10 March and join him for a holiday in the Far East; and when that date passed without a call from him, she naturally began to grow apprehensive.

She was working as a receptionist for an electronics repair company, and had arranged to take a few weeks off, from the evening of Wednesday, 9 March. So, having said goodbye to her colleagues in the firm, she went home, expecting, any minute, to get a telephone summons from her husband, saying that she should go to Heathrow and buy a standby ticket for Hong Kong. By Sunday the 13th – Mother's Day – she was extremely worried; she had lunch in Gloucester with her daughter Kerry and her little granddaughters Jade and Christie-Anne. The lunch proved a festive occasion, but she could not shake off her anxiety, and she told Kerry's friend Brian Janneh so as he drove her to lunch that afternoon. On Tuesday morning, fed up with hanging around, she decided to return to work.

That evening, back at home, she was having a drink with two friends, Pete and Wendy Hill, who as usual had given her a lift from work, when the doorbell rang, and there on the step was Major Dean Hale, from the RLC vehicle depot at Ashchurch. 'Mrs Foster?' he said, 'I'd like to speak to you about your husband.' In a shaky voice he explained that he had been trying to contact her since 0830 that morning, calling in person at the house every hour, to tell her that Ron was overdue. . . .

That night, the full scale of the crisis suddenly hit her. Unable to go back to sleep, she got up at 3 a.m. and began cleaning everything in sight – cobwebby corners, silver photo frames, the bathroom. By morning she felt 'like an old rag', and was finding it difficult to concentrate. One person with whom she often exchanged views was Fiona Neill, whom she had never met. Throughout her ordeal, she clung to the fact that Ron was exceptionally strong, and would last as well as any of the missing party – provided he had not been injured. She became increasingly distraught, walked miles by simply wandering around the house, and spent much time gazing skywards, thinking, 'Please, Ron – wherever you are, hang on. Don't you dare leave me here without you.'

So began a period of intense anxiety, which she survived by talking frequently to family and friends. She asked Ron's sister Pat to tell their mother before his name was released by the press and, despite her own distress kept in daily contact with her mother-in-law Dorothy, endeavoring to placate her anxieties.

188

Despite her own busy schedule as a mother of two, Kerry spent most of her time in a supportive role, making sure that Jeanette ate regularly, and reading passages to her from magazines. She was a great source of comfort. Her son Vaughan, temporarily abandoning his car-repair business at the weekend, moved in for a few days to filter the endless telephone calls, and once surprised his mother with his prowess as a cook.

* * *

In the Gully the morning of 18 March brought a blessed change in the weather. At last the sky was clear enough for helicopters to fly, and Foster was out early on chopper-watch. Neill felt lethargic and weak, and stayed in his sleeping bag until 0900; then, when he moved clothes across to the rocks to dry them, he found it a severe effort. Kevin was in reasonable shape, and Victor not too bad, but Neill paid particular attention to Chow, who showed no outward sign of being any the worse for his assault by rock, beyond the cut on his cheek, but had begun to complain of feeling weak.

At 1100 the usual clouds and mist swept in, finishing their hopes of helicopter activity that day. Morale plummeted, and Neill wrote sourly: 'An awful lot of people are doing nothing, it would appear.' Their only food that day was a biscuit apiece and the last of the chicken soup, which they brewed up on a flattish rock in the open, staying in the sun as much as possible and absorbing its rays to keep up body temperature. Their remaining stocks amounted to four biscuits, some Dextrosol tablets, a few drink-powders, a tin of meat paste, and some sachets of beef stock. Foster had developed persistent diarrhoea, which he was combating with various remedies, but which inevitably eroded his morale as well as his strength.

Repeated searches had revealed no obvious natural food in the Gully. (Fruits, berries, vegetables and animals normally thrive at much lower levels, not more than 1,000 metres above sea level.) Grass and leaves abounded, but Neill cautioned everyone to leave the vegetation alone: the plants were all strange to them,

189

and might easily be poisonous. He did try one leaf, but when he found it tasted bitter, he rapidly spat it out, knowing that bitterness probably indicated poison. (In tropical jungle most leaves contain poisons as a form of protection against parasites.) To writhe to death in agony would be infinitely worse than simply fading away in their sleeping bags.

None of the group had completed a long jungle survival course, although both officers had read numerous books on the subject. They knew that finding edible plants in the jungle is a laborious process, and that before you eat anything, you must test it by smell, and by touching it on skin, lips, mouth and tongue. Warning signs include a definite bitter taste, like that of almonds or unripe peaches – evidence of prussic acid – and milky sap. Red plants are also liable to be dangerous. They knew that boiling poisonous leaves may render them harmless, but that some need boiling twice to make them safe, which destroys most of the nutritional value in the plant. In any case, because they could not get a fire going, the survivors had difficulty in boiling water at all.

Neill remembered that some forms of bamboo shoots actually used up more energy from the digestive process than they gave to the body, so that eating them would be counter-productive: eat yourself to death. At 1,950 metres above sea level, their searches for worms had resulted in a grand total of three, and very small ones at that. Nor did there seem to be any fish in the river: higher up, when the rock pools had been still before the rain, they had seen tadpoles – but now there were hardly any. Had the rest been washed downstream, along with Foster's trousers?

The thought gave Foster an idea. During his first week in the cave he had suggested to Neill that he should put a note in a plastic water bottle and throw it into the river. Neill had rejected the plan, because water containers were precious, and might become all-important if the party did break out through the jungle. But now Foster wrote a note in pencil, using large capital letters, on a piece of the graph paper which he habitually carried for making sketches. He gave details of the group's size, position, state of health and so on; also he drew a sketch map of their location, and put the rolled sheet into a clear plastic bottle which had held mineral water and had been saved after the hike up over the Col into Easy Valley. Having screwed the cap tight, he threw the bottle over the falls, and saw it bob away across the rocks towards civilisation. Of course he knew that it might be punctured, or become wedged between rocks; but since there was only one direction in which it could travel, he hoped it would have a better chance of finding someone than the bottle thrown into the sea by Robinson Crusoe.

At 1500 misty rain drove them back under cover. Neill then decided that he could not stand any more of his knobbly rock, so in an effort to improve their cramped sleeping area still further, the two men tried to prise more rocks from the floor. While they were labouring, a chunk of granite rolled over and crushed the top of one of Foster's fingers, causing it to split open: soon the finger started to swell, and although Neill dressed the wound, it became extremely painful.

Neill emptied his pack and stripped it down, stashed his possessions in cracks and crevices around the cave, and laid the pack down as a mattress. The act was an open acknowledgement of the fact that he had become too weak to try any more escapes: he was not going to use his pack for its original purpose again. The Hong Kong soldiers had also stopped using their packs, so Neill borrowed these as well to help level his bed space. 'Most placid day yet,' he wrote. There had been no crises, no physical danger from floods or rock-slides.

He and Foster had been regaling the Chinese with stories of other feats of survival, including that of the Australian trekker James Scott, who had held out for over six weeks in the Himalayan foothills during the depths of winter, with nothing to eat but two bars of chocolate and one caterpillar. His feat had been all the more remarkable in that he had been alone, with no companion to give him psychological support – and the survivors in Low's Gully drew strength from their numbers. In Neill's view, the fact that five of them were sharing their ordeal, and in harmony, was 'worth many, many days of rations'. He assured Chow, in particular, that their own problems had not yet reached epic proportions, and that, with unlimited clean water at hand, they had plenty of time left.

Far from despairing, the officers pointed out the advantages of their situation. Apart from the water, they were in a temperate climate, with no extremes of heat or cold to sap their remaining strength. There were no leeches or mosquitoes, or any other creatures to annoy them. Things could have been a lot worse – and they all had a single goal: to stay alive. Besides, every day that went by increased their chances of rescue. But a deep worry which Neill nursed was that civil unrest might have broken out in Sabah as a result of the elections, and that the white helicopter they had seen had been flying for political reasons. His innermost fear, which he did not yet confide to Foster, was that a search had already taken place, and that the would-be rescuers had concluded that nobody could still be alive.

On Saturday 19 March, a dry day, he had what he called his second 'big walk', or bowel movement, of the entire expedition. He and Foster had been joking about it – because a major effort was needed to walk far enough downstream from the overhang to find a spot in which to squat down. Now, when the moment came, Neill was amazed by the fact that his insides seemed perfectly normal: his body had evidently absorbed and used almost every scrap of ten days' rations, and he took it as a tribute to the high calorific value of Army rations.

Some time during that day Foster, whose physical condition was the best of the five, resolved to make one last attempt at a breakout. 'I can't just lie here and rot while I've got strength for another go,' he said. 'And besides, you keep beating me at chess.' Privately, he had visions of the others all dying round him, while he himself survived longer just because he was more solidly built. Rather than that, he felt compelled to go in search of rescuers. Neill wanted to go with him, but had become too weak. Survival was all he could hope for: energy conservation had become his principal objective, and he tried to dissuade Foster from expending a high proportion of his remaining strength on an attempt which he feared would be futile.

Yet Foster believed in his own ability to break out – and once he had decided to try again, he became more cheerful. He, too, had lost a lot of weight. From childhood he had always been heavily built, and at the start of the expedition his muscles had been covered by a layer of fat. But during the long hours in his sleeping bag he had started to feel his bones sticking out, and he no longer had any natural padding to give him a reasonably comfortable night. It came home to him that the clear physical deterioration visible in the others had debilitated him too, and that his body must be feeding off protein from legs, buttocks and abdomen.

That Saturday afternoon, in dry weather, he put in a four-hour reconnaissance of the slopes on New's side of the Gully, and came back confident that he had found a good line leading in the right direction – quite possibly the one that New himself had taken. He spent the remaining daylight in minute study of their map and aerial photographs, trying to glean every possible scrap of information about the lie of the mountain. He also took names and telephone numbers of people he should ring when he broke out. In his diary he wrote:

Gave paper to Hong Kong soldiers to write notes. Victor has been writing in his diary for quite a while. Can't read it – looks all Chinese to me! Realise now that the HK lads reduced to one biscuit a day early on, so that they still have rations. Robert and I will last till Sunday. Raid medical box. Robert finds half packet of Dextrosol. I find Throaties and stomach tablets and Diarolyte (replacement salts). They will help for a few days.

He set off at 0930 on the morning of 20 March. In his journal Neill wrote, 'Well done Ron for having the strength to go for it. Although it's rained and the water level is up, it's still a bright afternoon, and clear, so he should have a good start in that respect.'

By now he was becoming preoccupied with his own physical condition: 'My pee is still a good colour, but very smelly – ammonia. It's strange.' Doctors later told him that this was

193

caused by muscle breaking down, but at the time he was reluctant to acknowledge that his body was surviving by feeding on itself. Any fat he had carried had long gone, and now the muscle was on its way as well. His legs felt seriously weak: all the survivors had taken to moving slowly, afraid that otherwise they would fall and hurt themselves on the rocks that formed the floor of their prison. Above all they wanted to avoid perspiring, as that would clear their bodies of badly needed salts and minerals. Gradually it dawned on Neill where he had seen this slow, zombie-like form of perambulation before: in films of Nazi concentration camps. The memory enabled him to tell the Hong Kong soldiers how the inmates of the camps had been in an infinitely worse state than they were, and yet had survived, real matchstick men.

Foster, meanwhile, was locked in a life-and-death struggle on the eastern wall of their prison, as his own notes tersely recorded:

Recce route took one and a half hours. Slowed a lot, then vertical rock 4m high. Used vine to climb, then pulled up pack. Pack fell, but OK. Pulled it up again. Must keep going! Eventually got to furthest point, with only six or seven metres to climb. Very tired. 1718 decided to try in morning.

His day was one of all-out effort and (often) acute danger. Had he fallen and injured himself, he would have been in severe trouble: once off his recce route, he knew that he was in virgin territory, struggling on 70-degree slopes that no human had ever tackled before – and he found it a humbling experience. After climbing the rock face on the vine, he clawed his way up narrow gullies choked with vegetation, 'full of that thick, musky smell that pervades undisturbed forest'. Then came a dire struggle across the bed of a steep watercourse matted with coarse grass which, when standing, had been two or three metres tall, but by then had become bowed downwards to form a dense mat. Again he cursed his lack of a parang – but at least the grass was firmly rooted, and when grasped in handfuls gave him good support.

After an hour's battle he had wrenched his way to the far side of the watercourse, through this 'awful tangled mass', and had come to the base of another cliff. He followed this rock-band to the right and up the side of a moss-covered waterfall. At the end of the vegetation he reached a single rhododendron bush, perched above a 100-metre fall of bare rock, and tied a fixed rope to its trunk while he contemplated possible routes ahead. He realised that, in his state of exhaustion, it would be dangerous to go on. Disappointed as he was not to have reached the ridge which he had set as his target for the day, he knew that it was time to make plans for the night – so he retraced his route to a large tree by the waterfall, and prepared to settle there:

Bivvied in small shelter by tree, by moss-covered waterfall course. Uncomfortable. Shelter was enough for two-thirds of me. Big tree root protruded from ground. I took half an hour to chop it off – hard wood – with lump of sharp stone. I then filled in the hole remaining and had to use my rope back and forth across the gap where my legs were going. Putting my empty rucksack as a base, and dive sack under my knees (secured to the rope), I laid out my bivvy bag and sleeping bag and after my evening meal of a swig of water I settled down for a very disturbed and uncomfortable night.

Chapter 14

To the Rescue

In the early hours of Tuesday, 15 March messages began to whistle back and forth between the Far East and the United Kingdom by fax and telephone at the highest possible priority. At 0525 local time Lieutenant-Colonel David Kerr, with whom Brittan had been in touch by telephone, signalled from Hong Kong to the Operational Headquarters of the Royal Logistic Corps in Andover, with copies to relevant offices of the Ministry of Defence:

> Subject is RLC adventurous training exercise Gully Heights to Mt. Kinabalu in Sabah. You should be aware that five persons on subject exercise are overdue at final RV by some seven days. Search party activated and following reverse route up Low's Gully to summit of Mt. Kinabalu.

After giving the names of the men in both groups, the signal concluded: 'It is stressed that they [the second group] are overdue on an arduous route, carrying heavy packs, but food will be a concern.' That afternoon the defence attaché at the British High Commission in Kuala Lumpur, Colonel Jonathan Seddon-Brown, signalled the Ministry of Defence in London, adding more detail:

> The remaining five are now thirteen days overdue. Neill and Foster are the most experienced members of the team, and Neill has been on the mountain before. Local advice is that the next seventy-two hours are critical if survivors are to be found.

The Ministry took instant action. Within minutes,

196

authorisation from a high level sanctioned the immediate deployment of Royal Air Force mountain rescue teams. Trained to locate and rescue the crew of crashed aircraft in mountainous or remote areas, search-and-rescue personnel are based at RAF stations around the country, on permanent standby and at various degrees of notice. Early that afternoon the national co-ordinator, Warrant Officer Alister Haveron, stationed at RAF Kinloss in Scotland, received a terse call from London: 'Go to six hours' NTM [notice to move] to help five servicemen lost on a 14,000-foot mountain in East Malaysia. Take the strongest group you can assemble – the leader and deputy leader of every team in the UK, plus others as you see fit.' Minutes later Haveron learned that his composite force would fly out from Heathrow that evening: they were to be at the airport by 2200.

Haveron instantly alerted the team at Kinloss, and contacted those at Leuchars (Fife), Leeming (North Yorkshire), Stafford, Valley (on Anglesey) and St Athan (South Wales). As luck would have it, every station had its best men on base, so that the ablest possible group was assembled. At once they prepared to take off for the other side of the world, collecting all the equipment that they could conceivably need. Their main difficulty was lack of information about Kinabalu: they knew that it was near the equator, and that jungle had been mentioned. But because of the great height of the mountain they threw in ice-axes, crampons and other equipment for climbing ice and snow, and as they were flinging things together, Haveron telephoned the Royal Geographical Society for further information. In the early evening an RAF Nimrod was scrambled to collect personnel from the most northerly stations and fly them to Heathrow.

Another urgent telephone call alerted Flight Lieutenant Richard Mowbray, chief instructor at the RAF School of Combat Survival and Rescue at St Mawgan, in Cornwall. An expert in all aspects of survival, Mowbray had had previous experience of the jungle in Brunei, and now advised that, in the absence of precise information about where the missing men were, the rescue team should include a couple of jungle specialists, besides the

197

mountaineers. The result was that he and another instructor, Flight Lieutenant Richard Mason, were asked to make for Heathrow with all speed. Luckily they both had their jungle kit in the office, and within four hours they were on their way by air from Newquay.

Meanwhile in London Lieutenant Commander Mike Elesmore, a fifty-year-old, who had retired early from the Royal Navy, had received a considerable shock. He was sitting in a classroom, twenty minutes into a turgid week-long course on Health and Safety at Work, when a man came in and handed him a message urgently requesting him to ring the Ministry of Defence. Excusing himself from the lecture, he made the call, and found himself talking to Major Stuart Hepton, who dealt with adventurous training. According to Elesmore, Hepton was 'at 50,000 feet and rising'.

'We've got a hell of a problem here, Mike,' he said. 'Five soldiers are missing on some bloody mountain called Kinabalu, and we're trying to jack up a rescue. Can you help?'

Elesmore could – but when he heard what the expedition had actually set out to achieve, he was taken aback. He had been Commandant and chief instructor at the Joint Services' Mountain Training Centre in Wales; but his particular value now derived from the fact that he had spent a year at the Outward Bound school near Kota Kinabalu, and had often climbed the mountain. Still better, he was one of the few people in the world who had seen Low's Gully from House Boulder which he had visited with Pinfield in 1986. He had married a Sabahan, and had bought a house in the shadow of the mountain. Rapidly he put Hepton right on essential points, in particular the severity of the Gully – and was asked to pack some gear and make ready to catch the flight that evening.

So it was that he joined the rescue team, already numbering twenty: seventeen mountain rescue specialists, the two jungle survival instructors from RAF St Mawgan, and Major Tony Williams, an army doctor from the RAMC training centre in Surrey. Having been on a Joint Service expedition to the Antarctic, Williams was judged a useful recruit, and spent a frantic afternoon ransacking a hospital dispensary for the medical stores he thought appropriate. As he recorded later, he 'stripped the shelves of Paludrine, Nivaquine, Imodium, Doxycycline, and Ciprofloxacin, grabbed some Morphine and Cyclimorph, snatched some fluids and bandages from Casualty on the way out and headed for the airport'. The mountain rescue team had already been briefed by the Ministry on the basis of information sent from Kuala Lumpur, and was still expecting almost Himalayan conditions; but on board the Malaysia Airlines 747 Elesmore disabused them of some of their wilder notions, and Mowbray began giving them a crash course in jungle survival.

From his own perambulations on and around Kinabalu, Elesmore felt certain that the missing men must still be in Low's Gully: he knew that the jungle on the northern side, to which the ravine led down, was frequented by local hunters, and that many tracks ran out to villages. As he put it later, 'there was no way that five men in the jungle there would not crawl out somewhere in the end'. For this reason, he insisted that the search should concentrate on the Gully itself.

In the Far East, the Malaysian officer in charge was Brigadier General Hussin bin Yussof, Commander of 5 Brigade. A graduate of the Royal Military Academy, Sandhurst, speaking excellent English, he had many English friends. Reacting with commendable speed, he deployed a reinforced company of 16 Royal Malay Regiment, about one hundred strong, to Melangkap Kappa, to prepare for a wide-ranging sweep upriver. Because the men were not trained or equipped for rock-climbing, the plan was that they should search the jungle on either side of the river for as far upstream as they could go, and that the RAF mountain rescue teams should work down towards them from the top. The Malaysians set up a base in the village, began sending out patrols, and made contact with local hunters who had first-hand knowledge of the tracks.

On the British side, the senior officer was Major General John Foley, Commander of British Forces in the Far East, based in Hong Kong. Luckily he was familiar with the Borneo jungle, having served in it as a young man during Confrontation in the

1960s. Now he appointed Major Tony Schumacher, commander of the jungle warfare training team in Brunei, to lead the rescue operation, and immediately appointed him to the local rank of lieutenant-colonel, to give him more clout.

Brittan and Page spent 15 March helping the Malaysians. Brittan twice went up in an Alouette helicopter, searching the river and lower parts of the Gully. He was able to chart some of his own route down the ridges, hoping that Neill's group might have emerged from the ravine, as he had done; but although the weather was clear, he saw nothing.

Lieutenant Commander Cliff Williams, the Assistant Defence Attaché, recently arrived from Kuala Lumpur, took charge and put Shearer into the modern Sabah Medical Centre on the outskirts of Kota Kinabalu. He was suffering from bruised and infected legs, as well as from dehydration and lack of food; but he was well looked after, and his condition soon improved. That same evening Mann and Mayfield reached Hong Kong by air; they had paid for their own tickets out of expedition funds, because they had booked before Cliff Williams reached Kota Kinabalu. In Hong Kong they were admitted to the British Military Hospital suffering from exhaustion and malnutrition, as well as multiple cuts, lacerations and bruises. Their condition was described as 'poor', and although they were debriefed, they were in no state to give a clear account of where they had been or a chronology of events. When doctors operated to repair the severed tendons in Mann's hand, they were amazed by the way in which the Sabah medicine woman's potion had stifled the infection: reckoning that it had saved his hand, they became eager to discover what its ingredients were.

Meanwhile, the Defence Attaché at the British High Commission in Kuala Lumpur had been keeping the United Kingdom informed of progress, formally notifying the Malaysian police authorities about the missing personnel, seeking diplomatic clearance for the RAF rescue team, arranging for the importation of medical supplies, and gaining special permission for the arrival of Mike Elesmore, technically a civilian equipped with a temporary passport. The attaché also warned the Ministry of Defence that Sabah was full of newspaper and television reporters, covering the elections, and that the story of the rescue would probably break as soon as the RAF party arrived.

That evening Schumacher flew into Kota Kinabalu, bringing 250 ration-packs for the search-and-rescue team. He joined Cliff Williams at the five-star Hyatt Hotel, which rapidly became the headquarters of the British rescue effort. (Cool and comfortable as they were in the air-conditioned bar of the Hyatt, the rescue co-ordinators were delighted to read in the press that their headquarters was somewhere in the middle of the snake- and insect-infested jungle.)

When the RAF team landed at Kuala Lumpur in the evening of Wednesday, 16 March, their passage through the airport controls was smoothed by staff from the High Commission, who had them shuttled swiftly from one terminal to another for the domestic flight to Sabah. In a few minutes they were airborne again for the last leg of their marathon trip, and reached Kota Kinabalu at 2330.

Schumacher, who himself had been there only a few hours, met them at the airport, and Malaysian Army transport took them straight to the Hyatt, which they reached just before midnight. After twenty-six hours on the move, they immediately went into the conference room for a briefing from the search commander, with Brittan giving his own version afterwards, and Page in attendance to answer questions.

Richard Mowbray was shocked by the survivors' appearance. Both were very thin and a good deal the worse for wear; Page in particular had cuts and bites everywhere, and his skin was 'all roughed up'. Even after three days back in civilisation, he was 'definitely not with it'. Brittan, on the other hand, struck Mowbray as 'looking pretty sheepish at having brought twenty-odd guys half-way round the world to sort out something in which he'd been involved'.

There was doubt as to whether the lost five were still in the Gully, or whether they had broken out into the jungle. Mowbray was afraid that they had been swept down the ravine to their deaths: with his wide experience of the jungle, he knew how difficult it would be for the missing men to find any natural food. Listening to Brittan's account of conditions in the gorge, he concluded that the missing party must have become trapped, unable to go up or down, and had been pushed by desperation into some rash move, like jumping over a waterfall. He thought that the chances of rescuing anyone alive were very small. One man even advanced the theory that the Hong Kong soldiers had mutinied, murdered the two officers, and legged it into the jungle.

After considerable discussion, Elesmore repeated his advice that the only sensible thing to do was to make a complete transit of the ravine, top to bottom, and this was adopted as the plan. At last, about 0300 on 17 March, most of the team crashed into bed, exhausted by the long flight and the eight-hour time change, but Mowbray stayed up all night, endlessly discussing possibilities.

That morning, after breakfast, Schumacher met General Hussin and heard what the Malaysians had done so far. Their troops were scouring the jungle at the mountain's northern base, reinforced by two rangers from the National Park, and two local guides. Word had gone out into all the villages that a party of British soldiers was lost. Various items of equipment had already been discovered, but it was assumed – rightly – that these had been discarded by the recce party on its way out. Helicopters were searching the lower reaches of Low's Gully, but because of the altitude and hazardous flying conditions the air search had not been able to cover the upper third of the gorge. Schumacher reported that the Malaysians' assistance, advice and support had been 'exemplary', but that so far no search had been launched from the top of the mountain downwards.

That was the obvious role of the RAF. Besides, the need for action – and visible action – was urgent, not just from the point of view of the missing men, but to satisfy the publicity machine, which was already gearing up. Elesmore suggested that it would be sensible for the rescue team to spend twenty-four hours shaking down and recovering from their flight, but by then media interest was so intense that a feeling of tremendous pressure had built up, and the men went straight into action.

To secure an advanced base for them on the mountain, Elesmore went ahead to Park Headquarters. In the middle of the peak holiday season, all normal accommodation was full, but Elesmore sought out Eric Wong, the Chief Warden, whom he knew well, and who now offered him the use of the old warden's house, outside the main gate. This proved ideal, as it was set apart from the tourist areas and had plenty of space, as well a telephone of its own.

Moving out of the Hyatt after only a couple of hours in bed, the mountain team split into two groups. The first hoped for a helicopter lift up to Park Headquarters, and on up to Panar Laban if possible, while the second sorted out the heavy gear and came on by truck. In the event, foul weather meant that aircraft could not fly up the mountain at all, and the first group landed in the grounds of a village health centre, outside the Park, whence they were given a lift by two teachers who happened to be passing.

Schumacher himself decided to stay down in Kota Kinabalu, so that he could liaise with General Hussin, keep Hong Kong informed, and fend off the press. It was agreed that he would send out a sitrep (situation report) at 1630 every day, when failing light would bring search activity to an end. The international time difference meant that his reports reached Britain at 8.30 in the morning, and for everyone caught up in the developing drama, life came to revolve round the information that arrived in London then.

During the afternoon of Thursday, 17 March – as Neill and his fellow-survivors were battling with the flood which burst through their cave – the RAF team established itself in the old warden's house, which became known as Forward Control Headquarters. By late afternoon, when Group A was ready to leave, cloud had descended to that level, and rain was pelting down. Nevertheless, the eight-man team set off up the tourist track which had proved such a trial to members of the expedition, and by a phenomenal effort reached the Panar Laban huts at 2100, having gone most of the way in the dark.

On the morning of Friday, 18 March, they were off again

before first light. The weather was still foul, but they made excellent progress, and by 0900 were on Easy Valley Col. There they left one man behind to act as a radio link with Elesmore in the Forward Control Headquarters. The rest descended into the huge bowl, searching as they went, and soon found the first of the expedition's abseil points, just beyond House Boulder. Having gone down the fixed ropes left behind on those drops, they found further progress blocked by a waterfall, and because the light was already failing, they decided to climb back up to House Boulder for the night. By then they were very tired, having had little sleep since leaving London, and having made extraordinary efforts to achieve so much in one day.

Meanwhile, more of the team's equipment had been ferried up the tourist trail by porters, some of them old women wearing flip-flops. The mountain rescue men, used to humping all their own gear, were uncomfortable at the idea of hiring people to carry things for them, but Mowbray told them to take advantage of the fact that porters were available, and to save their energy for the formidable task ahead.

Conditions at Panar Laban were far from ideal. For their accommodation, the rescue team had been assigned the luxurious-sounding Burlington House – but this turned out to be a little, rat-infested hut with bunks for four people. Already there were fourteen RAF men at or above 3,390 metres: rain was deluging down, and they had brought no tents, so all of them were soon soaked through and short of proper sleep. On the second night some of them crashed out on the floor of the cooking area in the big hut, which was full of tourists – and indeed they gave two Chinese visitors medical attention, one for hypothermia and the other for a twisted ankle.

From what they had already seen, the leaders realised that 'Easy Valley' was a dangerously misleading name, and that in the Gully itself they would need far more rope than they had anticipated. Back went a radio request to RAF Leeming, where 100-metre lengths of 100 metre pre-stretched rope were promptly dispatched in the direction of Borneo. During Friday two members of Group B had flown on a helicopter reconnaissance of the lower reaches of the Gully: some good photographs had been taken, but mist, rain and spray from the waterfalls obscured some stretches, and because the weather was so murky the Alouette had not been able to fly as high as they would have liked. The upper reaches of the Gully had still not been reconnoitred from the air. In the jungle to the north a second company of soldiers, from 16 Royal Malay Regiment, had joined the search, but progress was constantly frustrated by the harshly steep terrain on either side of the ravine, and the patrols had been unable to find any winching sites into which helicopters would be able to lower men and stores.

North of the mountain on the morning of 19 March helicopter flights began again at first light; but as usual cloud soon came in, and by 1100 the mist was so bad that all aircraft were grounded. On the low ground either side of the Penataran the search continued throughout the day, without result, and General Hussin decided to deploy further troops on the southern flank of Kinabalu, to search the ground on either side of the tourist track, in case the lost men had somehow struggled back over the Col and were trying to come down there.

* * *

In Hong Kong, Mayfield and Mann had recovered sufficiently to be put on a flight to London. They flew overnight, and so urgent was the need for accurate information that Major Tom Parker, Commandant of the Adventurous Training School at Ripon, went to meet them at Heathrow, together with Colonel Ossie Hall, who had authorised the expedition in the first place, and who now came down from Yorkshire. Parker interviewed the two survivors at length in a Special Branch police office the moment they arrived, at 0600 in the morning of Sunday, 20 March. Part of the aim was to elicit information which might narrow the area of the search; but Mayfield could not produce any definite idea of where the lost men might be. Nor could Mann contribute much: he merely agreed that Mayfield's account was substantially accurate.

* * *

On top of the mountain a clear dawn had allowed two men of Group B to leave Panar Laban early, with the aim of continuing the climb down into the Gully; but all too soon the mist came in, and abseiling became highly dangerous. Water from the previous days' rain sluiced down the ropes, drenching the climbers and making every surface treacherous. The descent was a desperate task, and put the mountain rescue specialists at the limit of their endurance. When at last the leaders caught sight of the bed of the Gully, all they could see was a thundering mass of white water. Quite apart from the fact that they were running short of rope, they knew that no human could hope to survive in that maelstrom.

Shaken by its concentrated power and violence, they jumared back up their ropes, climbing 300 metres in the most difficult conditions imaginable, with flash floods bouncing from the granite walls and cascading over them. By the time they rejoined their colleagues in the tents at House Boulder, they were exhausted. Brittan, talking to them over their radio link, confirmed that no such flood had been running when he and his companions had gone down the gorge three weeks earlier. Wet, tired and disconcerted, the RAF men spent a miserable night in the lee of the boulder, exactly where New and Pinfield had camped during their epic descent. In the words of the team leader, Flight Sergeant Jim Smith, Easy Valley was 'like a huge amphitheatre, but black and foreboding. It's oppressive and dark – these domineering walls stretch for thousands of feet above you, and you feel shut in.' Whoever gave Easy Valley its name, he added, 'obviously had a sense of humour'.

That evening Brittan was admitted to hospital in Kota Kinabalu with a high temperature and suspected malaria. His relapse was no doubt a reaction to the strain of leading his group out of the jungle, and to the pressure he had been under ever since: he badly needed a rest.

Tony Schumacher's life was made easier by the arrival of Arthur Murray, a member of the Joint Services Public Relations staff in Hong Kong, who flew in to help handle the media. Press reporters were besieging everyone remotely connected with the rescue, and a few of the more intrepid had even heaved themselves up the mountain as far as Panar Laban, before sinking back to the lush pastures of the Hyatt or the Shangri la. Daily press briefings were given at the Hyatt, but the regular meetings between the British and Malaysian military took place at the fire station in Kota Kinabalu.

On 21 March the weather in Easy Valley was still unspeakable, and the RAF climbers knew, without looking over the waterfalls, what conditions on the abseils would be like: all the rain pouring into the huge catchment area at the top of the mountain was being channelled into that one ravine. Low's Gully, they saw, was nothing but a colossal drain. Immense volumes of water would have come crashing on to the head of anyone trying to abseil – and any man who started out, but then tried to unclip himself from a rope to seek shelter, would almost certainly be swept away and battered to death on the boulders below.

In this frustrating situation, Group B climbed back over the Col and went down to Panar Laban to meet Haveron and try to plan a way ahead. Haveron, for his part, was seriously concerned for the safety of his men, and wanted to confer with them before they committed themselves further. He was also worried about the risks of crossing the steep rock slabs leading to the Col. Such had been the urgency of the search that no safety ropes had yet been laid across the slabs, and in the continual rain they were as slippery as ice.

In the jungle to the north the Malaysians brought two platoons of the Police Field Force into the search, together with twenty Frontier Scouts. These men – a unit of the police force – were recruited from indigenous tribes, and had the best knowledge of the forest in that area, besides being experts on survival. They were sent to the east and north-east of the Gully, into an area through which, it was thought, the lost men might be trying to fight their way if they had managed to escape from the ravine.

207

Chapter 15

Sinking

Down in the Gully, on the morning of Monday, 21 March, Day Twenty-Six, Neill thought he had nothing to get up for. But shortly after 0800 the whole party was galvanised into action by the sound of a helicopter. This time there was no doubt: the thudding flutter of blades and engine was unmistakable.

Out they all tottered, as fast as their shaky legs would carry them, to see an aircraft of military appearance – drab green in colour – flying only three or four hundred metres downstream of them but very high – certainly above the level of the ridge. Soon it disappeared in a westerly direction, leaving them bitterly disappointed. Neill jotted down in his diary that probably it had nothing to do with them: certainly, it had not appeared to be searching the river or the jungle. Secretly, he felt sure that it had been looking for them; but had he allowed himself to believe this, the disappointment would have been hard to bear – and difficult to explain to the Chinese. So he sought to rationalise the helicopter's movements by deciding that it had been taking part in a military exercise.

High on the side of the ravine above him, Foster had decided that he must make one last effort to reach the ridge. So he packed up his kit and started doggedly climbing again, up the fixed rope which he had left dangling from the rhododendron bush the night before. Reaching the bush, he put down his pack and looped his second rope round the branches, to form a double. Scarcely had he attached his Shunt to the ropes when the entire patch of moss on which he was standing gave way, and he was left dangling 100 metres above bare rock.

Having scrambled to safety, he sat down, drank some water and ate a glucose tablet. At 0810 he was still trying to recover from the shock when he heard and saw the helicopter which had

208

alerted the survivors below. Finding an open spot, he rapidly set out his space blanket and dive-sack and began firing the flash on his camera. But although the helicopter seemed to be searching, it stayed much too far away to see him, and did not come up the Gully itself. Nevertheless, the sight of it made him hope (and believe) that rescue was imminent, so he decided to retrace his steps and rejoin the stranded party – especially as the mist had put in its usual blanketing appearance.

Down below, after their brief excitement, the whole party remained on chopper-watch, sitting outside in the sun and attempting unsuccessfully to get a fire going. When the mist came in at midday, they retired to their sleeping bags. Neill's legs felt very weak, and his stomach had begun producing loud noises as the gastric juices churned round with nothing to work on. He made his daily drink of hot lemon, and was pleased that his inner core, his upper body, still felt warm and reasonably strong. In some ways it was almost a relief that the last of their food had gone, because the absence of anything to eat meant that there was one less decision to take, and he no longer had to pretend that one biscuit a day – or its equivalent – was going to keep him alive indefinitely.

At 1345 he was under the overhang when he heard a commotion outside: Foster had returned, blocked in his attempt but jubilant, because he felt convinced that rescue was coming. Neill was delighted and relieved to find that he was safe. 'Welcome back!' he said. 'Bloody marvellous to see you. Thank God I won't have to play chess against myself any more.'

The appearance of the military helicopter had renewed everyone's hopes, and together with the Chinese the officers spent hours discussing the possibilities of rescue. Assuming that an operation had only just been launched, and that the morning's helicopter had been conducting an initial recce, Neill calculated that it would be Wednesday, two days hence, before anything more happened. Foster spent the afternoon washing his clothes and tending to minor sores. The finger crushed by a boulder had swollen to double its normal size, and his ribs were still aching; but his leg wound, which he kept wrapped in a soaking-wet bandage, was not giving any trouble.

That night the officers squeezed into their original sleeping positions, jammed so tight up against one another that if one wanted to turn over, the other had to as well. But Neill did not mind, because he was elated by Foster's safe return. By midnight the Gully was bathed in brilliant moonlight – a sight they had rarely seen – and Neill roused Foster to tell him that it looked as if the next day would be clear.

A clear day meant there was a chance of a helicopter – and so, long before first light on 22 March, they were all awake and listening. Sure enough, just after 0700 the noise of gurgling water suddenly changed into the sound of an engine, which Chow detected first. Rushing out, the party became tremendously excited: Foster flashed his camera, and as they watched the aircraft sweep over the entrance to the Gully, about 300 metres up and a kilometre downstream of their position, they tried to will the pilot to fly in their direction. But once again, after a minute or two, the aircraft went away over the west ridge without flying any obvious search pattern, exactly the same as the one the day before. Once more they set up a chopper-watch, and in this Foster took the lead, as he found the overhang oppressive during the day and preferred to be outside. Kevin also remained on the alert; in the past few days he had become more active, probably because his build was more powerful than that of his compatriots; they, feeling ever weaker, stayed in their sleeping bags.

Neill reckoned that his calorific output was about the same as that of Victor and Chow – very low. Foster had deliberately slowed his movements, but was still active. It was only a matter of time – and not much time, at that – until he too must succumb to inertia. Yet there was still some flesh on him – an energy reserve for which he was now very grateful. He felt twinges of guilt at being stronger than the rest, but thankful for all the puddings he had eaten in Bavaria during the winter.

With no further action in the sky, the day seemed interminably long. Some of their clothes dried out, but very slowly. Even now hunger was not a major preoccupation: they could not forget it, but equally, there was nothing they could do to appease it, so they tried to put it from their minds and concentrate on the business of keeping warm. In the afternoon Neill and Foster played chess, and swallowed a drink of lukewarm, heavily diluted chocolate – but immediately regretted adding so much water to the brew, as it tasted disgusting.

They had set themselves little goals: the warm evening drink became the high spot of the day. They still had one or two packets of powdered beef stock, and although each represented only 13 calories, they drank one just before settling down for the night, in an attempt to persuade their stomachs that they had had a meal. They sipped at the liquid slowly, for it was psychologically important that whatever they drank should linger in their mouths as long as possible. In Foster's absence Neill had delved ever deeper into his pack and had discovered a packet of Polo mints which Fiona had managed to smuggle into the first-aid box. In the circumstances this was a major find: the officers limited themselves to one Polo each a day, and as the sweets had been made in York, they seemed a real taste of home. As Neill remarked when he returned to the United Kingdom, Polos were 97 per cent sugar, sugar was energy, and energy was life. Foster decided to use the Throaties (throat pastilles) which he had found in his first-aid box to supplement the diet of Polos. He and Neill also chewed up a packet of antacid tablets designed for stomach upsets, on the off chance that they contained some form of nutrition.

Neill noticed that during the day five hours usually passed between the time at which he had a drink and the moment at which the need to urinate drove him out of his cocoon – a process which now took about five minutes (out of sleeping bag without getting wet, out of bivvy bag, find footwear, stagger out over the rocks without falling or tripping over any of the others, proceed far enough from the cave to be hygienic, relieve self and return). He had begun to be troubled by a powerful stink of urine in his sleeping trench, and although he said nothing about it, he became convinced that someone was relieving himself in the overhang. Then, much to his embarrassment, he realised that the smell was his own, and was emanating from the place which he used as a lavatory: the ammonia from broken-down muscle was so strong that its fumes invaded the cave. After this he expended even more effort in tottering still further away when he wanted to have a pee.

For much of the night both men lay awake in the green glow of their incredible light-stick, making mental notes about future plans. With the helicopters had come real hope of rescue, and they were so excited that sleep was impossible. Chat about things they hoped to do, once rescued, helped enormously to pass the time: anything to get through the interminable still watches. Some time after midnight Neill announced that he had just completed plans for a major alteration he proposed to carry out at his home in Yorkshire – and this set Foster thinking how he would build the conservatory he had been promising Jeanette for years. From about 0200 he was designing it in his mind, and as soon as first light came, he got up and drew it.

* * *

In Yorkshire, after the initial public announcements, Fiona stopped watching television, so terrified was she of hearing bad news. The worst she could imagine – worse even than hearing that Robert was dead – was that the search had been called off, and that the men would never be found. She had arranged with David Bentley what he should do in any such emergency. She most certainly did not want Robert's Commanding Officer and a padre to make an official visit – as army regulations laid down that they should. She told David to give her the bad news, as briefly as possible, over the telephone, and then to come round an hour later.

There was nothing that she herself could do to influence events: she could only pray that the missing men were still all right, and had enough strength to hold out until they were found – but with every day that passed, the strain increased. Like Jeanette Foster, she derived enormous comfort from closing her eyes and concentrating with her whole being on communication with Robert, willing him to survive.

There was one piece of information which she badly wanted to know: *who had seen Robert last?* In an attempt to find out why the party had split, she telephoned Paul Hughes, the friend in Plymouth who had suggested Mayfield and Mann as members of the expedition. He promptly rang Hong Kong, managed to bypass the entire army system, and spoke direct to Mann, who by then was in the British Military Hospital. Mann told him that the last time he had seen the rear group they had been perfectly all right – and this brought some small relief. Hughes also assured Fiona that the rations (which he himself had provided) would last much longer than the ten days intended.

By Wednesday, 23 March things looked so grim that she could no longer bear to listen to the daily situation report which David telephoned through at 1100. Instead, on that day her father took the call, only to hear that the RAF team had retreated, and that the Malaysian Army had found nothing. Desperate for more information, and for reassurance, she again telephoned Hughes, who by then had recovered Mann and Mayfield from Heathrow, and brought them back to Plymouth. It was a shock to hear how he had changed from the cheerful, optimistic person she had spoken to a few days earlier: he sounded depressed, and described how, when he went to fetch the two men, he had found them in the charge of an officer, who seemed reluctant to discuss the expedition. It seemed to him that there was more to be explained about how and why the party had split. Clearly Hughes was despondent, and did not feel able to talk to her any more.

By now James was becoming deeply depressed, and even Alexander, who had been compulsively tidying the house, was retreating to his room for long periods. Then, at 0045 on 24 March, came what Fiona remembered as 'a hideous call'. Waking suddenly, she stumbled to the answerphone, dreading bad news: the caller had already gone, and she could not immediately remember how to replay the taped message. Panic-stricken, she rushed round the house, rousing the others. But when one of the boys ran the tape back they found that, as usual, it had been a reporter, who had left no message.

* * *

That morning in the Gully the survivors were outside by first light, on the alert for helicopters. Foster gave Kevin his camera to flash, and primed Victor with the Morse code for SOS: . . . - - - . . . Victor was planning to flash his headlamp at the next aircraft that appeared, even though its battery was failing: he was also preparing to wave any bright object or garment.

When no helicopter came, the disappointment was intense, especially for Neill, who had worked out that this was the most likely day for the Malaysians to react. He was worried by his own increasing general weakness and lack of mobility: even to leave his sleeping bag had become an exhausting task. He and Foster discussed at length what they would do when they were too feeble to accomplish it any more: they decided they would use bottles in which to relieve themselves, and the strongest one would empty them as far away from the overhang as possible.

Foster had begun compiling a video diary which, in conjunction with their written diaries, would tell their story if they were found dead. That morning he spoke to the camera for several minutes, describing their plight, their state of weakness and morale. He also recounted his puzzlement at the failure of the two groups to meet up, and described his own escape attempts. He then went into the cave for his and Neill's last cup of coffee, sugar and whitener. Apart from that, breakfast consisted of one tablet each of Dextrosol. Foster wrote in his diary:

> *Robert says I'll outlive him because I've got more meat on me. He says he looks as though he's out of Belsen. I said, 'I will soon.'*
>
> *Told the Hong Kong soldiers to keep writing notes. They seemed to cheer up. Perhaps the difference in culture has made their attitude different from Robert's and mine. Lads have been brave – no trouble.*

Keeping warm had become the overriding priority for all five of them: anything to stop the core of the body getting cold. Neill reckoned they would die very quickly if their upper bodies

214

became chilled, and as he lay there, the day again seemed interminable. Yet one strange fact gradually became apparent: although he was growing weaker physically, at the same time he was becoming more aware mentally. His mind seemed to move at lightning speed.

Next morning, 24 March, they were all awake well before first light, listening intently for any change in the noises whistling up through the rocks. At 0715 Foster went across to the boulder, and soon after that they were rewarded. At 0740 Chow gave a squawk of excitement from the cave, and a few seconds later Neill, still in his sleeping bag, also heard the telltale sound. Bundling outside, they saw a helicopter, very high and flying in apparently random fashion. Again Kevin fired the flash of Foster's camera up at it, and Victor flashed SOS in Morse with his headlamp. Foster thought they had been spotted, because the helicopter continued to circle for a few seconds, but then it floated away.

The survivors remained in the open, praying that it would return, until the chill drove Neill and Chow inside again. Then, at 1020, as Neill was writing his notes in the warmth of his sleeping bag, he suddenly heard what was clearly an overpass: even though he had not seen it, a helicopter had flown over the Gully. The others had caught a glimpse of it, and had flashed frantically – but they could not fathom why the pilots were staying so high, and why none had apparently flown up the line of the Gully itself: the whole point of staying where they were, in the bed of the ravine, was that they were in the open, where they could be seen from the air.

Although this second visitation caused a scramble of excitement, Chow did not take part in it: he remained in his bag, saying that he felt too weak to get out and that his back had become very sore. Naturally this worried Neill, and he gave Chow another physical check. He could still find no sign of injury, so, apart from reassuring him and making him as comfortable as possible, there was nothing he could do to help. Foster, in contrast, took advantage of the fine day to remain in the open, drying his and Neill's clothes. In fact, he took all his kit out on to the rocks, to be ready for evacuation. 'He is a tower of strength,' noted Neill – but he could not help thinking how disappointed his ever-eager Number 2 would be if help did not arrive:

He's a lucky chap, being built so much more beefily than the rest of us. He will survive me by quite a few days. So far he doesn't appear to be badly affected by the starvation diet.

I discovered today that Kevin still has a little food left, which he had secreted away. I admire his self-control. Obviously this is his lifeline to sanity. As long as he has something left, he knows that he is one-up on starvation.

The sun made one of its rare, full-blooded appearances. Foster stripped off to let the rays soak into his skin. Soon feeling better, he began to think about trying yet again to make a fire. Together with Kevin and Victor he collected some wood, which was drying out, and the Chinese built a fireplace out of stones, on which to pile broken sticks in a little wigwam, with shavings and scraps of precious paper beneath – but they did not try to light it until there seemed to be a chance of a helicopter coming close. Neill stripped open his camera, in an attempt to dry out its innards and resuscitate the flash mechanism.

Sitting out on the rock, examining his own torso, Neill decided that it looked 'pretty pathetic'. Writing his diary outside, he noted: 'If this is the best the rescuers can do, they're not going to find us. I'm convinced they have not done a full overpass of the Gully yet.' Nearly two weeks before, during the joint escape bid, he and Foster had both noticed that they could easily see the reflective aluminium space blanket from a distance of over 300 metres above the floor of the Gully. How could the airborne searchers keep missing it?

At 1400 everyone returned to the overhang disappointed; and as if to deepen their gloom, the light became very dim in the afternoon. For Neill, the low point of the entire expedition came when Foster beat him at chess in four moves. 'Unfortunately I must be right,' he wrote (meaning that no rescue activity was in progress). 'Another wasted day, bringing us nearer to whatever fate has in store for us.' Yet although he wrote these grim thoughts down, he did not inflict them on the others.

Foster, on the other hand, found some comfort in the improved morale of the Chinese. As he put it, they seemed earlier 'to have gone into a state of suspended animation', but now had livened up again, and were actively looking forward to being recovered.

Again the night seemed endless, and Neill was driven up once by the need to relieve himself. He had been trying not to drink too much water in the afternoon, but in the morning he noticed that his urine had turned from dark yellow to a sinister yellow-brown, and he resolved to step up his intake of water again, to keep his kidneys functioning. He also noticed how difficult it had become to rest on the rock: earlier, he had always managed to make himself comfortable somehow, but now every single bone in his body seemed to be in contact with the granite. All the padding had gone from his body, and his vertebrae were particularly uncomfortable. Nor could he escape the horrible smell of decaying clothes and rotting boots: no matter how frequently the survivors washed their garments with soap, they quickly took on the same stench of decomposition – an unwelcome reminder of how in the jungle decay is rampant, as everything constantly feeds on everything else.

Chapter 16

Closing In

By Monday, 21 March the rescue teams knew that time was desperately short. The lost men were now seventeen days overdue, and it was assumed that their food must have run out many days earlier. If they were alive at all, they must be perilously weak.

And yet at the top of the mountain the weather continued so foul that further attempts to abseil were out of the question. Schumacher gave a graphic account of conditions at the front: 'The water is falling in such quantity that the Gully team describe the situation as a battle against large waves of many thousands of gallons.' Implicit in this description was the suggestion that if the missing party were still in the gorge lower down, the chanceomef them surviving such a torrent were minimal. To add to the discomfort of the rescuers, the temperature at high altitude had fallen sharply. At least the filthy weather had driven the tourists and reporters off the mountain – but Schumacher feared that he would have to bring his team back to Kota Kinabalu at the end of the week, before they became so exhausted and weakened that one or more of them had a fatal fall.

In the jungle to the north the Malaysians deployed four of their best men, with local guides, on to a ridge east of the river which was thought to be a possible escape route: Eric Wong had himself completed a traverse of this ridge some years before, and now he sent men to search the whole length of it. On the river itself the Malaysian soldiers had penetrated to within three kilometres of the bottom of the waterfalls, and had put out piles of food and fuel along the hunters' trails, in case survivors at their last gasp should stagger on to them. On the south side of the mountain soldiers completed their search on either side of the tourist track, right up to Panar Laban, without success.

Meanwhile Mowbray, finding that as yet there was no role for him in the jungle, quickly metamorphosed into a liaison officer and co-ordinator, particularly concerned to improve the erratic communications between the advance base at Panar Laban and Schumacher's headquarters. On the evening of 21 March he went down the mountain with Haveron to give Schumacher a full briefing, and managed to arrange a helicopter reconnaissance flight for Tuesday morning.

This took off at 0630 on 22 March – a clear morning – and quickly exposed the limitations of helicopters in that environment. The twin-engined Sikorsky (known in the United Kingdom as a Sea King) was in good condition, but elderly, and its ceiling in that climate was about 3,400 metres: furthermore, it lacked the power to hover at that altitude, and could maintain height only by continuing to fly forward. Thus, when it took off, it went up over Panar Laban in a spiral climb, but was unable to clear Easy Valley Col, so that the pilot had to fly clockwise round the summit of the mountain and approach the top of Low's Gully from the west.

Urged on by Elesmore and Mowbray, who was hanging out of one door to take photographs, he did six or seven wide orbits over the Gully, descending about 600 metres on each; but he was not keen on going close to any of the rock faces, where unpredictable winds and fierce down-draughts were liable to be blowing. The result was that although the observers looked into the Gully, they did so only from a distance, and could not even spot the RAF climbers, who they knew were in there somewhere, and who saw them going over. Schumacher's sitrep for that day concluded:

Due to the altitude, wind and poor visibility, the helicopter had to make a pass from a one-kilometre standoff, which did not afford a comprehensive or successful look at the Gully. Nothing of significance was identified, but the flight confirmed the difficulty of helicopter operations at this altitude.

One of the most encouraging features of the entire search was the whole-hearted generosity with which the Malaysians gave help. In spite of the political difficulties between their country and Britain, they identified closely with the rescue attempt on every level. Thus when General Foley sought authority to visit Kinabalu, it was granted immediately, and at grass-roots level one woman who heard that the RAF team had no sun cream insisted on taking Elesmore and Mowbray home and turning all the old tubes out of her cupboards. Several Sabahan people were admitted to hospital suffering from acute anxiety on behalf of the missing soldiers.

On Tuesday with the weather eventually settled, and rain no longer falling, the water level in the Gully dropped quickly, and the mountain rescue teams resumed their descent. Both RAF groups made an early start. Two men remained at the headquarters in Panar Laban to provide communications downwards; four were positioned on Easy Valley Col to act as a radio relay and give forward logistic support; six covered the upper reaches of the 600-metre drop into the Gully, and the remaining four became the Gully team proper. On the way down the cliff the climbers came on the remains of a bivouac site: two empty sardine cans, and a green food bag with the name NEILL on it (this had been the party's overnight bivvy spot, after their rope had jammed). The RAF men were jubilant at finding this, the first concrete evidence that the missing men had travelled that far down the Gully – and Brittan confirmed that the Chinese were ace eaters of sardines. The news was flashed back to Kota Kinabalu, and thence to Hong Kong and Britain.

Forging on with renewed hope, the team at last reached the Gully floor at 1330, after six days of intense effort and frustration. The waters had fallen dramatically, and now the men were confronted by a series of huge, smooth boulders stretching ahead. With plenty of daylight left, they were able to reconnoitre a short distance forward, but they soon saw that progress would be slow and difficult, and that they would again need more rope. Having found a reasonable site, they camped in the Gully for the night.

North of the mountain, the ground search had continued fruitlessly, and Elesmore had flown further helicopter missions, without seeing anything. Although on one sortie they had gone up the Gully for its whole length, they could not penetrate into the very narrow part where, it turned out, the men were stranded. For a single-engined Alouette, it was exceedingly dangerous to go into the ravine at all, for if the engine failed, the pilot would have no chance of saving himself, as he would need space in which to autogyrate down.

Elesmore realised, of course, that the missing men could have met with an accident and might have been 'swilled down the watercourse', so that nothing would be found except 'a horrible log-jam of bodies'. Nevertheless, his intuition kept telling him that they were still in the steepest and least visible part of the gorge. General Hussin was trying to procure a fixed-wing aircraft equipped with Skyshout (a large loudspeaker system), to fly over the area and broadcast assurances to the missing soldiers that they were being looked for.

The fact was that the RAF team was reaching what Mowbray described as, the 'prudent limit' of endeavour. Not only were the men very tired: their supply lines were extremely long, and they had gone so far down the Gully that recovery of bodies or weakened survivors in an upward direction would be extremely difficult. If the lost men were unable to climb ropes, they would have to be manhandled upwards for nearly 2,000 metres.

This consideration made the search organisers decide to switch their attack, and start upwards from the bottom end of the Gully, beginning at the point beyond which the Malaysians had been unable to penetrate. More and more, Schumacher and his men became convinced that if there still *were* any survivors, they must be trapped in the gorge section of the Gully, which was only about one and a half kilometres long, with a drop of some 700 metres.

The urgent need was for a second search team, to take over while the RAF had a rest – and in England the Ministry of Defence had begun assembling a second group of climbers and specialists. Since these men were mostly from Special Forces, their movements were cloaked in secrecy.

That morning, at 0600 local time, Shearer flew into Heathrow, much recovered, and was immediately debriefed by Tom Parker, again in a Special Branch office. His account of the expedition was substantially the same as Mayfield's, though sunnier; but when Parker tried to pin down the spot at which the recce party had last seen Neill and his group, the standard 1:50,000 map which he had proved so vague as to be useless. Shearer reported – quite correctly – that the contour lines and other features were mostly figments of the cartographers' imagination, rather than substantiated fact. All he could do was describe how, on the morning of 28 February, they had looked back and seen one of the rear group on a rope – although whether the man had been going up or down (he told Parker), they could not be sure. Brittan, also now recovered, had been released from hospital, but had been kept in Sabah, not only to advise the searchers, but also, if the worst came to the worst, to identify bodies.

At dawn on Wednesday, 23 March two members of the RAF back-up group abseiled down to the bed of the Gully with another 150 metres of rope. The lead pair, Sergeant Dan Carroll and Corporal John Roe, then resumed their search, scrambling and sliding over the boulders just as members of the expedition had done, except that they were not encumbered by heavy packs. At another obvious bivvy site they found more sardine cans, and they also came across Mayfield's cut ropes, which had somehow survived the furious floods. They were halted again by lack of rope: they had descended almost to 2,000 metres, and reckoned they had reached the waterfall section proper. Had they but known it, the two-man lead team were no more than 200 metres above the stranded party: if they had stood on the right boulder, they might have seen the trapped group's aluminium space blanket. As the light was failing, they made their way back up the boulders, and met their support team in the bed of the Gully at 2030, well after dark.

The day's progress made it clear that, if any survivors were still alive in the ravine, they must be in the waterfall section. All effort therefore needed to be concentrated in that area, to close the gap between the top and bottom search parties. In Kota Kinabalu that day Schumacher learned that the group of specialists, now fifteen strong, was to fly from Heathrow that evening; but privately, some of his men were wavering. As one remarked, 'Who was going to be the person to suggest calling the search off? We were getting nowhere, and things were getting more dangerous all the time.'

In Hong Kong Foley was well aware that hope was fading. Further, he had gained the impression – partly from press reports – that the Malaysian military authorities were losing heart. They had made immense efforts, put hundreds of men into the field, and spent a very large amount of money – all in an attempt to resolve a crisis not of their own making; but after more than a week they had found no sign of survivors, and now, it seemed, they were on the verge of pulling out.

On 23 March Foley flew to Sabah to see the rescue operation for himself, and to lend the Malaysians his personal support. From the moment he and General Hussin met in Kota Kinabalu, things went well. The local commander's Sandhurst background enabled them to establish an immediate rapport, and he agreed to fly Foley over the Gully first thing next morning.

Thursday, 24 March dawned brilliantly clear, and at the earliest possible moment Foley was airborne in an Alouette flown by a Malaysian pilot, Captain Izhar bin Hassan, generally known as Michael, with Schumacher and Brittan also on board. As they climbed over the jungle on the north side of the mountain, the corporal did his best to point out his party's escape route; but the General was disconcerted to find that they were just cruising about, not conducting a systematic search. The aircraft had no intercom system, and the noise level inside it was high, so he had to shout instructions at the pilot, urging him to go in close and creep up the Gully to as high a level as possible. Early as it was, cloud was already forming.

The pilot did as he was asked, and they began to climb the great ravine – only to get a sudden demonstration of how hazardous it was to fly in such a place. All at once the rock walls on either side of them appeared to be moving upwards at considerable speed: a freak down-draught, blasting down the Gully, was blowing them backwards and downwards. Just as they noticed this alarming phenomenon, Foley looked down and saw something straight below them: a flash. Brief though it was, he felt sure he had seen something flash. The pilot had seen it too. Foley shouted and gestured at him to go round and come in again – but even as the helicopter was wheeling away, the wretched mist closed in and obscured everything.

* * *

In the Gully they heard the helicopter coming. By 0715 Foster, Kevin and Victor had transferred their kit to boulders in the middle of the river. Then they saw the Alouette circle, almost above them, and Kevin fired Foster's flash at it repeatedly. Whenever he looked like desisting, Foster yelled at him to keep going.

> *Convinced he has seen us* [he wrote]. *Waited with HK lads for hours. Chopper appeared again at 1021, briefly, then vanished. Sun was out until about 1230 – quite hot. Got all my things dry and some of Robert's. He feels quite weak. I'm still OK, but hungry. Repacked kit at 1315 as mist had come up the valley. Looked like rain. Went into shelter and had three games of chess. I WON TWO!*

Back on the southern side of the mountain, Foley's helicopter landed on the football field in the village below Park Headquarters, where Elesmore and Mowbray met him. At first they had not been pleased by the idea of a visit from a senior officer, since it threatened to deflect energy and resources from the task in hand. That's all we need, Mowbray had thought. Is there anybody else we can invite? Can we get the Girl Guides in? But now, with the General among them, he realised that he could profit from the occasion. 'Using the General's clout', he commandeered one of the Alouettes while Foley was being briefed by Haveron, and together with Elesmore nipped away for another look at the bottom end of the Gully, which he felt was long overdue (a second Alouette had joined the search a couple of days earlier).

For days he had been wanting to 'get down in the weeds' – to go in at really low level over the jungle – and now was his chance. His primary aim was to find a 'winch-hole' or opening in the forest canopy, into which men could be lowered, so that they could fell or blast down enough trees to make space for a helicopter to land. By this means he could establish a forward base, close to the bottom of the unsearched section of the Gully, which would save the new search team hours of trekking in. A secondary objective was to identify a site for a new headquarters beside the football pitch at Melangkap Kappa, next door to the one which the Malaysians had already established.

He and Elesmore flew round, made one reconnaissance flight, landed, and again flew towards the mountain, going as high as the little aircraft would climb, just above 2,000 metres (this was the sortie which Foster logged at 1021). Mowbray found that from the air the terrain did not look nearly as bad as from the ground, but there was still a good deal of mist around, and as soon as the helicopter started doing turns, he saw how easy it was to become disorientated about which valley was which – sometimes he was not even sure which river was the Penataran. At 2,000 metres the Alouette was 'almost falling out of the sky'; nevertheless, on one pass, with a jolt of excitement, he saw two climbers roped together. From their posture, and the fact that they were waving cheerfully, he concluded that they were members of the mountain rescue team, retracing their route towards Panar Laban.

He thought that the sides of the gorge proper were far too steep, and too thickly covered with trees, for the helicopter to approach close enough to winch men down; but in the bed of the Penataran, about 12 kilometres upstream from Melangkap Kappa, they identified a possible winch-insertion point – a small clear space that would allow the new team to abseil in and blast away enough trees to open up a helipad. Bolts would be needed

225

to climb the Gully, and explosives to blast them into the rock –
but the specialist climbers had been forewarned of these
requirements, and were coming fully equipped.

Having found and photographed the winch-hole, Mowbray
and Elesmore headed back to Kota Kinabalu in time for a press
conference which Foley was giving at the Hyatt. The General
had already told Haveron about the flash in the Gully: analysis
of the position showed that whatever had made it, it could not
have been either of the search teams. Foley also reported his
impression that, in spite of all the sorties that had been flown,
the Gully had still not been systematically searched from the air.
The effect of his visit was to endorse the opinion of Elesmore
and Mowbray, that if the missing men were still alive, they could
only be in the Gully's remaining unsearched section.

The paramount need, now, was to brief the new group of
climbers, due in Kota Kinabalu that evening, so that they could
go into action with maximum effectiveness and minimum delay.
The team had been drawn from the Special Air Service and the
Special Boat Squadron, with a handful of airborne forces
personnel and cavers thrown in. When they flew in at 2230, they
were driven off, out of the public eye, to the Outward Bound
school, where Elesmore had set up a small headquarters, and
could talk without interruption. There he gave an admirably
clear brief and put forward his plan of action. He had no power
to issue orders, but his idea of going in from the bottom was so
obviously sound that it was promptly accepted as the only one
feasible. Apart from difficulties of supply, to have renewed the
assault from above would have meant a delay of two or three
days before the new team could put itself in position.

The gorge section of the Gully had been likened to a cave
without a roof, and the new team's caving experts included Tony
Flanagan, who had briefed Neill at the School of Adventurous
Training at Ripon during his visit the previous year. Cordless
drills had been bought in England and taken to Heathrow by
Sergeant Chris Jackson, a standby caver who – to his huge
disappointment – had to remain behind in the United Kingdom.
Another caving expert, Chief Petty Officer Wally Wallace, had

226

brought with him a thermal imaging camera which he hoped would pick out live bodies beneath the jungle canopy.

During that day the RAF teams had climbed 600 metres of rope, out of the Gully, leaving a marker to show the lowest point of their descent, and gone on over Easy Valley Col to Panar Laban for rest and recuperation. They had given their all, and really were hanging on their chinstraps.

Chapter 17

Saved!

Friday, 25 March was the thirtieth day of the expedition, and the party's twentieth in Kevin's Cave. They had had no food to speak of for the past two weeks. At first light all five of them were awake, hoping fervently that dawn would again bring a helicopter. They had agreed that the strongest members of the group would go on chopper-watch, and Foster was outside first, with his video camera at the ready.

Their hopes ran high, as the day had dawned crystal clear, and for once they could see blue sky. The crucial time was about 0730: it was then that there had been action on earlier days. But, to their intense disappointment, no helicopter appeared, and at 0800 Neill once again made a gloomy note to the effect that no search seemed to have started. With the weekend coming up, he told the Chinese not to expect any more activity. 'Oh well,' he wrote with a sudden spark of irony. 'There's always next week, and I'm sure we'll last till then, even if it won't be pleasant.' His urine had turned an even more sinister colour, dark yellowy-brown.

Foster was also starting to lose his normal robust good humour, as frustration gnawed at him. 'What are they playing at?' he demanded in his journal:

Chow is quite ill, with his back and lack of food. Kevin quite strong. Robert spends all his time in his sleeping bag. Many thoughts go through your mind about chances of rescue. Have the Malaysians searched yet? Have they told the UK they have, and found nothing?

The idea of starting a fire was still attractive – 'If we could set fire to the whole damn jungle, we would do,' Neill wrote – but it

228

had been so wet that they could not make anything ignite. 'Feeling strong in myself, but walking is a bit zombie-like,' he added. Foster still seemed incredibly little affected by the lack of food, and was able to carry his pack across on to the rocks with only limited difficulty. Whereas Neill preferred to do his writing in his sleeping bag, wedged against a boulder beneath the overhang, Foster liked to be in the open.

Foster had enough medical knowledge to be aware that, with plenty of water, he and his fellow-survivors would not die for some time; but he also knew that if they did not get food soon, they would risk sustaining irreversible physical damage. Even at rest, as they were, their bodies needed between 1,500 and 2,000 calories a day to maintain themselves – roughly the equivalent of half the daily rations which they had been carrying at the outset of the expedition. (The attempts he and Neill had made to climb out of the Gully had probably burnt up 400 or 500 hundred calories per hour.)

Foster later calculated that their average daily intake of calories went down from 120 on Day Sixteen to fewer than forty on Day Twenty-Eight. Now that they were eating next to nothing, they were living on their own reserves, and using up first glucose (found in blood, muscle and liver), then protein and lipids (oils and fats) in muscle and skin. Already they were suffering from weight loss and muscle wasting: further starvation might easily lead to oedema (retention of fluid in tissue) and damage to the digestive system. If their brains and nerve cells were deprived of glucose, there was a danger that they would become disorientated, suffer impaired vision and possibly go blind. Finally their bodies would suffer convulsions and they would go into a coma.

* * *

Driving through the night of 24-25 March, and several times becoming bogged down on the dirt roads along the way, Elesmore and Mowbray reached Melangkap Kappa at 0600. Their own plan was to start setting up communication links with

Kota Kinabalu, but to send the leader of the Special Forces team straight in to look at the winch-hole, the moment the first helicopter of the day arrived. The rest of the new search team were following round the mountain by four-tonner.

At 0830 two Special Forces officers boarded an Alouette on the pad at Kota Kinabalu and quickly flew round to Melangkap Kappa, where Mowbray and Elesmore greeted them. Michael, the Malaysian pilot, had just shut down his engine when Mowbray asked him if he had enough fuel to take three of them on a recce: the morning was particularly clear, and he planned to show the newcomers the exact nature of the problem. When Michael said he would have to shed some weight by leaving one man behind, Mowbray said, 'OK – I'll stay off. Go exactly where we went yesterday – to the same part of the Gully. Point out the winch-hole and the 2,000-metre contour.'

Away went the little aircraft, skimming over the jungle-clad ridges towards the mountain. A few minutes later, the four-tonner arrived and the rest of the team began laying out their kit.

In the Gully Neill was at his usual task, pencil in hand, and at 0930 he wrote:

Helicopter heard. Hope springs eternal, but Chow and I do not move from our bags. We've done it too often before. One flight appeared to be overhead. Mustn't get overconfident, as disappointment is bad. Helicopter's buggered off again. Everyone's listening intently.

In fact the miracle had happened – and Foster prepared to eat his disgruntled speculation. 'Spoke too soon!' he scribbled afterwards – but at the time he began leaping up and down and waving frantically as the Alouette spiralled above them. When the pilot flashed his landing lights, Kevin and Victor yelped in excitement. Surely this meant that he had seen them? At once they brought out the tinder they had been carefully hoarding for this very occasion, and, for the first time in twenty-three days, got a fire going. Soon smoke was billowing down the valley.

From the helicopter, just as he was about to turn away,

Michael had spotted a flash from the camera. As he made one more sweep, everyone on board saw three figures on their feet, waving desperately, and beside them the SOS distress signal set out in stones. Then a gust of wind buffeted the helicopter, and the pilot had to swing away. Immediately he tried to raise Melangkap Kappa on his radio, but he was so low in the Gully that no signal went through, and he headed straight for base with his amazing information.

The second he touched down, someone sprinted from the aircraft to break the news. Excitement swept through the embryo camp. Michael, normally a phlegmatic fellow, had become immensely elated by this, the greatest event of his career. But when Mowbray asked him if he could go in and 'get a leg down' – · hover, with one wheel on a boulder – he remained commendably objective. Much as he wanted to try, he decided that it would be crazy to jeopardise the success of the whole operation by taking such a risk. Nor did he have the power, at that altitude, to hover and winch the survivors out, one by one. The answer was to send for the more powerful Sikorsky. Immediately Mowbray got on to the high-frequency radio link and passed a message for Schumacher to the headquarters of 5 Brigade, calling for the bigger helicopter as soon as possible.

What Michael could do, meanwhile, was to make another run to drop the survivors food. While he was refuelling from the hand pump, Mowbray and others threw rations and a couple of radios into two yellow waterproof bags. At 1030 the Alouette was airborne again,

Already doubt had set in among some of the survivors, who were not entirely sure that they had been seen. At 1034, still gloomily scribbling, Neill wrote:

And again [more helicopter noise]. *Damned water drowns the noise of everything. Constant raising and dashing of hopes. This is really weird, recording our fate as it happens. 1035. RESCUE! And all in five minutes!*

As he was writing, he suddenly heard the 'incredibly loud

noise' of an engine, so close that he thought the helicopter was going to crash on the rock. Whipping out of his bag, he did not stop to pull on his boots. There, unbelievably, was the Alouette, hovering a few feet above the boulders.

When Foster saw it coming up the Gully, the hair stood up on the back of his neck, goose-pimples came out all over him, and a lump rose in his throat. The drumming of the rotor blades grew ever louder, until the down-draught was buffeting him. Inside the cockpit he could see three men. One of them began lowering a yellow bag on a thin nylon cord. Foster grabbed the cord, but by then the bag had landed in a pool a few metres below him. Heaving it up, he found it was quite heavy, and as he brought it in he saw a second bag land on a rock beside Kevin and Victor. Looking up at the winch-man, he indicated 'FIVE' with one hand, then showed two fingers and held his stomach with the other hand. He pointed into the cave to indicate that two men were lying under the overhang.

When the survivors ripped open the bags, to their amazement they discovered British Army rations. 'Funny,' thought Neill. He was not aware that the Malaysian Army had such stuff. Foster immediately thought that the helicopter must have come from Seria, in Brunei, where the British had a training base. In their euphoria, neither officer had thought to look for the helicopter's identification marks, which would instantly have told them that it belonged to the Royal Malaysian Airforce. Then Foster found medical supplies, Hexamine – small white blocks of dried paraffin fuel – and two radios. Best of all was a note, which had got wet when the bag fell into the water. 'HELP IS ON ITS WAY,' it said. 'ENCLOSED ARE RATIONS, RADIOS . . .' Then some words had been obliterated by water. There followed instructions for using the radios, and the exhortation, 'HANG ON IN THERE LADS!'

No Malay could have written that. At last it dawned on the survivors that the British Army was involved in the search. This meant that the initiative had come from the United Kingdom. It followed that the survivors' families must know that they were missing, and that the loop had been closed. Their exultation knew no bounds: they burst into laughter and tears simultaneously, clapping each other on the back as they frantically emptied the bags.

At once they dived in to get food inside themselves. Neill went for biscuits and chocolate. There was no nonsense about taking it easy, for fear of throwing the food up again: they just got as much down as their shrunken stomachs could stand.

The note asked that someone should talk to the helicopter crew, but neither of the officers was able to make contact. No matter: the relief of having been found was overpowering. Kevin and Victor piled more wood on the fire, together with Hexamine tablets, and coaxed up a more vigorous blaze. Mess tins were soon on the boil, heating up sachets of chicken casserole and corned-beef hash for the most wonderful meal that any of them had ever eaten.

In the village Mowbray was beset by numerous problems. The radio link was so bad that, even though he had passed a message direct to Schumacher, shouting, 'We've found them!', he was not sure that it had been understood. He therefore also called urgently for the Sikorsky. Then, as the Special Forces team were sorting their kit in a large hall made of corrugated iron with a stage at one end, and all the villagers were thronging round, two reporters suddenly appeared, 'mincing in, casual as anything'. They had come round to the kampong purely to see what was happening, but now suddenly realised that they had the scoop of the year. They could not immediately profit from their luck, since they had no communications – and in any case, with great presence of mind Mowbray banned them from the team building and ordered them to stay on the other side of the road.

The Alouette returned from its food drop. Still there was no sign of the Sikorsky. Mowbray went back on the radio and yelled, 'Get the bloody thing in here, or else you'll miss it. The weather's closing in!' Inevitably the reporters overheard him, and asked if they could speak to the man who had seen the survivors first.

'Sorry,' said Mowbray. 'He's not available.'

'When will he be available?'

'He won't be. You're not speaking to anyone here except me. All those people in there are out of bounds to you. I'll tell you what's going on. Those are the rules. Take it or leave it. If there's one mention of Special Forces in any article . . . *I* won't come looking for you. *They'll* do it.' As it was, the press in the United Kingdom had already caught up with the fact that Special Forces were involved, but Mowbray, being out in the jungle, was not to know that.

Michael, the Alouette pilot, was bursting to help, so they decided to send him in again with a trained medic, one of the Special Forces party. They were still not sure whether there were bodies to be lifted out of the Gully, or whether the survivors were fit to be winched. Foster's indication of two people lying down had been interpreted in various ways: some people thought it might mean two bodies, others that two of the survivors were ill or injured.

Luckily the medic was a compact man. To give Michael the maximum chance, they took out the helicopter's rear seats and offloaded as much fuel as they dared. They also left behind one of the crewmen, and forbade the medic to take his 60-kilo bergen with him. Normally it is a cardinal sin for a Special Forces man to allow himself to be separated from his kit, but in these circumstances it was inevitable. So, lightly laden, the helicopter took off yet again at 1115.

In the Gully, they saw it coming, straight as an arrow, apparently unaffected by altitude or the narrowness of the ravine, and as it hovered only seven or eight metres above them, a figure slid down out of it on a winch. The first question Neill shouted was, 'What about the first group?'

'All safe,' called the medic, who became known to the survivors as 'Wings'. 'It was they who raised the alarm.'

Relief seemed to drain away the colonel's remaining strength. Later he wrote, 'Life can now begin again', but for the moment he was close to passing out. So was Victor, although Chow suddenly seemed much stronger. Neill spent some minutes persuading Wings not 'to stick a bloody great needle into Victor' and put him on an intravenous drip: he felt sure that the Hong

234

Kong man was all right, and it was just reaction that had made him collapse. As Wings worked on Victor, he told Foster that his party had been given instructions from the highest level to stay in Sabah until they found the missing men, however long that took.

He also said that the Sikorsky was on its way to lift them out. While they waited, they put on a brew and made hot, sweet tea. As they swallowed the dissolved sugar, they could feel energy pour back into their veins – and in a matter of seconds they were able to walk more steadily. No sooner had Victor eaten than he was sick, but they restored him with the tea, and kept him sipping at it. Foster, in contrast, felt amazingly well, as did Kevin: taking care to eat in small mouthfuls, they suffered no bad reaction at all.

In the village, a radio report brought the bad news that for some reason the Sikorsky had been diverted. Soon it was midday. Clouds were forming round the upper flanks of the mountain. The rescuers felt increasingly desperate.

But at last the big helicopter appeared, touching down at Melangkap Kappa at 1325, piloted by Lieutenant Gabriel Joel. It was full of people, including three doctors, and as it sat there refuelling, with its rotors still turning, there was what Mowbray described as 'a gigantic cake-and-arse party' about who was to go and see the rescue site at first hand. Yelling through the din of the engines, he thinned out the passenger list, removing himself, among others. Away the helicopter went, with two winch-men and a Malaysian Army doctor on board.

To the survivors it was an unbelievable sight – this huge machine, also coming in true as a die to hover above them, with the tips of its rotor-blades almost touching the trees on either side. Fifteen tons of down-draught set the ferns on the rock faces thrashing and blew much of the party's kit away down the Gully – but nothing mattered now. Down came two crewmen, Corporal Aris bin Rahaba and Corporal Mohammed Noh bin Bidin. Foster filmed every second of their miraculous arrival. The stranded men gave the Malaysians a great welcome, and Neill's last diary entry read: 'Somebody must have been on our side after all.'

A stretcher followed the two men down. Neill had already told Foster that he wanted to be last out, for obvious command reasons; but the medic pointed at him, the crewmen grabbed him and helped him on to the stretcher. Up he went with a wave to the lads below. Coming alongside the open door, he was hauled inside by a major from the Malaysian Army Medical Corps, who made a great fuss of him and yelled out a few questions about how he felt. The stretcher went back down, and reappeared bearing Victor, who had recovered enough to sit in one of the seats and strap himself in.

The sides of the Gully were so close that Neill felt he could almost jump out on to them. There seemed to be plenty more room on board, but to his consternation the helicopter lifted away, turned and immediately went into cloud. He had not noticed, but once again the weather was closing in. As they pulled out, he got a brief view up the Gully, but he never saw the remainder of the gorge section because the mist blotted out the view. In a minute or two they flew into clear skies above steeply undulating, jungle-clad ridges, which gradually flattened out as they drew away to the north. Soon human habitations came into sight – huts with roofs of straw or corrugated iron, and then the village, where they landed on the playing field, opposite the large shed taken over by the search team.

Suddenly the temperature was 30 degrees Celsius – a breathtaking contrast with the cool air in the cave. For the first time in a month the survivors felt properly warm. The Malaysians left the helicopter first, then beckoned Neill out. Declining their offers of help, he walked down the steps, and picked his way carefully across the wide-bladed grass of the playing field towards a spot on which people were gathering, and staring, as if at a being from another world. Some of them came forward to meet him and shake his hand, among them Tony Williams, the doctor.

Inside, he was ushered on to a chair. People came to talk to him, Mike Elesmore, whom he had never met, said, 'I just knew you were there. I knew it all the time.' When asked what he would like to eat, Neill opted for rolled oats, on which he had existed for the early part of the expedition.

To Mowbray he looked in extraordinarily good condition, 'very thin but very happy, smiling and well-focused'. Yet the RAF man realised that Neill probably had no idea of the scale of the rescue operation which he had set off, and because he 'didn't want him to drop himself in it by saying things he might later regret', he warned him that members of the press were present, and advised him to keep his mouth shut. In private conversation, he found that Neill was 'quite bitter' about the way the expedition had broken up.

Victor was brought in and laid on a stretcher, covered by a blanket, and both men were given hot drinks. The Hong Kong soldier had become even more spectacularly gaunt than Neill: the skin of his cheeks was stretched tight over the bones, which looked sharp enough to cut through it.

The next few hours passed in a pleasant haze. People came and talked, among them the two journalists, who, in the few seconds before they were shooed away by Tony Williams, managed to construct a good enough story to make front-page leads in all the next day's British national newspapers. Belatedly Neill began to realise that his adventure had hit world headlines, and that a huge search operation had been going on for nearly two weeks. Never in his wildest dreams had he imagined that the RAF Mountain Rescue Service would have been involved (he later found that this was the first time they had ever been deployed outside the United Kingdom).

Every now and then he went out to see what the helicopter was doing. In fact it flew two more sorties in attempts to rescue the remaining survivors, making spiral descents into the Gully, and on the second it came within 200 metres of the stranded party, only to be driven off by the drifting mist. In the end the attempt was abandoned until the morning, and as the light began to fail, the Sikorsky headed back for Kota Kinabalu, with Neill and Victor on board, accompanied by Tony Williams, who had carefully made sure that they ate the right things, gradually finding out what their medical condition was – as well as gaining an idea of what shape the others were likely to be in. Quickly they skimmed through the gathering dusk to the Sabah Medical

Centre, and on their approach to land they saw floodlights, and a mass of people waiting.

As the rotors stopped turning, the door opened, and various people walked off. Then it was Neill's turn. Until then he had been quite capable of walking, but when he saw all the people, including nurses with stretchers, he knew it would be hopeless to resist the preparations that had been made for him, so he allowed himself to be helped down the steps and on to a trolley, amid volleys of camera flashes and a babble of questions.

With crowding nurses all around, the trolley party set off at a fast trot, through crowds of journalists shoving cameras and microphones into his face. So wild was their progress that the trolley threatened to overturn as it went round corners on two wheels, but it reached the hospital safely, hurtled into a lift, and up into a consulting room. Doctors had assembled to look at these men who had defied their expectations by surviving the jungle and starvation, and they were clearly curious to discover what medical problems they might have developed.

When nurses took off Neill's boots, the stitching came apart in their hands. A doctor examined his torso, and said there was nothing to be worried about – but Neill himself was appalled by his appearance, which did indeed resemble that of a concentration-camp inmate. His ribs were sticking out, and his upper arms had withered to the thickness of his wrists. When asked what he would like to eat, he chose an ice-cream and a milk shake, and was left alone to rest in a comfortable room, with a drip in his arm. Neither he nor Victor felt hungry for solid food, but realised that they must take in as many calories as they could.

Merely to lie on a soft mattress, without the damned granite sticking into him, secure in the knowledge that all his men were safe, was the utmost luxury. So was the shower which he took soon afterwards – a tremendous cleansing. Examining himself more thoroughly, he was amazed to see how much weight he had lost: in particular, he found that the cheeks of his behind had gone flabby, 'like deflated party balloons'.

Far too excited to sleep, he spent most of the night reliving the past month. Above all, he was relieved that all his party had survived, and would be able to do what they had talked about more than anything else – rejoin their loved ones. Victor would soon be able to hug his beloved Pansie, and sort out his motorbike. Kevin could start a family with Jessie, and Chow could eat Peking duck to his heart's content. With his mind whirling, Neill realised that numerous inquisitions must lie ahead, and that the only way to survive them would be to be as frank as possible about what had happened.

To keep the press at bay, doctors had forbidden incoming calls; nevertheless, one journalist came through in the middle of the night, asking for an interview. Neill stalled him by pretending that he was not yet well enough. Then he realised that he could make outgoing calls, and through the operator reached his home number in Yorkshire – only to hear it ring and ring. For the rest of the day he kept trying, without success, and then switched to an old office number in York which he had had a year before. (Those were the only two numbers he could remember.)

At last he got an answer, and immediately recognised the voice of a colleague, Mike Lentz. 'Hang on,' said Mike. 'Fiona's in the building.' Neill was astonished. What on earth could she be doing in York? But suddenly there she was, bursting with the news that she was on her way with Alexander and James, to fly out and meet him, either in Sabah or in Hong Kong, depending on how long it took him to recover. The sound of her voice was the best tonic he could have had. He also spoke to the boys, and to some of his army friends.

* * *

In Yorkshire the telephone had rung at 0630 that Friday morning. This time Alison, Fiona's stepmother, was first down, half expecting bad news, or at least the usual enquiry from some thoughtless reporter. But from the stairs Fiona, hot on her heels, heard her scream, 'Oh David! That's brilliant! Wonderful news!'

Fiona's knees gave way under her, and she slid down the last four steps, undermined by a mixture of relief and excitement. Then she heard her stepmother say, 'Three standing up, and two

239

lying.' My God! she thought, three of them are alive, and there are two corpses. Which are which? And why are there still bodies lying on the rocks? Surely they must have done something with them. But in a few moments everything became clear.

The television news, which she now felt able to watch, gave a fuller picture. Her stalwart neighbours, Nell Dunwell and Ruth Andrew, came in to offer congratulations and found the family still in their nightclothes, too excited to get dressed. The telephone rang constantly, as well-wishers bombarded them with happy messages. At 0930 David Bentley arrived with Gordon Williams, an army press officer from York, who warned Fiona she would now have to face the reporters who had massed in the pub car park. To work out a statement, she and Williams sat down in the quiet of the dining-room, away from the bedlam in the hall and outside the front door, where reporters and cameramen were clamouring.

When David suggested that she and one son should fly out to Hong Kong immediately, she at first refused, partly because she hated flying anyway, and partly because she wanted some time by herself, to recover from the trauma. Then, at Williams's urging, she decided that she would go, provided David went with her; during the crisis she had become dependent on his help, and could not face the journey without him. Determined to keep the family together at this supreme moment, she offered to pay for James to fly out with them.

With her press conference over, the family had less than two hours in which to pack and leave. The boys became wildly excited, and had their packs ready within minutes. 'Remember to take your suits!' their grandfather roared up the stairs, and with much groaning they went back to put them in. Cars sped the travellers to the army headquarters in York, where people were hanging out of windows, thrilled and jubilant at the news, smiling and waving as they arrived. David's wife Fay had brought his suitcase along, and as Fiona sat in her car for a few moments, thanking her for her support over the past weeks, someone rushed over calling, 'Robert's on the phone! Quick!' Leaping out, she ran into the front entrance, up the stairs two at a time, past landings full of people, and found an ecstatic Sylvia Dicks, whom she had several times spoken to during the preparations for the expedition, proffering a telephone. There was his voice, loud and clear, sounding perfectly all right: to her inexpressible relief, she realised that he had not suffered any permanent damage.

Her journey to reunion began in nightmarish fashion. One of the party's two cars sustained a puncture, and as time was short they all squashed into the other. Then the plane from Leeds to London seemed to bounce around all over the sky, and when they reached Heathrow they found the airport's road system at a standstill, paralysed by a terrorist scare. So chaotic was the traffic that it was barely possible for the authorities to transfer the travellers from one terminal to another. At last, however, they were escorted into a smart departure lounge.

Against her better judgment, Jeanette Foster had given an interview to Sean Rayment, a reporter from the *Daily Mail* who had rung her doorbell at 7.50 one morning; but the article proved far more sympathetic and accurate than she had expected. The Foster family had remained in good heart, confident that Ron's well-known resourcefulness and knack of hoarding would have helped him survive, and accurately predicting that he would have been carrying extra rations, which he would have distributed to his fellow survivors.

At the family home in Tewkesbury Vaughan had startled numerous telephone callers when he answered in what they took to be his father's voice, so alike did the two sound. The answerphone was still set with Ron's usual message, and in spite of well-meaning suggestions, Jeanette steadfastly refused to replace it, saying, 'He's not dead, you know – only missing.' Dean Hale told her not to worry if she heard that the search was being called off, as the interruption would only be due to bad weather. One day when Kerry's children were watching television, Jade saw a picture of her grandfather appear on the screen, during the news. 'What happens when Grandad gets undressed at night?' she asked her mother in a worried voice. 'Everyone will see him without his clothes on.'

On 23 March Vaughan had to go back to his business, promising to return as soon as possible. The following night Jeanette unpacked the bag which had been standing ready for two weeks: as she went to bed, she was feeling very low, and wondering how much longer she could remain strong. But then she seemed to turn a corner: she resolved that if no news came by Easter, the following week, she would go back to work. With her mind eased by this decision, she slept for six hours, the longest since 15 March, and woke feeling refreshed, in good heart.

At 6.30 the phone rang. It was Pete Arnott an old army cycling colleague of Ron's, and when he heard Jeanette's lively 'Good morning!' he said, 'You've heard the news, then?'

'No.'

'They've found them.'

Stunned but elated, she clung to the receiver as he gave her the details and warned her to prepare for a fresh onslaught from the press. In spite of the report that three men were standing and two lying down, she felt convinced that Ron was all right,

From that moment the line was so jammed with incoming calls that she could scarcely dial out. Mary and Geoff Daff came across with champagne, and Geoff took charge of the telephone. Jeanette and Kerry spoke briefly to the reporters waiting patiently outside. Then came another surprise: an army officer rang and told Jeanette that she would be able to fly to Hong Kong that evening, taking one other member of the family with her.

Having decided to go on her own, she repacked her bag and had been ready for hours when the car collected her at 1600. Kerry went with her to Heathrow, and Brian Janneh met her there to help her check in. Then, in a first class lounge, someone thrust into her hand a copy of the *Evening Standard*: on the front page were photographs of Ron and Robert, beneath the headline JUNGLE TEAM FOUND ALIVE.

After a while she was moved to a different but equally luxurious waiting room. There, Fiona Neill was enjoying the most delicious gin-and-tonic of her life, when in walked a woman who, she knew instinctively, was Jeanette Foster. The two flung

242

themselves into each other's arms and 'screamed with delight' – which woke up the more staid passengers with a jolt.

Whisked smoothly on board the 747 at the last minute, the party was ushered into the club class section and given tremendous service. The Neill boys were in heaven, not least when they were allowed up the staircase to inspect the first class cabin on the upper deck. The wives found that the night passed swiftly in endless talk, and at dawn they were rewarded by the stunning sight of Mount Ararat, in eastern Turkey, whose summit, rising through clouds, was bathed in the early rays of the sun. As they stared at it, thinking of Noah and his ark, the steward came along and told Jeanette that the captain would like to speak to her. On the flight-deck he passed her a message which set the seal on the entire journey: Major Foster had just been winched safely out of Low's Gully. Glasses of champagne appeared, and other passengers toasted the survivors and their families until the whole of club class was in a state of 'total elation'.

* * *

On Saturday the 26th Neill looked out from his hospital bed over Kinabalu Bay onto a phenomenal dawn, and thought it the loveliest morning of his life. At 0715 he wrote down: 'Others should be rescued around now, God willing.' During the morning he moved, walking, to an ordinary room, and was pleased to find Victor next door, in good shape. On a beautiful sunny day, he sat around enjoying the warmth, and as he watched a hummingbird hovering outside the window, he thought how wonderful it was to be alive.

In the course of the morning he met several of the men who had directed the rescue operation, including General Yussof and Tony Schumacher. He was pleased and relieved to find that everyone was treating him with sympathy, and that there was no hint of condemnation. Still very wound up he asked for a couple of Valium tablets, as he had been too excited to sleep the night before, and under their influence he eventually dozed off.

Later, hearing helicopters, he rushed to the window (as did Victor) and saw the Sikorsky coming in with the Alouette behind it. He knew they must be bringing Foster and the others. (For months afterwards none of the survivors could hear the sound of a helicopter without the noise triggering hopes of rescue.) Someone came in to tell him that the rest of the party were all right – and soon Foster arrived.

He revealed that on Friday Wings, the medic, and the two Malaysian crewmen had been left in the Gully without any kit. During the afternoon Wings had hacked pieces off the dead tree stranded in mid-stream with a survival knife, and had got a good fire going. The Malaysians were given the sleeping bags of the men who had been lifted out, but in spite of them, and the fire, they were frozen, and passed a miserable night on rock mattresses. Foster spent half the night talking compulsively to Wings, constantly brewing up tea and soup, before at last managing a couple of hours' sleep.

Discussing items of equipment that might have helped them, Foster learned about mountaineering strobe lights, which would have sent out pulses of bright light every second, and would have been far more effective than his camera flash, and visible for several kilometres. But he discovered that SARBE (search and rescue beacons), which transmit via satellites, were accurate to within three kilometres only, so would have been of limited use to anyone searching for the stranded party. When satellites are not overhead, beacons also work on line-of-sight, which would have made them of limited use in the Gully.

In one of his last diary entries he recorded:

Everyone happy. Kevin strongest of the Hong Kong soldiers. Last few days he has been very positive. He asked Lord Buddha to send rescue, and this changed his attitude – stayed with me on rocks in middle of river for hours. All our prayers have been answered. The HK boys have survived with fortitude, and have not caused any trouble. Robert and I have discussed recommending them for awards.

In the morning, when the Sikorsky returned to lift the whole party out, Chow went up first with one of the crewmen, Aris bin Rahaba, then Kevin and Foster together on the same wire. But because of the altitude, the helicopter could lift only a light load, and they all had to leave their packs behind. That did not much worry Foster, since he had salvaged the items that mattered most: his passport, diary and beloved video camera. As he alighted at the Sabah Medical Centre, he managed to avoid most of the reporters by walking round behind them with Tony Schumacher, while they focused their attention on Kevin and Chow,

A sheaf of press cuttings, brought into the Medical Centre by Schumacher, was of burning interest. Neill was appalled to find that Brittan had already been speaking freely, before he even knew whether the colonel's party were alive or dead. The corporal had apparently given a general interview to the correspondents of several leading British newspapers, and had revealed many of the things that had gone wrong on the expedition, starting from the fact that Chow had had difficulty climbing the tourist track on the first day. He had mentioned the difference in fitness between the two groups, and other causes of friction.

Neill was horrified to read of the ordeals the recce group had gone through in their fight for survival. But he felt that he himself had been 'hung, drawn and quartered before he had even been found'. Yet two thoughts gripped him above all others: how seriously he had underestimated the severity of the Gully, and how glad he was that he had not surrendered to the desperation which had almost driven him to push on down the Gully below New's Pools once the water receded. Obviously, he reflected, it paid to listen to gut feelings.

He saw that the press had been enjoying a field day. With its usual verve the *Daily Mail* had reported that the 'crack RAF rescue team' was 'armed with guns and machetes', and described the missing men's ordeal as a 'battle with starvation and a billion mosquitoes'. References to 'jungle hell' had been numerous, as had descriptions of the wind 'howling through the vegetation-choked clefts of the mountain'. On 20 March the *Sunday Times* had led its front page with the headline TIME RUNS OUT IN LOST VALLEY KNOWN AS 'PLACE OF THE DEAD' and by the 24th hopes of finding anyone alive had been widely reported to be 'fading'.

Presently General Hussin returned, together with the British Defence Attaché from Kuala Lumpur and the Permanent Secretary to the Minister of Tourism for Sabah, Datuk Wilfred Lingham, who had taken up his appointment only twenty-four hours before news broke that half the expedition was missing. Two visitors whom Neill and Foster were especially delighted to welcome were Gabriel Joel (by now known as 'the Archangel Gabriel') and Michael Izhar, pilot of the Alouette; the latter apologised profusely for the fact that, when flying Foley on 24 March, he had seen the flash of Foster's camera, but had not realised that it came from the trapped men.

Schumacher warned Neill to prepare himself for major press conferences: like it or not, he had been in the UK headlines for the past fortnight, and would have to give an account of himself. Letters from media representatives, handed in via the nurses, offered vast sums for the officers' exclusive stories; but Neill knew that, as a Regular Army officer, the last thing he should do was to exploit his predicament by taking money from the press.

Foster was told that, as a member of the Territorial Army, he was in a different position. He learned officially that if he sold his story to the newspapers, he would be well advised to donate a substantial sum to the Malaysian rescue effort. This seemed to him to be an excellent idea, and in due course he was given every encouragement and assistance by various officials to settle with a national daily newspaper. It also appeared to those around him that if Foster did sell his story to the media, it would help to put his side of the story in view of the comments that Brittan had made to the press earlier in the week. The best thing to do, said Schumacher (himself a former journalist), was to retain a lawyer, to whom requests for interviews and information could be referred. Ringing the number which Schumacher gave him, Foster got through to London in the middle of the night and retained a rather startled solicitor there and then.

The news Neill most wanted to hear was of what had happened

to the other group, and why they had pushed on without waiting for him. But it seemed likely that he would have to wait until the Board of Inquiry, which he understood would be convened to investigate all that had happened. In the meantime, he learned that his expedition team had been scattered across the world, from the United Kingdom to Hong Kong and Sabah.

Medically, his own group of five had stood up to their ordeal extraordinarily well. The only one causing concern was Chow, whose back was still giving trouble. Neill's weight had dropped from 12 stone 4 pounds to 9 stone 11 pounds, and Foster's from 14 stone to 11 stone; but they were both in far better shape than the non-commissioned officers had been. Mayfield had gone home suffering from suspected malaria, but Mann's cut hand had continued its miraculous recovery, and no member of the expedition appeared to have suffered any lasting harm, physical or mental. Foster's elation was such that, for the second night running, he had difficulty sleeping, and was up at 0255, preparing notes for the press conference later that day.

On his second night in hospital Neill also was still so excited that he too could not sleep, and spent hours pursuing a mosquito that persistently homed in on him – the only one which he had seen on the whole expedition. But he was so relieved by the fact that his party was safe that nothing else seemed to matter. In the morning Schumacher introduced him to Arthur Murray, the Public Information Officer from Hong Kong, who suggested that he should prepare a press statement for when they came to leave Sabah, and offered to help work one out.

Then in came Brittan, bringing the kit which they had left at the Travellers' Rest before the expedition set out. When Neill asked why he had given the newspaper interviews, Brittan replied that he thought it was all right, 'as the Army had arranged the press conference'. Further conversation was cut short by Foster's urgent need for new trousers, and Brittan was sent out to buy him a pair. Neill's stinking clothes had come back immaculate from the laundry: when he shaved off a month's beard and looked in the mirror, he got quite a shock; his skull-like face reminded him so sharply of his father's, just before he died. Suddenly he saw how close was the resemblance between two generations.

His stomach took several days to recover its normal dimensions, and at first, though hungry, he was eager for snacks rather than large meals. But starvation did not seem to have affected his taste buds, and he was delighted when Robert New dropped in bringing some beer, which he had smuggled into the clinic, as well as the kit that Foster had left with him. The officers thanked him for all his help in the rescue – but felt it inappropriate to bring up the fact that they had formed a misleading impression of the Gully from his cheerful descriptions.

Schumacher had arranged a flight to Hong Kong for the Sunday; and in due course, after being pronounced fit to travel, they drove to the airport in a convoy of limousines, hotly pursued by carloads of reporters and photographers, one of which took a roundabout the wrong way in an attempt to snatch a picture. At the airport Malaysian dignitaries had foregathered, as had the RAF mountain rescue team, together with Mike Elesmore and officials from Park Headquarters. Neill and Foster had a few hectic minutes, striving to express their thanks adequately, and at the same time trying to find out more about the rescue operation. Though still not clear about exactly what had happened, Neill saw that a phenomenal effort had been made on their behalf, and privately began to regret all the disagreeable remarks about lack of action which he had written in the Gully.

During the reception General Hussin revealed that his own daughter had gone into hospital during the rescue, prostrated by nervous strain. At the press conference that followed, he made a generous speech, followed by one from Neill, who had embellished a skeleton text prepared for him by Arthur Murray. Aware that his clothes were hanging off him, and that he and Foster were the focus of international media attention, he found it a severe strain to face such a scrum of reporters and cameramen.

He began by paying tribute to the courage and resourcefulness of the search-and-rescue teams from the Malaysian armed forces,

the police and the Parks Authority. He also thanked local
people, and the British service personnel, all of whom 'rallied to
our plight so magnificently and generously'. Asking the
rhetorical question of whether he would do the same thing again,
he said that the descent of Low's Gully had been intended to
present a challenge, and that the challenge remained:

*I would still dearly love to conquer it. The expedition, in my
mind, presented a justifiable challenge, and met all the criteria
of army adventurous training. No – I would not do it the
same way again. But what we have learnt from this
experience will provide others with information which will
enable them to do what my team was unable to achieve.*

*When I and my colleagues were rescued thirty-six hours
ago, I was amazed by the extent to which our plight had
captured the attention of the world's media. They don't
deliver newspapers to the bottom of the waterfalls in the
Gully, and television reception is terrible. I want to thank
you, your readers and your listeners for your concern. But
most of all I want to say thank you once again to those whose
superb efforts, both in the air and on the ground, allow us to
be with you today.*

He went on to speak of the need for adventurous training. The
expedition, he agreed, had been 'an arduous undertaking, but so
is training for war, and in peace regular and TA officers and
soldiers train for war'. He pointed out that such training
'provides one of the few opportunities the Army has to see how
younger soldiers in particular react under pressure'; and as
evidence of the way in which it brings out latent qualities, he
cited the conduct of some of his men:

*I would like to pay tribute to Corporal Hugh Brittan, whose
leadership of the group which succeeded in breaking out and
raising the alarm led to the saving of all our lives.*

*I am also going to pay tribute to three very special and dear
friends – my three Hong Kong soldiers, whose personal*

249

conduct has been exemplary. They grew in stature daily, and are alive today because they exhibited the three basic military qualities of teamwork, self-discipline and courage.

Only after the reception had finished did it come home to Neill that his recce group had in fact achieved the purpose of the expedition. Until then he had thought that they used a different version of New's escape route. On the aircraft the press scrum continued. The officers had been allocated club class seats, but they sent two of the Hong Kong men to occupy them, and a kind journalist gave up her seat so that all three Chinese soldiers could sit, and be interviewed, together. Nobody asked awkward questions about why the expedition had broken in two: what fascinated the reporters were the mechanics and sensations of survival.

In Hong Kong it had been arranged that the survivors would meet their families in public at the British Military Hospital, with five cameramen present; that was the only way to satisfy the press, who otherwise would pursue them all over town. Neill considered this in the worst possible taste: but the others said they could handle it, and so the plan went forward.

As the cars drew up outside the hospital, Alexander and James ran out to greet their father. Then all five survivors went inside, and fell into the arms of their wives and families. As Neill later recalled, it was a highly emotional moment, but 'it was not our style to crack up or cry' – there were too many cameras around for people to let their guard down. Fiona was shocked by her husband's skeletal appearance, and by his pallor. She had expected that after so long in the open he would be weatherbeaten, rather than white. Seeing how slowly he walked, she thought he looked 'like a stick man in a Lowry painting'. Yet her spoken reaction was characteristically forthright: 'Another fine mess you've got us into!' she said by way of greeting, between hugs and kisses. Jeanette waited at one side of the room, and as Ron slipped in through the doorway, their reunion escaped the main flurry of attention. The families were allowed 30 minutes' peace in private rooms, where Foster looked through photographs of his grandchildren and demolished a whole plate of sandwiches.

Jeanette and Fiona had already been besieged by the press when they arrived in Hong Kong, and now, after the brief private reunion, the survivors moved into a formal press conference, at which Neill gave the same speech again, deferring questions about what had gone wrong until he reached the United Kingdom. Then they moved up into hospital rooms on a higher floor, and were told to rest – which was impossible.

Foster's first visitors were Major Peter and Angela Knoll, old friends who had just been posted to Hong Kong. Then in came General and Mrs Foley, joining the ranks of well-wishers: they found the three Hong Kong soldiers in a state of euphoria, proud that they had been through a fantastic experience.

The survivors were detained in hospital for a period of observation, until tests proclaimed them fit, and during this time the bonds which had been forged between all five in Kevin's Cave became, if anything, even stronger. For the duration the officers' families were allocated rooms in a nearby married-quarter block. The Hong Kong men's families, who lived in the colony anyway, could visit whenever they wished. The only man with a real problem was Chow: X-rays revealed that one of his vertebrae had been cracked by the rockfall which nearly redesigned Neill's head.

Neill was puzzled to find that he weighed less, four days after rescue, than he had when he was lifted from the Gully. It turned out that the body takes several days to revert from its emergency burning up of muscle to its normal method of using food. He was amazed to find that his neck measurement had shrunk from 16 inches to 14: never since he was a boy of 13 had it been so small.

On Tuesday 29 March, with the Matron, Lieutenant Colonel Maureen Mumford-George acting as minder, the two officers were shepherded into the Reuters' television studio for a live link-up with GMTV in London. Foster got a fine surprise in the form of a chance to speak to Vaughan and Kerry, for the first time since the rescue. Next day he was pronounced fit to travel. His spirits soared at the appearance of his last visitor, George

McGrellis, another old friend, together with his son Paul, who was stationed in Hong Kong. The Fosters were then whisked away to Kai Tak airport, anxious to rejoin the rest of their family in England.

One evening in the hospital Neill fell into conversation with an ultra-fit-looking young Gurkha soldier, whose wife was being treated in the hospital. The colonel was thrilled to discover that he was talking to Corporal Kushang Gurung, three times winner of the Mt Kinabalu Climbathon – the annual race from the power station to the summit and back. Gurung then held the record, with the astonishing time of two hours, forty-two minutes which he had achieved in 1991 – an extraordinary contrast with Neill's own painful, ten-hour slog up the tourist trail on the first day of the expedition.

On the Friday evening before he and his family flew home, Neill managed to convince the medical staff in the hospital that he was well enough to be allowed out to dinner. Off went the family to the restaurant at which they had planned to join the Hong Kong soldiers in a great feast of Peking duck; but as poor Chow was still flat on his back, the Neills went on their own, washing down delicious Chinese dishes with draught after draught of Tsingtao beer. The real celebration banquet, about which everyone had fantasised so often in the cave, would have to wait until later.

Chapter 18

Aftermath

It had been arranged in Hong Kong that the official United Kingdom press conference would take place in York on Wednesday, 6 April, a few days after Neill and Foster had returned home. By then, even though they had not seen all the newspapers and television coverage of the rescue, they realised that what people really wanted to know was why the expedition had split in two.

Over a hundred reporters and television cameramen gathered at Imphal Barracks for the conference. The euphoria which greeted the rescue had evaporated, and had been replaced by a critical attitude. When asked why the expedition had split, Neill stated his belief that he had not authorised his recce party to carry on down the Gully, and that there had obviously been a breakdown in communication. He added that he was 'personally extremely angry' about what had happened.

When reporters heard this, they assumed that he was attacking Brittan, who was sitting next to him. But when asked what he thought about Neill's comments, Brittan said that if he had been left behind, he would have felt exactly the same. 'Until we've collated all the information, we're not going to start shooting anybody,' he added – but this did not stop newspapers running stories to the effect that the leader of the expedition had criticised his recce group.

Neill and Foster were still on sick leave at home when official letters arrived informing them that the Board of Inquiry would assemble at Headquarters, Eastern District, in York, on Monday, 25 April 1994, to investigate matters arising from the expedition. The Board was to report its findings to Major General Patrick Cordingley, the General Officer Commanding Eastern District. All the members of the expedition were told

253

that, if they wished, they could be represented by solicitors, but because Neill and Foster had nothing to hide, they decided to dispense with any form of legal representation. Soon after the inquiry began, it became clear that extremely detailed personal accounts would be required, and that every conceivable point would be scrutinised in detail. Neill and Foster realised that their diaries – until then their lifelines to sanity and to their wives – had now become critically important as accurate records of events and thoughts as they occurred, to be used as evidence under oath.

The inquiry was held in a ground-floor conference room, in which the four members of the Board – a full colonel and three other officers – sat at a long table, faced by a single chair and small table for the individual giving evidence, with further chairs and tables for the other witnesses behind. Proceedings were formal, with all ranks in uniform, court orderlies present, evidence given on oath, and everything taken down both by stenographers and on tape. Chow was still in hospital in Hong Kong, being treated for his injured back, but Kevin and Victor had been specially flown to Britain, together with a staff sergeant from the Hong Kong Military Service Corps who acted as minder and adviser. The Board also had the benefit of a Chinese interpreter, recruited locally.

The Board dealt with events in chronological order, and much of the first week was taken up with Neill's evidence about the planning of the expedition. Since the inquiry opened only a month (to the day) after the rescue, he and Foster were by no means back to full strength, and both found the proceedings almost more stressful than being trapped in the Gully. Luckily, because Neill had written all his letters of organisation on a word-processor, he was able to produce copies of relevant documents, which showed every step that he had taken in his preparations. Interesting statistics emerged about army adventurous training in general. In 1992, when 645 applications for expeditions had been submitted, there had been two fatalities; in 1993, out of 623 applications, none. The Gully Heights application was said to have been one of the most comprehensive ever put in, and the expedition was described as one of the half-dozen or so projects every year which were truly challenging.

The inquiry continued for over a month, and ran on into June. In its findings, released in September, the Board concluded that the planning for the expedition had been conducted thoroughly and professionally, that the qualifications of the leader and team members met normal safety requirements, and that the correct authorisation procedures had been followed. The Board commended Neill for assembling a mixed group, including Regular, Territorial and Chinese soldiers. However, the Board considered that his judgement and leadership during parts of the expedition were flawed, and that the decision to take the less experienced members of the group into Low's Gully was over-ambitious. The Board decided that the orders given were too vague and unspecific to cope with the situation that developed and hence there was no deliberate disobedience, nor had the recce party abandoned Foster and Neill's group.

The Board recorded that at one stage during the expedition Neill had become ill, and that for a short period Foster had assumed command. The Board formed the opinion that certain decisions taken by Foster during this period, although completely in line with the general plan, subsequently contributed to the situation of jeopardy which developed. The Board also found that the conduct and performance of Brittan, Mayfield and Cheung were 'such as to deserve formal recognition'. As a result, General Cordingley was pleased to announce that these three NCOs had been awarded commendations for their actions during the expedition.

Later Neill issued the following brief press statement:

As organiser and leader of the expedition, I accept full responsibility for anything that went wrong. I am sure you will appreciate that it would be entirely inappropriate for me to comment further, except to say that the Board was entirely fair.

I would like to say how pleased I am that Corporal Brittan, Lance Corporal Mayfield and Lance Corporal Cheung have been commended for their conduct on the expedition. They are all very brave young men.

The five of us who were winched out of the Gully remain eternally grateful for the courage, professionalism and tenacity of our Malaysian and British rescuers, and all those others who contributed to the success of the operation. We are extremely conscious of the fact that they risked their lives in appalling weather conditions to help find us.

Lastly, I hope that the lessons learned from our experience will benefit others in the future.

Being a serving officer, Neill was, and remains, unable to comment on the Board's findings. Foster, a Territorial Army Officer, who had kept himself out of reach of the national press, later expressed his disappointment with the Board's findings to a Gloucestershire newspaper.

Yet criticism did not stop the leaders speculating about what might have been. Neill remains convinced that if he had pushed on down the Gully with his party of five, beyond New's Pools, he would probably have killed them all, and certainly the Hong Kong soldiers, as he would not have been able to get them out of trouble without his rock-climbing instructor. If, on the other hand, he had not taken the Chinese into the Gully at all, the other seven members of the expedition would probably have reached New's Pools before the rain set in. He still would probably not have gone on down, as he reckoned it was too dangerous. But with the full British team, in particular with Mayfield present, he felt sure they would have found a way out: with their combined equipment, expertise and strength, they would undoubtedly have broken out of the Gully by finding New's escape route.

For Neill and Foster, it was acutely embarrassing to have had their expedition end in rescue. Apart from anything else, the huge operation obscured the fact that the expedition had achieved its objective – the first descent of Low's Gully. Yet some crumbs of comfort could be salvaged from the wreckage. No lives were lost, and no serious injuries sustained, either among the expedition members or among their rescuers. The RAF Mountain Rescue Service gained invaluable experience in mounting an extensive operation overseas, and in future crashed pilots may well have cause to be grateful for the lessons learned as a result of Operation Gully Heights.

Certainly, future adventurous training expeditions mounted by the armed forces in remote areas will have the benefit of a complete package of rescue-emergency equipment, information and advice. The fact that the five trapped men came through their ordeal was a testament to the soundness and value of military survival training, as well as to the dedication and professionalism of their rescuers. These qualities were publicly acknowledged in November 1994 when the highest award of the Guild of Air Pilots and Air Navigators went to the crew of the Royal Malaysian Air Force Sikorsky, who winched out the survivors. The presentation was made by King Hussein of Jordan, himself an experienced pilot.

It was also reported that the close cooperation between the Malaysian and British armed forces during the rescue helped improve the diplomatic atmosphere, and did something to accelerate a return to more cordial relations between the two countries. It was early in September 1994, two weeks before the findings of the Board of Inquiry were announced, that Datuk Seri Dr Mahathir Mohamad, the Malaysian Prime Minister, announced the lifting of the embargo on trade with Britain.

On a personal level, Neill and Foster emerged with a more philosophical view of the future, with the importance of life, family and health strongly re-emphasised in their minds. Both also maintain their firm belief in the value of adventurous training as a means of character development.

Only the expedition members can fully understand the conditions and the atmosphere under which vital decisions were made. The authors have done their best to recreate an extraordinary experience, and are profoundly grateful to have survived their brush with death in that lost world on the north flank of Mount Kinabalu.

Exercise Gully Heights

Opening Statement to the Press following the Board of
Inquiry
by Major General Patrick Cordingley DSO
General Officer Commanding Eastern District

Exercise Gully Heights was a British Army adventurous training
expedition which took place in Sabah, East Malaysia between 16
February and 25 March. The aim of the expedition was to
descend the north side of Mount Kinabalu by way of a deep
ravine, known as Low's Gully, exiting the mountain area along
the Penataran river.

The expedition was conceived, planned and led by Lieutenant
Colonel Robert Neill, a member of the staff of my headquarters
here in York. Members included Major Ron Foster, a Territorial
Army officer, five British army non-commissioned officers and
one NCO and two soldiers from a British Army unit in Hong
Kong.

During the course of the expedition, the party became split,
initially into two and eventually into three groups. Two of the
groups, consisting, in total, of five British NCOs, eventually
reached safety on 12 March. The remaining group, consisting of
two British officers and three Hong Kong Chinese soldiers,
became trapped and were rescued from Low's Gully on 25 March
after a major search involving elements of both the British and
Malaysian armed forces.

As the General Officer commanding Lt Col Neill, the leader of
the expedition, I ordered a Board of Inquiry to be convened to
investigate the planning of, preparations for and conduct of the
exercise. The president of this Board was a senior army officer
currently serving in Hong Kong and the members were chosen
for their knowledge of adventurous training and of the jungle

environment. One of the staff from my legal branch was also a member of the board.

The Board sat, here in York, from 25 April until 24 May. The president and members of the Board subsequently visited both Hong Kong and Mount Kinabalu. All members of the expedition were in attendance throughout the Board proceedings in York with the exception of one of the Hong Kong Chinese soldiers, Pte Chow who was in hospital and unable to attend.

The aim of this press conference today is to brief you on the findings of the Board of Inquiry and the actions which have been taken as a result of it.

However, before doing this, I wish to make a few general comments about adventurous training. Such training has, for many years, been an important and integral part of the process of development of our soldiers, non-commissioned officers and officers. It provides an invaluable method of developing many highly desirable skills and attributes. Self-discipline, self-reliance, the willingness to take the initiative and the ability to overcome fear are all qualities which are essential in combat and which we therefore prize in our soldiers and officers. They are characteristics which can be developed and honed by involvement in adventurous training.

Hence, the importance which the army attaches to adventurous training activities which, over the past two years, have involved some sixty thousand soldiers on two thousand expeditions of which some one thousand two hundred have been undertaken overseas. Nothing which has come out during this Board of Inquiry has cast any doubt on the continuing value of adventurous training as a method of development for soldiers in the army and therefore our commitment to it remains as strong as ever.

Turning now to the findings of the board of inquiry and the actions which have been taken as a result of it. I will divide these into two parts. First I will cover the recommendations concerning procedures, equipment and qualifications and, second, I will cover the findings of the board which relate to those who took part.

259

First, procedures, equipment and qualifications. The Board of Inquiry concluded that the regulations and procedures were fully followed during the planning of the expedition and that there was nothing absent from those regulations or procedures which could have prevented the expedition from going wrong. I would stress that the qualifications required for this expedition were met in full.

However, we learn by experience and we are continually refining our procedures for the planning and approval of adventurous training exercises. The Army Adventurous Training Compendium will be amended to include the recommendations made by the Board of Inquiry.

These amendments are relatively minor and are designed to ensure that those responsible for approving expeditions can be sure that the degree of difficulty and element of risk in any adventurous training activity has been fully assessed during the planning stage and, further, that it is reflected in the qualifications, training and experience of those taking part and the safety equipment which is available to them.

Finally in this section, the Board recommend that a review of the qualifications required by those conducting abseiling should be carried out. This has been done and it has been decided to introduce a two stage system to ensure that those supervising abseiling are correctly qualified. This will involve attendance on two courses – the rock climbing proficiency course and the rock leader training course. The details of the more stringent qualifications will also be included in the amendments to the Adventurous Training Compendium.

I would now like to cover the findings of the board which concern the individuals who took part in the expedition.

The Board formed the opinion that the planning for the expedition was conducted thoroughly and professionally, the qualifications of the leader and team members met the safety requirements and that the correct authorisation procedures were followed. The Board commended Lt Col Neill for his plan to assemble a mixed group including regular, territorial and Chinese soldiers. However, the Board considered that Lt Col

Neill's judgement and leadership during parts of the expedition were flawed and that the decision to take the less experienced members of the group into Low's Gully was over-ambitious.

Lt Col Neill has been interviewed by myself and by the Deputy Commander in Chief of the United Kingdom Land Forces and these findings have been pointed out to him and discussed with him.

At one stage during the expedition, Lt Col Neill became ill and, for a short period, Major Foster assumed command. The Board formed the opinion that certain of the decisions taken by Major Foster during this period, whilst completely in line with the overall plan, subsequently contributed to the situation of jeopardy which developed. I have interviewed Major Foster and pointed this out to him.

Finally, the Board recommend that the conduct and performance of Cpl Brittan, LCpl Mayfield and LCpl Cheung was such as to deserve formal recognition. I am pleased therefore to announce that these three NCOs have been awarded commendations for their actions during the expedition.

That ends my formal statement. I am now willing to answer any questions which you might have. I would however point out that my Board of Inquiry did not examine the conduct of the search and rescue operation therefore I do not have the knowledge which would enable me to answer detailed questions on this aspect. However I would like to take the opportunity to pay tribute to the magnificent efforts of the Malaysian armed forces and the assistance from the government of Malaysia which brought this rescue operation to a satisfactory conclusion.

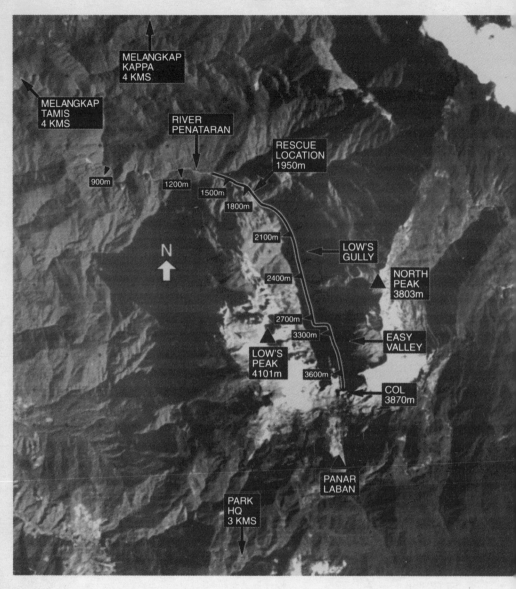

MELANGKAP
KAPPA
4 KMS

MELANGKAP
TAMIS
4 KMS

RIVER
PENATARAN

RESCUE
LOCATION
1950m

900m

1200m

1500m

1800m

N

2100m

LOW'S
GULLY

2400m

NORTH
PEAK
3803m

2700m

3300m

EASY
VALLEY

LOW'S
PEAK
4101m

3600m

COL
3870m

PANAR
LABAN

PARK
HQ
3 KMS

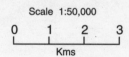

Scale 1:50,000

0   1   2   3

Kms

Kinabalu – based on aerial photography taken from 13,000m
(Gully bed in shadow)

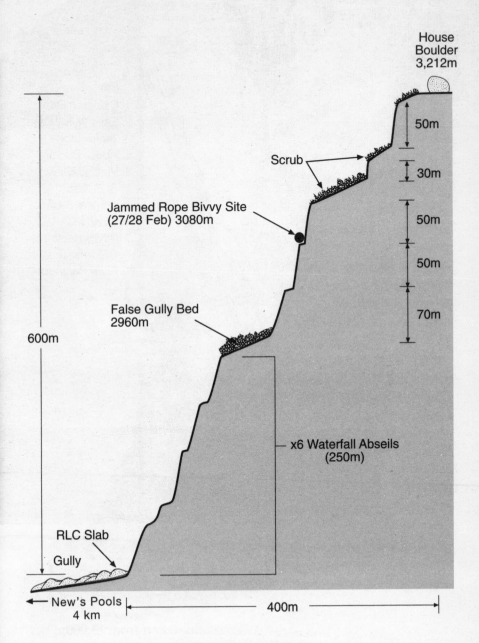

House
Boulder
3,212m

50m

30m

Scrub

Jammed Rope Bivvy Site
(27/28 Feb) 3080m

50m

50m

False Gully Bed
2960m

70m

600m

x6 Waterfall Abseils
(250m)

RLC Slab

Gully

New's Pools
4 km

400m

Abseils into Low's Gully

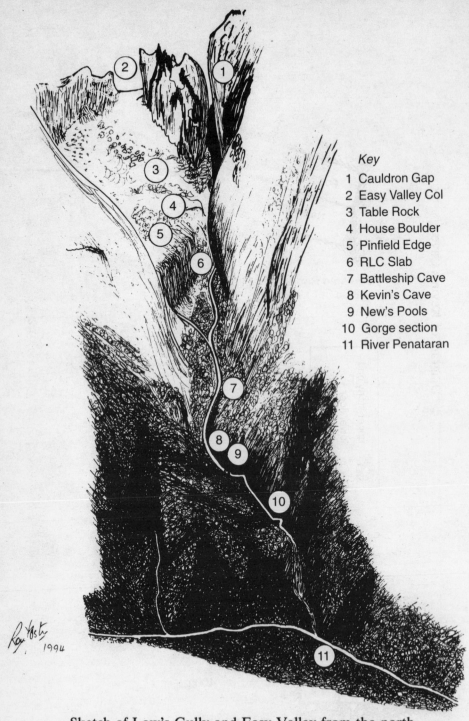

Key
1 Cauldron Gap
2 Easy Valley Col
3 Table Rock
4 House Boulder
5 Pinfield Edge
6 RLC Slab
7 Battleship Cave
8 Kevin's Cave
9 New's Pools
10 Gorge section
11 River Penataran

Sketch of Low's Gully and Easy Valley from the north

264

Diagram of Kevin's Cave

Foster from 15 March

Neill from 17 March

Neill before 17 March

Foster before 15 March

Chow's position under rock fall – 16 March

The Pit

entrance

upper stony bed

lower floor

boulders

direction of floods – 14 & 17 March

Chow

Chow's boulder

direction of rock fall – 16 March

Kevin

Victor

roof sloping 30° to floor

edge of overhang

265

Operation Gully Heights

Composition of the First Rescue Party

RAF Mountain Rescue Service personnel:

WO	Alister Haveron	HQ 18 Group
FS	Jim Smith	RAF Kinloss
Sgt	Dan Carroll	RAF St Athan
Sgt	Andy Church	RAF Kinloss
Cpl	Carl Vanderlee	RAF Kinloss
Cpl	Fletch Fletcher	RAF Kinloss
Cpl	John Roe	RAF Leuchars
Cpl	Dave Taylor	RAF Leeming
Cpl	Ray Shafren	RAF Leuchars
Cpl	Ponch Linnitt	RAF Leuchars
Cpl	John Williams	RAF Leeming
Cpl	Jimmy Clitheroe	RAF Stafford
Cpl	Graham Stamp	RAF Valley
Cpl	Bren Dunn	RAF St Athan
SAC	Larry Caulton	RAF Stafford
SAC	Pete Caulton	RAF Leuchars

Specialist advisors:

Maj	Andy Williams
Lt Cdr	Mike Elesmore
Flt Lt	Richard Mason
Flt Lt	Richard Mowbray